W9-CDD-191

Six Seasons

A NEW WAY WITH VEGETABLES

Joshua McFadden

with Martha Holmberg

Foreword by Barbara Damrosch
and Eliot Coleman

Artisan | New York

Published by Artisan
A division of Workman Publishing Co., Inc.
225 Varick Street
New York, NY 10014-4381
artisanbooks.com

Artisan is a registered trademark of Workman Publishing Co., Inc.

Published simultaneously in Canada by Thomas Allen & Son, Limited

Library of Congress Cataloging-in-Publication Data

Names: McFadden, Joshua, author.
Title: Six seasons / Joshua McFadden with Martha Holmberg.
Description: New York : Artisan, [2017] | Includes index.
Identifiers: LCCN 2016038070 | ISBN 9781579656317 (hardback, paper
    over board)
Subjects: LCSH: Seasonal cooking. | LCGFT: Cookbooks.
Classification: LCC TX714 .M3826 2017 | DDC 641.5/64—dc23 LC record
    available at https://lccn.loc.gov/2016038070

Cover design by Michelle Ishay-Cohen
Jacket photographs by Laura Dart
Design by Toni Tajima
Printed in China

10 9 8 7 6 5 4

Contents

Foreword

In fall 2008, our farm stole Joshua McFadden away from a really good job at Dan Barber's New York City restaurant, Blue Hill. Dan's loss, for which he has forgiven us, was certainly our gain—the following February we turned the running of the farm over to Joshua and a fellow enthusiast for most of the growing season so that we could take time to build a barn. They brought in two young cooks as farmworkers, and it was like turning over your garage to a budding John, Paul, Ringo, and George. This was before we had a real commercial kitchen, and soon the concrete floor at one end of our main greenhouse had more small cooking appliances than Broadway Panhandler. On weekends, our farm stand in the adjacent orchard was transformed into a restaurant. Strands of little white lights, strung through the apple trees, made it look like a festive gypsy camp.

Farmers and chefs are natural collaborators. Both work insane hours, although at different times of day. During that stretch of time when both are awake, they salute what the earth has to offer. Chefs are thankful when we give them great produce, and we love them when they enhance it with their art—even the picky ones. Especially the picky ones.

Put a chef in the garden and amazing things can happen. Joshua and the crew grew everything from celtuce to saltwort that summer, and he was even bolder as a cook, grilling outside in the dark and throwing fistfuls of whole herbs into exquisitely dressed salads. People flocked to eat his food, and still do, though now the ingredients that inspire him are from West Coast fields and waters. We've had the good fortune to taste some of his current fare and are overjoyed that we now have his wonderful book to show us how it's done. We're happy that a chance to play in the dirt at Four Season Farm gave him the deep understanding of seasonality that imbues so many of the recipes in *Six Seasons*. We like to say that there are 365 seasons of the year, when each day finds certain ingredients in their absolute prime state, but even going from four to six is a sign of enlightenment.

Lots of cookbooks these days celebrate vegetables, we're glad to say, but Joshua has an extraordinary gift for preparing them, and for making it easy for any cook to do the same. His directions are absolutely clear, and he is, above all, realistic. Even as he pours all his inventive ideas from the cornucopia of his brain into yours, he seems to know that we are all busy and need ways to make meals wonderful without going crazy. It's desirable to have a larder full of quality items—such as simple homemade breadcrumbs—that you can grab in a hurry. It's even okay to start your mayonnaise with a glob of Hellman's, whisk in an egg yolk, and keep going from there. It's pleasure we're after, not purity. Life, like Joshua's excellent croutons, should never be rock hard, but should have "a little chew in the center."

—Barbara Damrosch and Eliot Coleman

How Getting Dirty Helped Me Become a Cook

I grew up in Wisconsin in farm country, among rural beauty, large farms, but not a lot of terrific food— at my house anyway. Oh, my family cooked: big Sunday dinners and holiday parties, with spreads of vegetable salads, mountains of corn with butter and cheese, the grill going all day with burgers, steaks, and sausages. Some of my relatives even put up the end-of-the-year produce as pickles and preserves. But in our kitchen, you could still find the box of mac and cheese, processed foods, and out-of-season vegetables and fruits.

Prowling around my neighbors' gardens gave me a hint that there was more to food than what was in the cupboards. Some early moments are etched on my palate, maybe even on my soul: Biting into a sun-warmed, plucked-from-the-vine tomato with a saltshaker in my hand. Pulling a stalk of rhubarb from the ground, blowing off the dirt, and dipping it into a sugar jar. The elemental pleasures of those close-to-the-earth foods have stuck with me.

In the same way everyone finds a path through school and work, I wandered a bit, starting out studying film in Chicago, but deciding that rather than stories on film, I connected to the stories told every night at restaurants. I knew that's where I should be, so I ended up at Le Cordon Bleu in Portland, Oregon, in 2001. After months of reading, eating, and absorbing as much as I could from instructors (which wasn't as much as I needed, I knew), I headed into the pro world.

My skills weren't great, but my energy and passion were obvious, and I worked my way into some of the big kitchens in the big cities: Lark Creek Inn and Roxanne's in the Bay Area; North Pond in Chicago; Franny's, Momofuku, Lupa, and Blue Hill in New York.

After those stints, I was adept at working in kitchens, but I also knew that the magic didn't start in restaurants, it started on the farm. In the orchards. Off the coast. In the mossy soils of the forest. It started with nature.

And so, in the way that life unfolds for you when you're truly passionate about your pursuits, I found a job working for Eliot Coleman on Four Season Farm in coastal Maine. Eliot and his wife, Barbara Damrosch, are legendary. She's an amazing gardener and writer, he's a pioneer in both organic farming and farming throughout the whole year— which in the harsh climate of Maine is quite something.

Eliot writes too, and they both love to nurture people who choose a life in food, hosting interns on the farm, teaching, sharing. I was farm manager for a stretch, during which time Eliot let me integrate good cooking into the farm operations. I conducted weekly farm dinners inside the candlelit produce stand. We'd welcome guests at sunset with seasonal cocktails in a greenhouse, conversing among the cucumbers, tomatoes, and herbs, mingling with each other and the makings of their dinner.

It was an experience that marked me indelibly. The sign on the dirt road that leads to the farm reads, "Real farming, real food." When I took that dirt road on my first day, it was a big step toward understanding food in a whole new way, truly understanding the process of transforming a tiny seed into food that not only nourishes but delights, a process about the cycle of life that was life changing for me.

From Maine I went to Rome to work at the American Academy, an Alice Waters project. Cooking in Italy with Italian produce—well, that pretty much sealed my fate. I needed to work with real food, simple food, in season. Which is how I ended up as the chef and now owner of Ava Genes, in Portland. A nice full circle, right?

How This Book Can Help You Become a Better Cook

Writing a book is hard and time-consuming, so I didn't do it for fun (though plenty of fun was had along the way). My goal in writing this book was to encourage and energize cooks of all skill levels—that means you—in your efforts at seasonal and local eating. I want to show you how to eat tomatoes in August, peas in April, butternut squash only when there's frost on your car windshield. Cherish the vegetables when they're at their best, and then wait until their season rolls around again. The impact will be profound, in your own kitchen and in the community at large.

The best way to eat with the seasons is to frequent and support local farms, markets, and grocery stores that are doing good things. It's a virtuous cycle that nourishes the simple things that make life taste great.

Throughout the book, I praise small farms as the best places—other than your own garden—to get ingredients worth celebrating. But I'm not on a mission to point out the ills of industrial farming (though I believe there are many). My intent is to celebrate all the positive changes that have unfolded over the past couple of decades. Many more small farms, an explosion of farmers' markets, big grocery chains responding to peoples' desires for real, fresh food—an earnest, gentle, delicious revolution toward a new way of growing and consuming food.

So while you're free to cook any recipes in the book whenever you want, I'm begging you to jump on the joyful ride of eating with the seasons. When you begin with fresh, ripe ingredients, your cooking will improve right off the bat.

But what's a season, anyway? Winter, spring, summer, and fall don't adequately reflect what's truly happening in the fields, so I divided the book into six seasons instead of the traditional four. In this book, summer is three sections, because summer is where the action is, with waves of new families of vegetable arriving every few weeks, almost like microseasons. June brings fresh and delicate colors from light greens to ivories to yellows; an August market basket will vibrate with supersaturated reds, oranges, and purples. And of course seasons are different in different parts of the country, so you need to adapt to the rhythms of your latitude, soil, and climate.

In spring, you'll find plenty of dishes with raw vegetables, fresh from the newly warmed earth and needing not much more than a slick of olive oil and a sprinkle of salt to showcase their green goodness. English peas piled high (and tumbling off) grilled bread slathered with fresh cheese. Raw asparagus sliced to emphasize its crunch, tossed with walnuts, Parmigiano, and olive oil. That's what I want to eat in the first weeks of the regenerating earth.

When the sun grows stronger, more vegetables join the party—raw cauliflower crumbled to look like couscous, dressed with such a perfect balance of sweet, spicy, salty that you can't stop eating it. Charred broccoli, dipped in creamy, dreamy tuna sauce. Sophisticated fennel, iced to make it crisp, dressed in crème fraîche and garnished with pristine seafood.

The golden days of late summer are like Eden—vegetables that came on line earlier in the summer are still looking good, all the Mediterranean vegetables are luscious and ripe, so many awesome vegetables joined by herbs, stone fruits, melons. It's hard to go wrong when you can just toss chunks of melon with ripe tomatoes of every color, basil leaves torn to release their perfume, creamy burrata cheese, and a kick of chile and you've got dinner on the patio.

EVERY STAGE

As each microseason unfolds, my impulse is to start out using the new vegetables raw, when textures are juicy-crisp and I can taste the full essence of the thing itself. I recommend you do the same, even if you've never considered eating a particular vegetable this way. Raw winter squash? When sliced thin, drizzled with brown butter, and tossed with pecans and currants, um, yes, please.

As weeks progress, I'll turn up the heat, maybe bring in some fire from the grill to get some char. (And please note—when grilling or charring, skip the oil. Cook your vegetables naked, which will allow the sugars to nicely caramelize and avoid the awful taste of burnt oil.)

EVERY PART

And as chefs are recognizing the old farmhouse virtues of eating nose-to-tail with meat so as not to waste any part of the animal, I aim for eating leaf-to-root with many vegetables. When you think "carrot," you may think orange, but I also think green. Early in the year, carrots come with lacy tops that are delicious, such as in my Pan-Roasted Carrots with Carrot-Top Salsa Verde, Avocado, and Seared Squid. All roots have edible greens, so catch them early when they're tender.

MY FLAVOR SIGNATURE

All the recipes in this book, no matter how simple, present the vegetables in a context of complexity. I make sure that every dish has more than just balance—it must have tension,

a dance between sweet, sour, spicy, salty, creamy, crunchy. I use textural ingredients such as toasted breadcrumbs, nuts, croutons; flavor bursts from dried fruit, capers, pickles; and the all-important bright acidity from good vinegar and fresh citrus juices. These are some of the hallmarks of my cooking, and the means to make ordinary vegetables extraordinary.

INDISPENSABLES

Let's pause for a moment to talk about oil and vinegar. Real extra-virgin olive oil is almost more than an ingredient—it's a force of nature, and I wouldn't be a chef without it. Incredibly healthful (full of phytonutrients and monounsaturated fats), olive oil and humans go together. And oil carries and marries flavors, adds great moisture, and just finishes a dish in a way nothing else can. You can read how I dial in the final flavors with olive oil in my cowriter Martha Holmberg's section (page 15).

It's critical that you use a good-quality true extra-virgin olive oil. The world of olive oil is confusing, not well regulated in the United States, and frankly full of fraud. I use a California extra-virgin made by Albert Katz for everything I do in the kitchen—sautéing, frying, making sauces, drizzling over dishes . . . even making cakes (see the yummy Parsnip, Date, and Hazelnut Loaf Cake with Meyer Lemon Glaze, page 361). Albert is a wizard who has learned through passionate trial and error to do what many people think is impossible: make great olive oil in California. He's a stubborn guy and would rather make less money but better oil, so he nurtures every small batch of oil from grove to bottle, and it shows. His oils aren't inexpensive, but they're worth the cost (www.katzfarm.com).

So olive oil is my yin, and my yang is vinegar. Again, quality matters, and I use vinegars also made by Albert Katz. Almost all of his vinegars have a sweet-sour character to them, what the Italians call agrodolce. As I said above, that tension between sweet and acidic is key to my cooking, especially with vegetables. I find it brings out their own natural sweetness, plays off their earthiness, just makes them sing. In My Larder (page 17), I recommend a few brands of vinegar to use if you can't find KATZ.

Words to Cook By

- Visit farmers' markets often and always ask questions.
- Things that grow together in a season go very well together in a dish.
- Start with raw vegetables. Take a bite so that you understand their flavors before you begin making your dish. Do this as each season progresses to learn how vegetables change.
- If you haven't read My Larder (page 17), read it and act on as much as you can. Building a larder will help you cook faster and better.
- Don't be a slave to a recipe. Add different herbs, use a new spice, omit something you don't like— you're in charge.
- Be organized. Read the whole recipe first, gather all the ingredients, do the messy prep first. Clean as you go. Your food will really taste better, I promise.

- Eyeball it. Get comfortable cooking without measuring cups and spoons. Your mouth, nose, eyes, and hands will tell you the right amounts.
- Cooking times are simply guidelines. Use your senses, including common sense.
- Build layers into your dish, like you're making nachos. Hide things on the bottom. Sprinkle things on top.
- Use a pepper mill if you want to make good food.
- Leave fresh herb leaves whole most of the time. I want my guests to enjoy an herbal explosion.
- Texture is king. Use dried breadcrumbs, nuts, and seeds liberally.
- Make mistakes. Oversalt, use too much vinegar, make something too spicy, burn something—and then don't do it again. That's how you learn.
- Find the fun in cooking. Don't be scared.

EVERYTHING YOU NEED FOR GREAT VEGETABLE DISHES

Though my recipes are mostly simple, real cooking takes time . . . but less time if you plan ahead, break up the work, and have everything on hand. In My Larder (page 17), I recommend my indispensables, such as anchovies, cheeses, and canned tuna, with my favorite forms and brands. In Go-To Recipes (page 29), I share the basics like croutons and roasted almonds, but also yummy condiments like Green Garlic Butter, Whipped Ricotta, Caper-Raisin Vinaigrette, Charred Scallion Salsa Verde, and Pistachio Butter. Each one is super versatile and keeps for weeks; I suggest ideas for using them beyond the recipes in this book. And we can't forget pickles—I make quick refrigerator pickles out of everything that enters my kitchen; I've mapped out a few favorites for you on page 57.

ANY WHICH WAY YOU WANT THEM

One brilliant aspect of vegetables is that you can feature them in every place in the meal, from appetizers like my Rainbow Chard with Garlic and Jalapeño, to salads like Little Gem Lettuce with Lemon Cream, Spring Onion, Radish, Mint, and Breadcrumbs to slaws—please try the Beet Slaw with Pistachios and Raisins. It will change your life. Soups in every season, main dishes that are vegetarian . . . or not (I do use meat and seafood in some recipes, and I use anchovies and fish sauce), even desserts, like the parsnip cake mentioned earlier and a perfect-for-Thanksgiving Carrot Pie in a Pecan Crust.

I hope you'll like my food and find it delicious, even revelatory—who knew you could make pesto from fava beans and pistachios, cook celery root as you would a steak, grill unripe tomatoes to pair with watermelon? But I hope you never find it to be fussy. I hate chef books that presume home cooks have the time, money, and skills—and desire—to replicate restaurant-style recipes. Not to mention the dishwashing staff! We serve a lot of the dishes in this book at my restaurant, Ava Gene's in Portland, Oregon, but the techniques and ingredients are mostly quite ordinary. You'll need to do some prepping and cooking and seasoning, but the soil and rain and sun will have done the rest for you. Embrace the seasons and good cooking will follow.

What I Learned While Writing This Book with Joshua

The most important concept was the simplest—how to season a dish.

I always considered myself a "good seasoner." After all, I learned to cook in France, where no one is afraid of salt or fat or flavor. But as we worked together in the kitchen, I noticed that his versions of the recipe were always better than mine. Grrr. He would taste my dish and follow up with a flurry of grinding, sprinkling, squeezing, grating, and tossing. I would then taste my dish and find it was now sparklier, more vivacious.

Here's what I learned: Season (usually with salt, pepper, chile flakes, some kind of acid) *before* you add the fat, which in 95 percent of the recipes in this book will be olive oil. Dial in the flavors through a few rounds of tinkering, tasting, and tinkering again. The goal, says Joshua, is for the dish to taste "like a potato chip." Meaning so tasty and savory that you can't help but take one more bite . . . and then another.

At that point of perfect tension among the salty, sweet, spicy, zingy elements of the dish, add the oil. This brings a flavor of its own but acts mainly as a moisturizer and a vehicle to carry and marry all the other flavors.

I have now trained myself to take a serious moment of final seasoning, even when I'm rushed. I focus only on what I'm tasting and feeling in my mouth, then adjust the dial to bringing everything into sharp flavor focus. Such a simple step can truly help you get to delicious . . . always my goal in the kitchen.

—Martha Holmberg

My Larder

Cooking begins with shopping, or "sourcing" as chefs like to call it. Stock your larder with high-quality, versatile foundational ingredients and you can prepare fantastic meals without having to make a trip to the market. Here are my recommendations.

Salt

Simple fact: Salt makes food taste good. No question, salt is the *most important* ingredient in your larder, period. In the right amount, salt brings out the natural flavors of other ingredients, making them taste more like themselves. Though it's fun to collect salt in all its different colors and varieties, at minimum you should have kosher salt and a finishing salt. Add kosher salt to water for blanching and cooking pasta, and use it for seasoning everything. Use a finishing salt for, well, finishing your dish with a final hit of salt and in some cases added crunch. Most of the salt in my cabinets are shades of white to gray, with a sprinkling of pinks and black. A salt's color is determined by its other mineral content as well as by the method used to process it. I don't care as much about color as I do about the overall flavor of the salt and how the texture interacts with my dish.

For kosher salt, I prefer Diamond Crystal, available at most grocery stores. Morton also makes a kosher salt, but Diamond Crystal has a larger grain that's very crushable, which gives me more control over the amount I add.

For finishing salts, Maldon is wonderful, with a delicate flake in a pyramid shape (www.maldonsalt.co.uk). I also love Jacobsen pure flake salt (www.jacobsensalt.com), which I use on everything; Jacobsen's is made in Oregon, which is where I live. French *sel gris*, which has a coarse, gritty texture, is great with meat. Find salts for every occasion at www.themeadow.com.

STORAGE Salt lasts forever. I keep salt in jars and saltcellars so I can pick it up with my fingers. Be sure to keep salt next to your pepper mill and use it often. Those little shakers on the table are of no help when you cook; you need to feel the salt with your fingers as you add it, so you'll begin to understand how much does what.

Black Pepper

One of the most important ingredients in the kitchen is black peppercorns. A few twists of good black pepper is the easiest way to step up just about any dish. A perfect example of the beauty of black pepper is the pasta dish *cacio e pepe*. It's loaded with flavor even though the "sauce" is just black pepper, pecorino cheese, and pasta water. (Check out my Cacio e Pepe Butter, page 34, which also gets its delicious kick from black pepper.)

As with all spices, freshness is key, so buy from a good source and replenish frequently. I prefer Tellicherry whole black peppercorns. Left on the vine to ripen completely, they have a full flavor in addition to their peppery kick. I order peppercorns for home and for my restaurants from Reluctant Trading (www.reluctanttrading.com).

The pepper mill you use is of great importance. It should have a range of settings from fine to very coarse. Never buy preground or precracked pepper, ever! You want the fresh, intense flavor and aroma of freshly ground or cracked black pepper. (I lean toward very coarsely ground pepper for seasoning a dish; the slightly larger grains produce flavor explosions in my mouth.) I am a big fan of the mills from Fletchers' Mill (www.fletchersmill.com); they are adjustable from fine to coarse, and they last forever.

STORAGE Keep peppercorns in an airtight glass container, like a mason jar, so you can pour them quickly from the jar into the mill.

Spices and Dried Herbs

I actually don't use many spices—and I'm partial to fresh herbs—but they do have their merits. I'll add toasted whole coriander seeds to pickles and fennel seeds to some salads. I do use dried herbs occasionally, especially dried bay leaf and dried oregano along with abundant amounts of fresh. Oregano is the perfect mate for tomatoes, both cooked and raw. I use earthy, mellow dried bay leaf in beans, soups, and broths. Be sure to remove the leaves from a dish before it's served.

I always toast whole spices first and then, when not using them whole, grind them in a coffee grinder that I keep just for that purpose. For a coarser grind, I use a mortar and pestle. I add dried spices at the start of cooking and then adjust with more at the end. I don't "dust" finished dishes with spices much, as some chefs like to do, with fennel pollen being the exception. Though fennel pollen does add a slight anise note, its flavor is delicate and has a remarkable ability to wake up other flavors in a dish.

My favorite sources for high-quality spices and dried herbs are Penzeys (www.penzeys.com) and Reluctant Trading (www.reluctanttrading .com).

STORAGE I buy only small amounts at a time and store them in little glass jars that I refill often. Don't store in plastic containers, because the plastic can absorb the spice oils and eventually impart stale flavors.

Extra-Virgin Olive Oil

Olive oil is a huge reason I enjoy cooking. I really would have no idea how to make food taste good without it. I even take a nip straight from the bottle now and then.

Like wine, the flavor of the oil depends on the variety of olive, the climate and soil where it's grown, the processing method, and the "vintage" of the oil. One look at my recipes and you'll see the many ways I use olive oil, including the fact that I sauté and deep-fry in it. Though olive oil can be more expensive than other oils, I want all my ingredients to contribute to the quality of the dish, so why use an inferior oil? I cook with modestly priced olive oils and save the more expensive ones for dressing and finishing. Some cooks worry that extra-virgin olive oil will degrade at high temperatures, but the smoke point of extra-virgin olive oil is about 400°F, and most frying takes place at around 375°F, so it's all cool.

It is so important to support local farmers, and olive oil producers are farmers. Albert Katz is such a farmer in California, and a great friend of mine; I've used KATZ oils and vinegars for years (www.katzfarm.com). Other notable small California producers are Grumpy Goats Farms (www.grumpygoatsfarm.com), Bondolio Olive Oil (www.bondolio.com), Pacific Sun (www.pacificsunoliveoil.com), and Enzo Olive Oil (www.enzooliveoil.com), as well as California Olive Ranch and Corti Brothers; from Spain, I like Unio. These last three are widely available in grocery stores.

STORAGE Keep olive oil away from light, from heat, and from too much air, meaning don't buy a large can and let it sit for months while you slowly use it. If you buy in bulk, transfer the oil to smaller sealable containers. It's tempting to keep your bottle of oil right at the stovetop, but the heat there will hasten its deterioration. (Though if you use as much oil as I do, that bottle will be empty in a few days, so you'll be fine!) Try to buy the youngest oil you can: Harvests are in late fall and early winter, and the dates are often marked on the label.

Vinegar

I use a ton of it—vinegar is critical to my cooking—and yet you'd never say my food is sharp. Any type of acid, judiciously used, simply brings brightness and delicious tension to a dish. I use it in dressings and vinaigrettes, and in salads, of course, and I plump dried fruit in vinegar. Balancing the vinegar or citrus is one of the final adjustments I make to any dish. Unlike many chefs, I prefer a vinegar that's slightly sweet because I like its agrodolce complexity and the gentler flavor, especially when it comes to vegetables.

As with their olive oil, KATZ (www.katzfarm .com) makes exquisite vinegars; it is my gold standard. KATZ uses traditional methods and only late-harvest grapes with a high sugar level

(measured in units called Brix) and natural bacteria that promote fermentation.

Unio vinegars from Spain are also excellent, widely available, and reasonably priced. (Not all Unio vinegars are sweet-sour, so look for their "agridulce" line, including Merlot, Riesling, and Moscatel.) If you can't find Unio in your local market, order from Corti Brothers (www .cortibrothers.com). Italian Volpaia vinegars, which are not sweet, are also well made; find them at Manicaretti (www.manicaretti.com). Making vinegar requires great grapes and a lot of skill. Just like olive oil, there are plenty of mass-produced, not-great vinegars on the shelves, but if you buy one of the real ones, your cooking will forever be changed.

BALSAMIC

This type of vinegar is legendary, of course. The high-end stuff should never be used in cooking, which would be a waste of a precious substance. I rarely use the traditional aged balsamic, even at the restaurant, but when I do add a drizzle to finish a dish, my favorite brand is from Villa Manodori. For everyday use in cooking, Lucini is a very good, value-priced option; it's more of a balsamic-*style* vinegar than a traditionally crafted one, but perfectly fine.

SABA

Saba is an Italian syrup made from cooked grape must (the juice and skins before fermentation). It looks and smells like balsamic but is sweeter, grapier, and much less acidic. And it's less expensive because it's not aged. Saba is wonderful with cheese, nuts, bitter greens, and roasted vegetables.

STORAGE Store vinegars in their original bottles in a dark, cool place. They will last and last and improve with age. Beware of fruit flies in the warm months—they love vinegar, so never leave the caps off.

Dried Beans

There is nothing better than a bowl of perfectly cooked beans napped with bean cooking liquid and a healthy glug of extra-virgin olive oil. I always have multiple varieties in my larder, including these four go-tos:

Chickpeas (aka garbanzos) are for me the most versatile of the beans. I'll puree chickpeas to make dips, such as hummus, or toss them into pastas. They also play nicely in vegetable salads, adding a hit of protein. And, of course, fried until crisp and salted, chickpeas are fantastic as a snack.

Borlotti (aka cranberry beans) are my favorite bean. They are soft-skinned, dense and meaty but creamy, and good all by themselves with a splash of olive oil. I use borlotti in pastas, soups, and stews, and I love to pair them with fish—grilled, sautéed, or poached on a bed of warm beans and lemon.

Dried fava beans are not common in the United States, but I am a fan. Big in the Middle East, you may have eaten falafel made from ground fava beans. They're also big in Roman cooking, added to soups and pastas, mashed and spread on garlic-rubbed toast, or—my favorite way—pureed and served with wilted bitter greens on top.

Black turtle beans, with their dense, earthy flavor, are my go-to black bean. I like them for baked and braised bean dishes, as well as bean salads and refried beans, and I love them in summer salsas.

The age of the beans you buy is important, because very old beans will not cook evenly. They may not even soften at all. If you're buying them in a bag, older beans will look slightly dusty and you may see cracks or splitting skins. Definitely look for beans less than a year old, though very old beans are great as pie weights! Knowing the actual age of beans is tricky, though, unless you buy them freshly harvested. If possible, buy beans directly from a farm when they are in season, when the beans are still quite tender. Fortunately, I have a wonderful relationship with a farmer who grows exceptional beans. Using a quality-minded retail source is also a guarantee for fresh, flavorful beans. Two excellent sources are Rancho Gordo (www.ranchogordo.com) and Zürsun Idaho Heirloom Beans (www.zursunbeans.com).

Be sure to plan ahead because beans need to soak in water overnight before cooking (unless they're freshly harvested and cook very quickly without soaking). For my cooking method, see Perfect Shell Beans (page 254). Contrary to cooking myth, salt does not inhibit beans from softening during cooking. I lightly salt the cooking water at the beginning so the salt can penetrate each bean, and then adjust the salt during the final preparation. What *will* keep beans tough, though, is acid, so never cook beans in wine, and limit tomatoes as well. I love beans and tomatoes, but I only unite them after the beans are fully tender.

The "liquor" left over from cooking beans is fantastic, full of flavor and body. Use it as a base for soups or for moistening pasta, and when you're reheating a simple bowl of beans, always include some of their cooking liquid. I let the cooked beans cool in their liquid and I store them with their liquid in the refrigerator.

STORAGE Store dried beans in an airtight container in a cool, dry place. Mark the date you bought them so you'll know their "vintage." Freshly harvested dried beans freeze well, or store them in a loosely closed paper bag in a place with good ventilation so they dry out evenly.

Grains

I'm gratified to see more grains such as farro, freekeh, kasha, quinoa, and barley on restaurant menus and home tables alike. I'm also happy to see old varieties and drought-resistant grains being grown, which will be so important to the future of good food. Whole grains provide good nutrition and are affordable and delicious.

Farro is my go-to grain; it's always in my larder. I usually make a large batch at home on the weekend to use throughout the week—as the base of a salad, to add to a soup or stew, or simply to eat with a drizzle of olive oil.

I cook farro the same way no matter its final destination, using a method that produces the best flavor and a nice, toothy texture. (See the basic recipe on page 50.)

Small mills that sell whole grains, as well as grind them into flour, are being established around the country. Look for them in your area. I order farro, rye, and wheat berries from Bluebird Grain Farms in Washington (www.bluebirdgrainfarms.com). You can also order grains and more from Anson Mills in South Carolina, which has some of the best dried corn, rice, wheat, and oats (www.ansonmills.com).

STORAGE Whole grains keep longer than ground flours. Store them in an airtight container in a cool place and replace them as needed. They'll last up to 6 months, even longer in a freezer. I tend to think in terms of harvest to harvest, and replenish every year.

Flours

All-purpose flour, as the name suggests, is the workhorse of flours. Its protein content is moderate, so the flour can do it all—make chewy bread, crisp cookies, moist cakes. I always go with unbleached all-purpose, which is slightly less refined than bleached and has a slightly higher nutritional content and protein level. However, I prefer the depth of flavor of whole wheat flour. This flour is made from the whole kernel of wheat, whereas white flour is made only from the endosperm of the grain, hence whole wheat has more nutrients and fiber compared to white flour. I use whole wheat in my flatbreads and crackers because of the flavor.

For any recipe that calls for flour, but especially in baking, it's important to know how to measure flour properly. I use a scale and measure by weight. If you're using measuring cups, be sure to spoon the flour out of the bag into the measuring cup and level off the top. (If you scoop the flour straight from the bag with the cup, you'll compress the flour and pack in too much.) Weights in ounces are included in the baking recipes in this book.

Finding a reliable source for freshly ground flour could change your life. If you become really committed, you can buy a small mill to use at home. Grocery stores are the more convenient option, of course, and many stores carry flours from regional mills. For any flour bought in the store, check the sell-by date and choose the freshest.

You can order amazing flours from Hayden Mills in Arizona (www.haydenflourmills.com). You can also find great flours at Anson Mills in South Carolina (www.ansonmills.com). Sunrise Flour Mill in Michigan (www.sunriseflourmill .com) is also another great source. Central Milling in Utah (www.centralmilling.com) is one of the biggest and best, and has a really wonderful selection of flours.

STORAGE Store all flours in airtight containers in a cool, dark spot. White flours will keep longer than whole wheat because the fat in the wheat germ can go rancid quickly. All flours will eventually lose their zing, however. Buy them in small quantities and replenish them often instead of having them sit around. Whole-grain flours have a shorter shelf life and are best stored in the freezer or the refrigerator, which will also prevent a flour bug infestation.

Pasta

Pasta is one of life's great pleasures. I always, always have dried long and short noodles in my larder. From spaghetti, bucatini, and linguine to ditalini, penne, and rigatoni, pasta can be quickly transformed into simple and satisfying meals. In addition to the obvious—starring them in pasta dishes—I like to include pastas in soups and stews.

A successful pasta dish is not only marrying the pasta with the right amount of sauce or condiment, it's also cooking the pasta properly— and there's more to it than simply throwing the pasta into a pot of boiling water. First you must use a pot large enough and full enough that the water won't lose the boil when you add the pasta. Second, the pasta water should be heavily salted, using a lot more salt than you think should go into the water. It should taste like the sea. (The pasta itself absorbs very little salt; it just helps boost the wheaty flavor of pasta as it hydrates in the water.)

And for the timing, never, never use the suggested cooking time on the box as anything more than a suggestion. If it says 10 minutes, I

set a timer for 7 and start tasting. By tasting, you can judge how much more time the pasta needs to cook, and when to put it in the sauce. I cook the pasta in the sauce for at least a minute but generally more like two, and always put a little of the pasta water in the sauce. It adds salt as well as the starch that leaches out while the noodle is cooking, which adds a tiny bit of body and helps marry the flavors of all the ingredients.

One of my favorite American pastas is Della Terra from Oklahoma (www.dellaterrapasta .com). I order it for my home and restaurants. I also like Rustichella d'Abruzzo from Italy.

STORAGE Store pasta in the container it comes in and use it up quickly. While dried pasta will look good for a long time, the flavor flattens out after a couple of months of being in an opened package. Just eat pasta often.

Cheese

Cheese shops are like butcher shops in that both seem to be making a comeback, and good cheeses can also be found in well-stocked grocery stores. When you find a store with a cheesemonger, engage her or him—taste several cheeses, ask questions. The following cheeses are my staples, always found in my fridge at home.

HARD CHEESES

With a hunk of cheese in the fridge, I can not only make quick pasta dishes, but I can also grate the cheese over roasted, grilled, or sautéed vegetables, or make a cheesy, salsa-style topping. And I use Parmesan rinds in soups, broths, and ragus.

I always have Parmigiano-Reggiano, SarVecchio Parmesan, Pecorino Romano, provolone, and an aged cheddar in the larder.

Parmigiano-Reggiano is, as Mario Batali dubbed it, "the undisputed king of cheeses." Perfectly balanced with sweet, salty, milky, and meaty notes, a twelve-month-old Parm has a slightly moist but grateable consistency. Older Parms become more grainy, crystalline, and crumbly and are deeply golden—delicious but best saved to eat out of hand, not as topping in a dish.

SarVecchio Parmesan, made in Wisconsin, is the cheese closest in flavor to Parmigiano that the United States has ever produced. Even Italy has taken notice.

Pecorino Romano is a hard, very salty sheep's cheese from Italy, with deep Roman roots. I use it when I'm looking for more salt, more tang, and less sweet. It pairs so well with sweet vegetables, spring peas, favas, beets, and mellow lettuces like romaine.

Provolone is an aged cow's milk cheese, which to me tastes like Italy. Look for the spicy (picante) version. I grate provolone on leaf salads, roasted and grilled vegetable salads, grain salads, and, of course, pizza.

A good cow's milk cheddar should be at least a year old, with a pleasantly sharp tang and slightly crumbly texture. I love aged cheddars from Grafton, Cabot, and Tillamook. Another firm cow's milk cheese is Pleasant Ridge Reserve from Uplands Cheese Co. in Wisconsin. One of the best cheeses made in America, it's an alpine-style cheese like Gruyère. It has a very deep, sweet, mellow, salt-and-grass flavor.

STORAGE/HARD CHEESES Cheese is a living thing that needs to breathe. Waxed paper or specialized cheese paper makes an ideal wrapping. If you must use plastic, be sure to use fresh wrap each time you re-wrap it. I store my cheese in a drawer in the refrigerator (or store it in a plastic storage container in the fridge). Cheese absorbs flavors, so keep cheese away from other strong-scented foods, such as onions or briny olives.

SOFT CHEESES

The soft cheeses I use most often are mozzarella, burrata, and ricotta.

Fresh mozzarella is to me the best expression of pure sweet milk. I use it in cold salads, with tomatoes, of course, and I tumble chunks of it into pastas and baked dishes.

Burrata—a tender oval of fresh mozzarella filled with a creamier version of more mozzarella—is perfect all by itself with just a drizzle of extra-virgin olive oil and a sprinkle of salt. I also serve it with a few condiments and vegetable purees. But I am not a purist and have no problem tearing it up and tossing it with melon and tomatoes or topping a hot pizza with it.

To my frustration, top-quality, real-deal burrata—*burrata di bufala*—is not yet available in the United States. This cheese is made from the milk of a water buffalo rather than an ordinary dairy cow. Super high in fat and very tender—and crazily perishable—it's meant to be eaten almost as soon as it's made. So while you'll see imported burratas, they are, at best, off-tasting and often actually spoiled. I wait until I get to Italy to enjoy them, but I wish someone in the United States would figure out how to make domestic water buffalo mozzarella.

Burrata needs no prep except to blot the liquid it comes in. If I'm using mozzarella in cooking, say in a baked dish, I will slice it, layer it between paper towels, and press it for a few minutes to squeeze out some of the water. I find this makes it less rubbery when melted. Both burrata and mozzarella should be served at room temperature, never actually cold.

Ricotta, which means "re-cooked" in Italian, is a fine curded cheese, a bit like cottage cheese. I mostly use it as a cooking ingredient, not a cheese to eat straight, though a bowl of pristine ricotta with a drizzle of honey can be a beautiful breakfast. I layer ricotta into my lasagnas, and I often whip it until it's very fluffy and creamy, season it with herbs and olive oil, and then spread a generous layer as a base for vegetable salads. I love the way the rich dairy flavor dances with the bright salads. Ricotta needs to be drained, to concentrate the creamy flavor and make it less runny.

I buy my fresh cheeses from Di Stefano in southern California (www.distefanocheese.com).

STORAGE/SOFT CHEESES Burrata, ricotta, and mozzarella are super perishable, so buy only what you need when you need it. Store them in their liquid in their original containers.

Canned Tomato Products

There are two kinds of tomatoes, each equally worthy: in-season fresh and canned. Canned tomato products come in several shapes, sizes, and consistencies, each one suited to a different purpose—adding acidity to a soup, body to a ragu, or sweetness to a sauce. At a minimum, you should have tomato paste and cans of whole peeled tomatoes on hand. Buying whole tomatoes is nice because you can control the final texture, from roughly chopped into pieces that stay intact to a smooth puree.

I use canned tomatoes in quick pastas as well as long-cooked ragus. I also use them for soups and stews and for pizza. I am a fan of Muir Glen Organic Tomatoes for long-cooked dishes and Bianco DiNapoli for quick pizza and pasta dishes. Pay attention to the labels to be sure you're not buying tomatoes with added herbs or other seasoning; you want pure tomato. For tomato paste, make your own *conserva* (see the recipe on page 272).

STORAGE No trick here, just stack the cans on your pantry shelf! If you only use part of a can, put leftovers in a zip-top bag and pop into the freezer.

Pickles

Everybody loves pickles. Pickled carrots, pears, green beans, beets—so many variations in flavor, color, and texture. I keep pickles around for quick snacks, condiments, and for mixing into salsas, vinaigrettes, and simple sauces. Just as breadcrumbs add texture, a pickle tucked away in a sauce or salsa will open up the flavors of everything around it.

I want you to make your own pickles (see "Pickles: Six Seasons in a Jar," page 57), because not only is pickling satisfying and a wonderful way to preserve the harvest, but homemade pickles are also the best way to control the ingredients in your pickle. If home pickling isn't right for you, store shelves are stocked with loads of interesting pickles, so acquire a variety.

STORAGE Though pickles are preserved in brine, refrigerate them for safety and maximum crunch.

Nuts

Nuts are essential to my cooking. They add tremendous flavor, texture, depth, and visual appeal, and nuts are so, so good for you. My favorites are hazelnuts, almonds, cashews, and walnuts. And although I use raw vegetables, I rarely use raw nuts. I roast them first, then finely or coarsely chop them and scatter them over salads and pastas or mix them into salsas. I also make nut purees, such as in Pistachio Butter (page 37) and as the base for Pine Nut Vinaigrette (page 39). A nut puree is incredibly rich and creamy and, of course, dairy-free.

I roast nuts without oil, for a long time in a fairly low oven, 325° to 350°F. I like the cleaner flavor of an unoiled nut, and it leaves them more versatile for adding to other dishes. Almonds get special treatment—brining in salted water before they're roasted (see page 30).

It's as important for a nut to be perfectly fresh as it is for a leaf of lettuce or sprig of basil. Nuts aren't as perishable as those delicate ingredients, but they don't have as long a shelf life as you may think. This means it's important to buy from a reputable vendor who has a high turnover. Bulk bins are fine when the store is well maintained and busy.

STORAGE When I buy large quantities, I store them in airtight containers in the refrigerator for up to a month or so. In the freezer they'll last longer, though not more than six months. Even frozen, nuts can slowly become rancid. You don't want to risk your whole dish by putting in even one nasty-tasting rancid nut. Use something heavier than a regular zip-top bag, because nuts—like all fatty ingredients—will absorb odors.

Dried Fruit

While dried fruit is a great snack, it finds its way into my cooking as well, in salads, salsas, vinaigrettes . . . anywhere I want a pop of bright sweet-tart flavor. I always have raisins, dried apricots, cranberries, figs, and dates on hand.

Before using dried fruit I rehydrate it in a bowl of water with a splash of vinegar (otherwise it can be too dense and chewy). The vinegar heightens its natural acidity and helps the flavor

blossom. Before soaking the fruit, cut it into whatever size you need.

I buy dried fruit in large quantities. As with nuts, it's good to buy it in the bulk sections of busy grocery stores. It's also good to check farmers' markets for dried fruit.

STORAGE Kept in airtight containers in a cool place, dried fruit will last and last. Most is treated with sulfur, which is why it has such a long life and keeps its color. If you're sensitive to sulfites, search out unsulfured fruit.

Preserved Fish

My larder shelves are always stocked with preserved fish in several forms: salt- or oil-packed anchovies, canned tuna, canned sardines, and salt cod. I add anchovies to salads, melt them in extra-virgin olive oil as a starter for pasta dishes, or add to marinades for grilling vegetables. A tube of anchovy paste is for when I'm lazy and just want to add a hit of umami, rather than full-frontal anchovy. Sardines and tuna on the shelf mean I can make quick pastas, dress a bowl of beans, make sauces, and top grilled breads. Salt cod is the only dried fish I use frequently; it requires advance prep, but once it's soaked and refreshed, I'll add it to soup, beans, or baked casserole dishes such as brandade.

Salt-packed anchovies are flavorful and meaty, but require attention. Packed in big tins in salt, they are the whole fish—bones, fins, and all. **To prep salt-packed anchovies**, gently prise a few out of the salt, rinse well, and soak for a few minutes until fully tender. Blot dry, then pinch a fillet at the tail end and gently pull the two sides apart. Lift off the spine and scrape away the guts, fins, or bits of bone. Lay on paper towels to dry completely, then use immediately or cover with olive oil and refrigerate. Cover the remaining fish in the tin with more of the salt, so they aren't exposed to air, and store in the fridge.

Salt cod also needs prep beginning a full day before it's used. **To prep salt cod**, rinse off surface salt, then soak in cool water for twenty-four hours, changing the water at least five times—you need to get rid of a lot of salt! Once the cod is de-salted, poach it gently in milk, broth, or water.

For salt-packed anchovies, I prefer those from the Italian company Scalia; for oil-packed I like Ortiz, a company in Spain. Matiz, another Spanish brand, produces beautiful, meaty sardines. You'll find these products at many good grocery stores and a number of online sources. My preference for tuna is naturally processed in its own juices, whether in a can or glass jar. I make sure the tuna comes from a sustainable fishery, as many tuna varieties are at risk of being overfished. Locally, that means albacore tuna caught off the Oregon and Washington coasts and packed by small fishing operations themselves. Wild Planet and American Tuna are widely distributed brands dedicated to sustainable tuna fishing. Salt cod can be seasonal, showing up at markets around Easter in particular. Italian markets are good sources.

STORAGE Canned ingredients are little miracles that can sit on your shelves indefinitely. Salt-packed anchovies need to be refrigerated once opened; be sure to cover exposed anchovies with salt. Salt cod often comes in a little wooden box; keep cool and dry.

Fish Sauce and Colatura

Fish sauce, an Asian condiment made from salted and fermented anchovy-type fish, is one of my all-time favorite flavors. It smells awful (don't spill it!), but the flavor of salty-sweet-umami elevates even the simplest dishes. Splash it into marinades, vinaigrettes, and killer dipping sauces for grilled meats and vegetables. (Make a batch of Spicy Fish-Sauce Sauce, page 43, and refrigerate at all times.) Red Boat is my go-to brand. It's made according to a 200-year-old artisanal process and is so nicely balanced. Three Crabs brand is also good.

Colatura di alici is an Italian fish sauce that's a bit more refined. It is pricey, but worth it. It's more concentrated than Asian fish sauce, so a little goes a long way. Used in a Caesar salad dressing, colatura can be life changing.

STORAGE Unopened bottles of fish sauce or colatura can last a couple of years in the cupboard. Once opened, they're best stored in the refrigerator. It's not a question of actual spoilage; refrigeration just keeps the flavor fresher. Use an opened bottle within a year.

Chiles: Dried, Pickled, and Preserved

Chiles are primarily a fruit, not just spicy fireballs, and their fruity, floral character is welcome in my cooking. My larder always has a few types of dried whole or ground chiles, pickled chiles, and oil-preserved chiles.

Of the dried chiles, chile de árbol is the most versatile. Dark red, two to three inches long, and warmly hot but not incendiary, árbols can be dropped whole into a pot of beans or a soup, or crushed and chopped into rough flakes, which I'll pinch and drop into pastas, soups, salads, dressings . . . pretty much anything but desserts. Crushed red pepper (dried chile flakes) from a store's spice aisle are a perfectly good substitute for home-chopped, and if you can find Aleppo pepper or piment d'Espelette, try them and experiment with their individual characters.

For cooked dishes, I "bloom" dried chile flakes in some olive oil during the first step of cooking, which softens them and coaxes out their flavors. For cold dishes such as salads, I sprinkle in chile flakes the way I use black pepper. Once you add acids such as lemon and vinegar, the chile flakes will also bloom and grow more dominant, so put in small amounts at first, and taste after a few minutes.

I do like to make pickled chiles, but I also use good old salad-bar pepperoncini. They bring tang and just a touch of heat to many of my dishes. Oil-packed Calabrian chiles, which are fiery crimson Italian chiles, are fantastic in very simple salsas, pastas, ragus, and stews. And they're dynamite in combination with nuts, breadcrumbs, and cheese. I also puree them and brush the puree on meats during grilling, or chop them up and toss them in vinaigrettes.

STORAGE Dried chiles will last in your cupboard in an airtight bag, but pantry moths like chiles, so for longer storage, pop them into a zip-top bag and freeze them. Opened jars of pickled or preserved chiles need to stay in the fridge.

Olives and Capers

I make quick salsas with smashed olives and capers to sluice over everything from raw vegetable salads to grilled and roasted meats. You can't beat classic brown butter with capers, parsley, and lemon. I'll also grab a mix of olives and infuse them with extra-virgin olive oil, fennel seed, coriander, dried chiles, citrus zest, and whatever else sounds good.

OLIVES

The big green Cerignola olives are mellow and sweet, while the black Cerignola are even sweeter. Castelvetranos are shockingly green, and they taste that way, almost crunchy, with a fruity, bright, clean flavor. Taggiasca are small dark olives, similar to Niçoise; they are well balanced, maybe the perfect olive, and often pressed into olive oil. The familiar Kalamata is deep, earthy, and a little more bitter than the others, yet still really versatile.

I prefer buying olives with their pits intact because I find it soothing to scoot out the pit by simply crushing one under my thumb or against the bottom of a small bowl. Hats off to the person who invented the olive bar at the grocery store; that's my go-to source for olives.

CAPERS

I prefer salt-packed capers to brined because you can taste more of the fruity, slightly vegetal caper and less of the brine. Salt-packed capers need nurturing to remove excess salt. Rinse and then soak in a few changes of cool water, tasting at each step until the salt balance is to your liking.

You'll sometimes find brined capers in grocery store olive bars, which is an economical way to buy them. Salt-packed capers are more often in the condiment aisle of a good grocery store, or you may buy them online.

STORAGE Store olives and capers in the refrigerator in their brine and they'll last for weeks. Salt-packed capers are happy to be on the shelf before being opened and in the fridge afterward.

Go-To Recipes

I use these recipes throughout the book to enhance, support, texturize, blend with, and otherwise collaborate with fresh vegetables to make wonderful dishes. A few hours spent cooking on a quiet Sunday will let you load your fridge or cupboard with some of these components, making executing an amazing midweek dinner both possible and fun. Many are also freezable, so you can consume them over time, but you'll find that most are so delightfully versatile that you'll easily incorporate them into meals. We share a few ideas to get you started.

CRUNCHY THINGS

Torn Croutons

There is no need to cut croutons into perfect little squares! Just tear the bread—it's easier and more fun, and most important, the croutons taste better because they have lots of raggedy edges that get crisp, and even slightly burnt. And stop cutting the crust off the loaf; the crust gives you more flavor, more texture.

What you don't want are hard croutons. You always want a little bit of chew in the center, not on every single one, but every third one at least; the lack of uniformity helps this. You also want the croutons to absorb the juices from vegetables, the extra-virgin olive oil, the vinaigrettes . . . All that flavor is carried into the crouton better through the torn edges.

» *Makes about 2 cups*

2 large, thick slices country loaf (about 4 ounces)

2 tablespoons extra-virgin olive oil

Kosher salt and freshly ground black pepper

Heat the oven to 400°F.

Tear the bread, crust and all, into bite-size pieces. Toss the torn bread with the olive oil and a light sprinkling of salt and pepper.

Spread the croutons on a baking sheet in a single layer and bake until golden brown, checking every 4 to 5 minutes and moving the outside croutons to the center of the pan so they cook evenly. Don't let them get rock hard; leave a little bit of chew in the center. The total baking time will depend on the type and density of bread you're using, but mostly likely will be 10 to 20 minutes.

Slide onto paper towels to absorb any extra oil and season again lightly with salt and pepper.

Store the croutons in an airtight container. (Be sure to make more than you need for your recipe because you'll find yourself eating these as a snack.)

Dried Breadcrumbs

I use breadcrumbs for extra texture and flavor. Make a big batch and store them in your pantry, ready to finish a pasta, salad, gratin . . . anything that wants a toasty crunch.

» Quantity is up to you

The better the bread, the better the crumbs; I like whole grain. Cut the bread into ½-inch-thick slices, leaving the crust on. Cut the slices into cubes and then spread them in an even layer on a baking sheet (or more than one pan, if making a lot; a 12-ounce loaf should fit onto one pan).

Heat the oven to its lowest setting, usually about 250°F. Bake the cubes until they are fully dry, but not browned. This could take an hour or more, depending on the bread's moisture and density.

Cool fully and then process into crumbs by pulsing in a food processor. The goal is small crumbs more or less the same size, though some bigger ones are fine—think Grape-Nuts. You want to avoid too much fine powder, however, so stop once or twice and pour off the finer crumbs or shake through a colander and then continue to crush the remaining big pieces.

Store the crumbs in an airtight container. If fully dry, they'll stay fresh for a few weeks.

Brined and Roasted Almonds

These are the best almonds ever, period. I learned to make these while working in Rome at the American Academy; it has become a staple in my pantry. You can easily scale up the quantities, but the more nuts, the more steam in the oven, and therefore the longer you'll need to cook them.

» Makes about 1½ cups

1 cup water

⅓ cup kosher salt

1½ cups raw skin-on almonds (8 ounces)

Bring the water to a boil in a saucepan. Add the salt and stir to dissolve. Add the almonds to the hot brine, remove from the heat, and let them soak for 30 minutes.

Heat the oven to 375°F.

Drain the almonds thoroughly and spread them evenly in a single layer on a baking sheet (use two sheets if you need to).

Roast until they are lightly toasted and fragrant, about 12 minutes. Take one out to test by biting into it—the interior should be a light brown, almost the color of a paper bag. The nuts will still be soft at this stage, but once completely cooled they will be very crunchy and nicely salty.

Store in an airtight container for up to 2 weeks (if you don't eat them all sooner).

Toasted Nuts and Seeds

You can toast nuts and seeds a number of ways—in the oven, in a dry skillet, with high heat or low heat (or brined and roasted; see opposite)—but in all cases, your goal is to go from raw, bland, and soft to fragrant and crunchy (pine nuts will stay slightly soft even when toasted). The color should be just a few shades darker than the raw nut or seed and should be even, not simply dark around the edges.

» *Quantity is up to you*

Heat the oven to 350°F.

Spread the nuts or seeds on a pan in a single layer. For a small quantity, a pie plate is good; for more, use a rimmed baking sheet.

Bake until you smell the nuttiness and the color is deepening slightly, 6 to 8 minutes for most whole nuts. Pine nuts will toast quickly, as will chopped or slivered nuts, and because of their small size, seeds cook the most quickly, so check early and often.

When the nuts or seeds are done, transfer them to a plate so they don't keep cooking on the hot baking pan. Determining doneness can be tricky, because the final texture won't develop until they're cool, so at this stage, you're mostly concerned with color and flavor. To be safe, take them from the oven, let cool, taste one, and if not done enough, pop them back into the oven.

Frico

Fricos are cheese crisps from the Friuli region of Italy. They're traditionally made with Montasio cheese, but I make them with Parmigiano-Reggiano. The cheese gets baked and then cooled, at which point it becomes very fragile and crisp. I like them simply in their flat, natural shape, but some people like to drape them over a rolling pin to give them a curved "tuile" shape. I'll add fricos to vegetable salads, either whole or broken into shards.

If you underbake the fricos, they will be more leathery than crisp. But of course if you overbake them, they'll be bitter, so pay close attention during the final minutes. If you have extra cheese, you could bake a test frico first. Have fun with them—just remember they shatter easily!

» *Makes 4 large lacy wafers*

1 cup freshly shredded Parmigiano-Reggiano cheese (if possible, use a rasp-style grater with large holes)

Heat the oven to 400°F. Line a baking sheet with a silicone baking mat or parchment paper, or use a nonstick baking sheet.

Mound the cheese in 4 evenly spaced piles. Using your finger or a fork, spread each pile out to a thin, even layer about 4 inches across.

Bake until the cheese has melted and is bubbling slightly and just starting to turn light brown, 6 to 9 minutes.

Remove from the oven and let cool for a few seconds to let the fricos set, then slide them off the baking sheet with a very thin spatula. Let them cool completely on a rack. You can make these ahead and store in an airtight tin, layered between paper towels.

MORE WAYS:

→ Serve as an accompaniment to a cheese course.

→ Break up and scatter on leafy salads.

→ Offer as a snack with Champagne.

Alla Diavola Butter

The Italians have a few dishes they refer to as alla diavola, which means "devil style"—in other words, spicy as hell. In this butter, I bring together layers of not just heat but all kinds of good chile and pepper flavors. You can adjust up or down, depending on how intense you like your heat.

» Makes 1 heaping cup

½ pound unsalted butter, at room temperature

1 tablespoon smoked paprika

1 tablespoon dried chile flakes

1 tablespoon cracked black pepper

½ teaspoon kosher salt

¼ cup finely chopped seeded pepperoncini (patted dry on paper towels after chopping)

1 tablespoon hot sauce, such as Tabasco

Fold all the ingredients together with a wooden spoon or rubber spatula and pile into whatever container you want to serve or save it in. Chill the butter for at least 1 hour to firm it up and to let the flavors marry and permeate the butter.

MORE WAYS:

→ Stuff in the center of a chicken breast and roast.

→ Swirl into a tomato soup.

→ Smear over grilled skirt or flank steak.

In the kitchen A neat option is to spoon the butter in a line onto a sheet of parchment or waxed paper and roll it into a neat cylinder. Wrap that up well in plastic or pop into a freezer bag and freeze until you're ready to use it. Then just slice off however much you need and keep the rest in the freezer.

At the market Smoked paprika is brilliant and should be in everyone's pantry. You'll find it in most well-stocked grocery stores now. It comes in sweet (*dulce*); semisweet, meaning medium hot (*agridulce*); and hot and spicy (*picante*).

Butters on a flank steak: Watercress, pickled vegetable, and mushroom

From left: Cacio e pepe, watercress, pickled vegetable, alla diavola, green garlic, and mushroom butters

Cacio e Pepe Butter

The inspiration for this butter comes from the classic Roman pasta dish of spaghetti with Pecorino Romano cheese and black pepper. I put those two ingredients—plus some Parmigiano to mellow the bite of the pecorino a bit—into a butter, which you can keep in your fridge for weeks. *Photograph on page 32*

» *Makes about 1½ cups*

2 tablespoons black peppercorns

¾ cup finely grated Pecorino Romano cheese

¾ cup finely grated Parmigiano-Reggiano cheese

½ pound unsalted butter, at room temperature

Put the peppercorns in a small skillet and toast over medium heat, shaking the pan or stirring constantly to toast the pepper evenly, just until you begin to smell a black pepper perfume, 2 to 3 minutes, depending on your skillet. Pour the pepper into another container and let cool completely.

Crack and grind the pepper, either in a spice grinder (or a coffee grinder you dedicate to spices) or with a mortar and pestle. It's nice to have uneven consistency, from fine to coarse.

Fold the pepper and both cheeses into the butter with a wooden spoon or rubber spatula and pile into whatever container you want to serve or save it in. Chill the butter for at least 1 hour to firm it up and to let the flavors marry and permeate the butter.

MORE WAYS:
→ Fold into hot brown rice or quinoa.
→ Drop a big spoonful onto pasta, spring peas, or smashed potatoes.
→ Toss with simple pasta, like spaghetti or angel hair.
→ Top a filet mignon.
→ Gild the top of an omelet with a slick of the butter.

Green Garlic Butter

Green garlic is the immature garlic plant before the bulb fully develops into separate cloves. It looks a lot like a thick scallion or spring onion, but the flavor is stronger and more, well, garlicky. You could make this same style of butter with garlic scapes (which are the curly green shoots that the garlic plant produces in early spring—catch them while they are still tender and young, or they'll be unpleasantly woody), scallions, or spring onions. *Photograph on page 32*

» *Makes about 1 cup*

½ pound unsalted butter, at room temperature

1 bunch green garlic (about 6 stalks), trimmed, including ½ inch off the green tops, cut crosswise into very thin slices

½ teaspoon kosher salt

Melt a spoonful of the butter in a skillet, add the sliced green garlic and the salt, and cook over medium-low heat. You want to soften both the texture and the intense flavor but you don't want to brown the garlic at all; this should take around 10 minutes.

Let cool and then fold this into the rest of the butter using a wooden spoon or rubber spatula, and pile into whatever container you want to serve or save it in. Chill the butter for at least 1 hour to firm it up and to let the flavors marry and permeate the butter.

MORE WAYS:
→ Serve with raw radishes and coarse salt.
→ Smear on good bread and toast to make the best garlic bread.
→ Toss with sautéed sugar snaps or snow peas.

Mushroom Butter

This butter is a bit more complicated than the other compound butters in this book, but it's a great use of mushroom stems. It's also a nice way to preserve an in-season wild mushroom. I make the basic version using the stems and trimmings from mushrooms, which makes it more economical. Stockpile the stems in the freezer until you're ready to use them in this butter or vegetable stocks. *Photograph on page 32*

» Makes 1 heaping cup

About 2 cups mushroom stems and trimmings, preferably wild mushrooms, wiped to remove any grit or debris

1 garlic clove, smashed and peeled

1 sprig thyme

½ pound unsalted butter, at room temperature

1 tablespoon finely chopped flat-leaf parsley

½ teaspoon minced fresh rosemary

¼ teaspoon dried chile flakes

½ teaspoon kosher salt

Put the mushrooms in a medium saucepan. Add the garlic, thyme, and water to cover by ½ inch. Bring to a simmer and cook until you sense that all the mushroom flavor has leached into the water (do a taste test), about 1 hour. Strain the mushroom cooking liquid into a bowl (discard the solids).

Return the mushroom liquid to the pan and simmer to reduce it to a glaze, about 2 tablespoons.

Cool the mushroom glaze and then blend it into the softened butter along with the parsley, rosemary, chile flakes, and salt, using a wooden spoon or rubber spatula, and pile into whatever container you want to serve or save it in. Chill the butter for at least 1 hour to firm it up and to let the flavors marry and permeate the butter.

Double-Mushroom Butter

To make the butter more mushroomy—and a fantastic topping for a steak—toss ½ pound mushrooms with a glug of olive oil and roast in a 400°F oven until they are shriveled and concentrated in flavor, about 20 minutes, depending on the size and moisture content of the mushrooms. Let cool and then finely chop (you should have about ½ cup). Fold that into the mushroom butter along with the mushroom glaze and seasonings.

MORE WAYS (FOR EITHER OF THE BUTTERS):

→ Use to scramble eggs, finish with fresh chives.

→ Spread on a grilled, sliced rib-eye steak.

→ Swirl into creamy polenta.

Pickled Vegetable Butter

Stay away from bread-and-butter pickles and the other basic cucumber-based pickles. Focus instead on a mix of vegetable pickles—such as carrots, green beans, fennel, radish, turnips, cauliflower, Brussels sprouts—which will give you more flavor and complexity. If you like heat, you can add some pickled peppers to the mix. *Photograph on page 32*

» Makes about 1½ cups

About 1 cup drained roughly chopped mixed pickled vegetables

½ pound unsalted butter, at room temperature

Drain the pickles and blot on paper towels. Put them in a food processor and pulse until fairly fine (you can do this with a knife if you like), but don't puree them.

Fold the chopped pickles into the softened butter using a wooden spoon or rubber spatula and pile into whatever container you want to serve or save it in. Chill the butter for at least

1 hour to firm it up and to let the flavors marry and permeate the butter.

MORE WAYS:
- → Pair with raw vegetables on a crudité platter.
- → Spread on the inside of your bread when making a grilled cheese sandwich.
- → Top a piece of steamed cod or halibut.

Watercress Butter

I like the peppery spice of watercress, but any herb or tender green with personality would be delicious in this type of compound butter. *Photograph on page 32*

» Makes about 1½ cups

3 garlic cloves, smashed and peeled

½ pound unsalted butter, at room temperature

1 teaspoon lightly packed grated lemon zest

1 big bunch watercress (about 2 ounces), dry ends trimmed, roughly chopped

Kosher salt

Put the garlic in a food processor and process until it's finely minced, stopping to scrape down the sides a couple of times.

Add the butter and lemon zest and pulse a couple of times to get the butter creamy. Don't pulse too much, however, because if you overprocess the butter it can separate.

Now add the watercress and a healthy pinch of salt and pulse again until the watercress is nicely incorporated—you'll still see flecks; it won't be completely pureed.

Taste and add more salt if you like, and pile into whatever container you want to serve or save

it in. Chill the butter for at least 1 hour to firm it up and to let the flavors marry and permeate the butter.

MORE WAYS:
- → Mash into potatoes.
- → Spread on bread for a chicken sandwich.
- → Swirl into a bean soup.

Brown Butter

Use this technique whenever you want to add a supernutty dimension to your butter, such as in crepes and pancakes, on fish, or as a final drizzle on a pureed vegetable soup. *Photograph on page 32*

» Makes as much as you want to make

Unsalted butter

Melt the butter in a small saucepan over medium heat. Keep cooking the butter, swirling the pan every few seconds, until all the water has evaporated, the milk solids on the bottom of the butter have turned deep gold, and the butter smells fragrant, 3 to 5 minutes—or more, depending on the amount of butter you use and the surface area of your pan.

Immediately (so the butter doesn't keep cooking) pour into another container. Some people decant off only the pure butterfat, but I like to include the toasted milk solids as well, unless I'm intending to use the butter as a cooking fat (in which case the solids would burn).

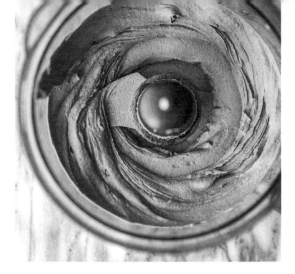

Pistachio Butter

This is a true nut butter—there's no dairy involved. When I worked at Lupa in New York City, we had a beet and pistachio butter salad that was famous—they could not take it off the menu for fear of riots. I've created my own version of that butter, and it's amazingly versatile. The flavor is super rich as is, but it's also really tasty with a squeeze of lime or lemon to cut through that richness.

» Makes 1 cup

1 cup (about 5 ounces) pistachios, lightly toasted (see page 31)

⅓ cup water

1 tablespoon red wine vinegar

1 teaspoon kosher salt

3 tablespoons extra-virgin olive oil

Process the pistachios in a food processor to get them as fine as possible. With the motor running, pour in the water, vinegar, and salt and process until smooth, scraping down the sides as needed.

Again with the motor running, drizzle in the olive oil. Taste and adjust with more salt or vinegar. Store in the fridge for up to 10 days.

MORE WAYS:

→ Pipe or spread onto celery sticks for an appetizer.

→ Smear on a plate and top with roasted root vegetables.

→ Drizzle over lamb meatballs, served on basmati rice.

Whipped Ricotta

Whipped ricotta is a spreadable flavor machine, incredible with tomato salads and perfect on the flatbreads in this book, either naked or topped with some wilted, sautéed, or roasted vegetables or greens. It keeps well, so store some in your fridge; you will always find ways to use it.

» Makes about 1½ cups

1½ cups whole-milk ricotta cheese

½ teaspoon kosher salt

Freshly ground black pepper

¼ cup extra-virgin olive oil, plus more as needed

Put the ricotta, salt, and 20 twists of pepper in a food processor and start to process. With the motor running, add the olive oil in a thin stream. Pause and scrape down the sides if needed. The mixture should get lovely and creamy. Taste it and adjust with more salt, pepper, or even a bit more olive oil—you should be able to taste the oil as well as the ricotta. Store in the fridge for up to 1 week.

Whipped Feta

Use the same process with feta cheese, adding 2 tablespoons lemon juice and a touch more olive oil. Adjust the texture and flavor with more oil and lemon.

MORE WAYS (FOR EITHER VERSION):

→ Spread on good bread and top with something savory: anchovies, peperonata, salsa verde.

→ Use as a dip for grilled vegetables.

Caper-Raisin Vinaigrette

This recipe is adapted from *Mr. Wilkinson's Vegetables* by Matt Wilkinson, a chef based in Melbourne, Australia. It's magically great with many things, in particular turnips, asparagus, broccoli, and cauliflower. Keep some around at all times; you won't have a problem finding things to do with it. *Photograph opposite*

» *Makes about ¾ cup*

2 tablespoons plus 1 teaspoon balsamic vinegar

⅓ cup golden raisins

3 garlic cloves, peeled

3 tablespoons capers, rinsed and drained

One 2-ounce can anchovy fillets, drained

¾ cup lightly packed flat-leaf parsley leaves

⅓ cup extra-virgin olive oil

Kosher salt

Put the vinegar and raisins in a little bowl and let the raisins plump for about 30 minutes.

Put the garlic in a food processor and pulse until finely minced, scraping down the sides of the bowl as needed.

Add the capers and anchovies and pulse until you have a coarse paste. Add the parsley and pulse until completely chopped, again scraping down the sides of the bowl as necessary.

Add the raisins and vinegar and pulse until the mixture is blended but still slightly coarse. Scrape

From left to right, top to bottom:
Caper-Raisin Vinaigrette, Pine Nut Vinaigrette, Green Herb Mayonnaise, Artichoke Mayonnaise, Pickled Vegetable Mayonnaise, Spicy Fish-Sauce Sauce, Salsa Verde, Spiced Green Sauce, and Tonnato

the mixture from the processor into a bowl and whisk in the olive oil to make a slightly chunky dressing. Taste and adjust with salt or more oil, if needed. Store in the fridge for up to 3 weeks.

MORE WAYS:
→ Spoon over grilled eggplant slices.
→ Fold into ratatouille.
→ Toss with steamed broccoli or broccoli rabe.

Pancetta Vinaigrette

This dressing is wonderful when served warm over sturdy greens, such as frisée or escarole, and it's also fantastic on anything starchy, such as boiled smashed potatoes or shell beans. Dress a tomato and butter lettuce salad with it, and you've got a BLT on a plate. *Photograph on page 40*

» *Makes about 1 cup*

Extra-virgin olive oil

3 ounces pancetta, finely chopped

3 scallions, trimmed (including ½ inch off the green tops), thinly sliced

2 garlic cloves, finely minced

¼ cup red wine vinegar

Kosher salt and freshly ground black pepper

Put a small glug of olive oil in a small skillet over medium heat, add the pancetta, and cook it slowly, stirring often, until the fat is rendered out and the pancetta is barely crisp, 7 to 9 minutes.

Take the pan from the heat and when the oil stops sizzling, add the scallions and garlic. Stir for a few minutes to soften the scallions.

Whisk in the vinegar, season with salt and pepper, and then whisk in ¼ cup olive oil. Taste the dressing and add more oil, salt, or pepper. It should be sharp, but it shouldn't make you cough.

You can store this in the refrigerator for a few weeks; the fat will solidify on the top. To use, let it sit at room temperature until the fat melts, then give a quick stir to blend the ingredients again.

MORE WAYS:
- → Update Lyonnaise salad, with frisée and a poached egg.
- → Sauté pork cutlets and deglaze the pan with the vinaigrette.
- → Toss with warm pinto beans and chunks of tomato.

Pine Nut Vinaigrette

This is an old recipe from my days at Franny's, a restaurant in Brooklyn where I worked for several years. It's such an incredibly tasty yet simple vinaigrette—my Italian version of an Asian peanut sauce, perhaps. The sauce packs a lot of flavor, so go easy with it when you're dressing your vegetables or greens. You can always thin it out with a little fresh lemon or lime juice to add more punch. *Photograph on page 38*

» Makes 1 cup

¼ cup red wine vinegar

1 tablespoon fish sauce

2 tablespoons water

4 ounces pine nuts, lightly toasted (page 31)

½ garlic clove, smashed and peeled

½ teaspoon dried chile flakes

¼ cup extra-virgin olive oil

Pour the vinegar, fish sauce, and water into a small bowl or cup.

Put the pine nuts, garlic, chile flakes, and about half the vinegar mixture into a food processor and process until you have a slightly smooth puree, scraping down the sides of the bowl as needed. With the motor running, drizzle in the olive oil and then the rest of the vinegar mixture. The ingredients should emulsify into a creamy, thick-but-pourable dressing.

Taste (watch out for the blade!) and adjust the flavors with more vinegar, fish sauce, or chile flakes. Adjust the consistency with more water if need be.

Store in the fridge for up to 1 week.

MORE WAYS:
- → Smear on a platter and top with roasted or grilled asparagus or broccoli.
- → Toss with grated carrots.
- → Drizzle on sautéed corn kernels.

MORE WAYS:

→ Dress a salad of shaved fennel and thinly sliced celery.

→ Drizzle over sautéed or grilled shrimp.

→ Toss with roasted beets and chopped walnuts.

In the kitchen Wake up this dressing, or any vinaigrette that's been in the fridge for more than a day or two, with a bit of fresh lemon, lime, or orange juice and another tiny pinch of salt.

Citrus Vinaigrette

Make this dressing with blood oranges when they are in season. The dressing is delicious cold, or you can gently warm it. It lasts forever in the refrigerator. Use it with leaf salads, root vegetables, celery, broccoli—the entire brassica family, really—plus asparagus, peas, snap peas, fennel, seafood, grain-based salads . . . shall I go on? *Photograph above*

» *Makes about 1½ cups*

1 orange	1 tablespoon Champagne vinegar or white wine vinegar
1 lemon	
1 lime	Kosher salt and freshly ground black pepper
1½ tablespoons honey	
	¾ cup extra-virgin olive oil

Using a rasp-style grater, zest all the citrus into a bowl. Halve the fruit and squeeze all the juice into the same bowl to get ⅔ cup juice (fish out the seeds). Whisk in the honey, vinegar, 1 teaspoon salt, and several twists of pepper.

Taste and adjust with more honey, vinegar, and salt and pepper, if needed, to make the flavor vibrant. Whisk in the olive oil a few drops at a time or put the juice mixture into a blender or food processor and drizzle in the oil while the machine is running; the machine method will make the vinaigrette creamier and emulsified.

Store in the fridge for up to 2 weeks.

Lemon Cream

This is a light, almost feminine dressing that is beautiful on a simple spring lettuce salad, but also on other green vegetables.

» *Makes ¾ cup*

4 garlic cloves, smashed and peeled	½ teaspoon grated lemon zest
½ cup heavy cream	About 2 tablespoons fresh lemon juice
Kosher salt and freshly ground black pepper	2 tablespoons extra-virgin olive oil

Put the garlic and cream in a medium bowl and let infuse for 2 hours in the refrigerator, so the cream takes on a gentle garlic flavor.

Fish out the garlic cloves from the cream, season generously with salt and lots of twists of pepper, and then add the lemon zest. Begin whisking the cream. Once it starts to thicken, add 2 tablespoons lemon juice and the olive oil. Keep whisking until it is light and airy. It won't be thick like fully whipped cream, but it will have a nice creamy texture. Taste and adjust with more salt, pepper, or lemon juice. Use this dressing within a day.

MORE WAYS:

→ Dress any type of green salad.

→ Drizzle over cold poached shrimp or scallops.

→ Toss with thinly sliced cucumbers.

Green Herb Mayonnaise

I do love a pure from-scratch mayonnaise, but they can be runny and they use up a lot of olive oil. Starting with good-quality store-bought mayo and then freshening up the flavor with a yolk and some oil is a fine compromise, and a time-saver. You can use whatever mix of fresh herbs you like—this is just a suggestion. *Photograph on page 38*

» *Makes about 1 ½ cups*

1 small handful flat-leaf parsley leaves and tender stems

1 small handful basil leaves

Healthy pinch of mint leaves

Healthy pinch of tarragon leaves

Healthy pinch of dill fronds

1 cup Hellmann's or Best Foods mayonnaise

1 egg yolk

1 teaspoon fresh lemon juice

½ teaspoon kosher salt

Freshly ground black pepper

¼ cup extra-virgin olive oil

Put the parsley, basil, mint, tarragon, and dill in a food processor and pulse 3 or 4 times to partially chop. Add the mayonnaise and pulse a few more times to blend. Pulse in the egg yolk, lemon juice, salt, and several twists of pepper, then, with the motor running, drizzle in the olive oil and process until the mayo is creamy and fluffy, scraping down the sides of the bowl as needed. Taste (watch the blade!) and adjust with more salt, pepper, or lemon juice. Store in the fridge for up to 2 weeks.

MORE WAYS:

→ Fold with boiled diced potatoes for potato salad.
→ Mix with shredded rotisserie chicken and roll up into a wrap sandwich.
→ Use instead of plain mayo when making a tuna sandwich.

Artichoke Mayonnaise

I love the flavor of artichokes and mayonnaise, but to be honest, I wouldn't bother prepping and cooking fresh artichokes just for this! Using a good-quality artichoke heart from a jar is a good idea. *Photograph on page 38*

» *Makes about 2 cups*

6 artichoke hearts (it's totally fine to use the ones in a jar, but drain them well)

1 small handful fresh basil leaves

6 medium fresh mint leaves

1 cup Hellmann's or Best Foods mayonnaise

1 egg yolk

About 1 tablespoon fresh lemon juice

½ teaspoon kosher salt

Freshly ground black pepper

¼ cup extra-virgin olive oil

Put the artichoke hearts, basil, and mint in a food processor and pulse 3 or 4 times to partially chop. Add the mayonnaise and pulse a few more times to blend. Pulse in the egg yolk, lemon juice, salt, and several twists of pepper, then, with the motor running, drizzle in the olive oil and process until the mayo is creamy and fluffy, scraping down the sides of the bowl as needed. Taste (watch the blade!) and adjust with more salt, pepper, or lemon juice. Store in the fridge for up to 2 weeks.

MORE WAYS:

→ Spread on good white bread and top with sliced spring onions for a new version of James Beard's favorite sandwich.
→ Sprinkle with Parmigiano and breadcrumbs, broil, and use as a hot dip for potato chips.
→ Spread on fish fillets and bake in a hot oven.

Pickled Vegetable Mayonnaise

The more, the merrier when it comes to adding pickles to this mayonnaise. Aim for a mix of colors and flavors. I don't usually use cucumber pickles, such as dill or bread-and-butter, but no harm in including a few if you like them.
Photograph on page 38

» Makes 2 heaping cups

1 cup Hellmann's or Best Foods mayonnaise

1 egg yolk

1 teaspoon finely grated lemon zest

About 1 tablespoon fresh lemon juice

¼ cup extra-virgin olive oil

1 cup chopped mixed pickled vegetables

1 tablespoon capers, rinsed and drained, roughly chopped

Kosher salt and freshly ground black pepper

Put the mayonnaise, egg yolk, lemon zest, and lemon juice in a food processor and pulse a few times to blend. With the motor is running, drizzle in the olive oil and process until the mayo is creamy and fluffy. Add the chopped pickles and capers and pulse just a couple of times to blend—you want to keep this quite chunky, like chunky tartar sauce. Taste (watch the blade!) and adjust with salt, pepper, or lemon juice. Store in the fridge for up to 2 weeks.

MORE WAYS:

→ Serve with fried fish instead of tartar sauce.

→ Slather it on good rye bread for a roast beef sandwich.

→ Blend into egg yolks for the best deviled eggs.

Spicy Fish-Sauce Sauce

When I lived in New York, a group of us chefs used to go to Queens to eat at SriPraPhai, a Thai restaurant where they serve a fried watercress salad dressed in a spicy, garlicky Thai fish sauce dressing. That dish made a big impression on me. I use Red Boat fish sauce, which is delicious and affordable, and it feels to me more artisan-made than mass-produced.
Photograph on page 38

» Makes about 1¼ cups

¼ cup seeded, deribbed, and minced fresh hot chiles (use a mix of colors)

4 large garlic cloves, minced

½ cup fish sauce

¼ cup water

¼ white wine vinegar

2 tablespoons sugar

Stir everything together in a small bowl until the sugar dissolves. Taste and adjust so you have an intense sweet-salty-sour-hot balance. Ideally, make this a day ahead, then taste and readjust the seasonings on the second day. The chile heat is likely to get stronger. The sauce will keep for a month or two in the fridge.

MORE WAYS:

→ Sprinkle over grilled fish or vegetables.

→ Use as a dip for salad rolls or lettuce wraps.

→ Mix with a touch of oil and marinate firm tofu to be grilled.

Classic Salsa Verde and a Couple of Variations

From an Italian perspective, a proper *salsa verde* should have just enough oil to bind and moisten the herbs but not so much that it pools out. Once you add the acid and salt, the herbs begin to "cook," so if you're making this ahead for a party, make the base, but don't add the lemon and salt until just before serving.
I love the classic version and often serve it just as is, but think of it also as a launch pad for other variations. *Photograph on page 38*

» Makes about 1½ cups

CLASSIC

1 bunch flat-leaf parsley, thick stems trimmed off and reserved, leaves chopped medium fine	1 lemon
	2 tablespoons capers, rinsed, drained, and chopped
1 bunch scallions, trimmed (including ½ inch off the green tops), thinly sliced	Freshly ground black pepper
½ cup extra-virgin olive oil	Kosher salt

Measure out half the parsley stems (compost the others or save for another use), trim off the dried end bits of the stems, and very finely slice them, as you would chives.

Put the parsley stems and leaves and scallions in a small bowl and pour in the olive oil.

Grate the lemon zest into the bowl, add the capers, and season generously with pepper. When you're ready to serve, halve the lemon and squeeze over about 2 tablespoons lemon juice. Season with salt.

Salsa verde is best eaten within a day, but it will keep for up to 3 days in the fridge.

Pickle Salsa Verde

Make the classic and fold in ¼ cup finely chopped pickled vegetables (such as carrots) along with 2 finely chopped Peppadews (sweet-hot pickled peppers).

Radish and Mint Salsa Verde

Make the classic and fold in 3 very finely sliced radishes and ½ cup chopped fresh mint.

MORE WAYS (FOR ANY OF THE VERSIONS):

→ Spoon over slices of roast pork, warm or cold.

→ Drizzle over steamed potatoes.

→ Serve with rich fish, such as salmon and tuna.

Spiced Green Sauce

This delicious sauce is similar to a classic Middle Eastern *skhug*, with its sweet spices and chile pepper. My friend chef Samuel Smith developed this recipe at Ava Gene's, where we use it on vegetables, grilled meats, and snacks of all kinds. It is a workhorse recipe, and you will find countless ways to use it in your own kitchen. To lower the chile heat, use milder chiles such as poblano or Anaheim. *Photograph on page 38*

» Makes 1 cup

½ teaspoon coriander seeds	2 cups lightly packed cilantro leaves
1 teaspoon cumin seeds	2 cups lightly packed flat-leaf parsley leaves
Seeds from 4 green or black cardamom pods	A pinch of ground cloves
½ cup deribbed, seeded, and roughly chopped fresh hot green chiles, such as serrano (2 to 4)	1 teaspoon finely grated lemon zest
	About 1 tablespoon fresh lemon juice
1 to 3 garlic cloves (to taste), smashed and peeled	Kosher salt and freshly ground black pepper
	½ cup extra-virgin olive oil

Put the coriander, cumin, and cardamom seeds into a dry skillet. Toast the spices lightly over medium heat, shaking the pan frequently, just until they become fragrant, about 4 minutes. Dump them out of the skillet onto a plate to cool, then grind finely in a spice grinder or with a mortar and pestle.

Put the chiles and garlic in a food processor and pulse a few times until they are fairly fine. Add the cilantro, parsley, toasted seeds, ground cloves, lemon zest, lemon juice, 1 teaspoon kosher salt, and a few twists of black pepper. Pulse until all is finely chopped into a rough puree. With the motor running, drizzle in the olive oil. Stop the processor before the sauce is completely blended and smooth—you want a slightly "bitty" texture.

Taste the sauce (be careful of the blade!) and adjust the seasoning with more salt, black pepper, lemon juice, or any of the spices—though show restraint with the spices because they can get overwhelming. Store in the refrigerator for up to 1 week.

MORE WAYS:

→ Season a pocket sandwich with pita bread and sliced leg of lamb.

→ Spread on grilled flatbreads as they come off the grill.

→ Drizzle over roasted red peppers, top with crumbled feta.

At the market For good chile flavor but not so much of the heat, choose an Anaheim or poblano chile rather than the quite spicy serrano or jalapeño.

Tonnato

Tonnato sauce is truly Italian, but you'll recognize the flavors from the tuna sandwiches of your youth. The sauce works so well with so many vegetables, from raw to grilled to pickled. *Photograph on page 38*

» Makes about 1½ cups

Two 5-ounce cans oil-packed tuna, drained

¼ teaspoon kosher salt

About ⅓ cup good-quality mayonnaise (such as Hellmann's or Best Foods)

¼ cup extra-virgin olive oil

About 1 tablespoon fresh lemon juice

Put the tuna and salt in a food processor and pulse until it's blended. Add ⅓ cup mayonnaise and pulse until the ingredients are getting creamy. With the processor running, drizzle in the olive oil and lemon juice and process until the tonnato is very smooth and creamy.

Taste and add more mayonnaise, olive oil, lemon juice, or salt. Store in the fridge for up to 1 week.

MORE WAYS:

→ Use as a dip for any raw, grilled, or roasted vegetables.

→ Spread on slices of cold roast pork or veal.

→ Thin it out with more lemon juice and toss with boiled and smashed new potatoes or add it to a romaine salad.

→ Spoon it on bread and top it with Soft-Cooked Eggs (page 52), tomatoes, and capers.

→ Use it in my charred broccoli dish on page 183.

Whole-Grain Carta di Musica

Carta di musica is a Sardinian flatbread whose name translates to "sheet of music," presumably because they are both thin and brittle. We make it at the restaurant every day, and we've found several nontraditional uses for it. The flatbread is addictive, super simple, and fun to make. Several recipes in this book use it, but you'll find so many things to put on it—even just olive oil and flaky salt is fantastic. If you can't find (or don't want to buy the small amount of) rye flour, just use more whole wheat.

» Makes 12 large crackers

1¾ cups (8 ounces by weight) whole wheat flour, plus a bit more for shaping

¼ cup (1 ounce by weight) light rye flour

¾ cup (4 ounces by weight) semolina

1½ teaspoons kosher salt

1 cup water

¼ cup extra-virgin olive oil

Heat the oven to 450°F. Place your heaviest baking sheet in the oven to preheat. If you have a pizza stone, this is a perfect use for it.

Mix the whole wheat flour, rye flour, semolina, and salt in a big bowl and whisk until everything's blended. Stir together the water and oil. Slowly add the liquid to the dry ingredients while you stir; you want to end up with a soft dough.

Scoop the dough onto the work surface and gently knead so that it comes together into a smoother ball of dough. Don't knead aggressively, use a gentle pressure, and only work it for a minute or two. If it feels really sticky, work in a bit more whole wheat flour.

Roll the dough into a fat log and cut it into 12 equal portions. Cup your hand on top of one piece and move it in tight circles against the countertop, which should shape the piece into a tidy ball.

Cover the dough balls with a kitchen towel. You'll work, shape, and bake only one at a time, because they bake so quickly.

Press a dough ball into as large a round as you can (don't worry about making the shape perfect—what's important here is to aim for an even thickness). Sometimes the dough is easiest to work on an unfloured counter, but if it's sticking for you, then lightly dust the work surface.

Take a rolling pin and continue working the round so it is as thin as you can get it. After every few strokes, gently slide your outspread fingers underneath to release the round from the counter and to ease and stretch it bigger.

Watch out for very thin spots, which will burn (though a few charred spots are just fine). You can press together any holes that may form. Shaping the crackers will take a bit of practice, so count on the first couple being not great. The ingredients aren't very expensive, so relax and enjoy the process, and if you have to make another batch of dough, so be it.

When you've rolled out one round, carefully take the heated baking sheet from the oven and set it down. Lift the dough round and lay it on the baking sheet. Don't worry if you have a few tiny pleats.

Pop the sheet back into the oven and bake the cracker until you see that the bottom is browning nicely and the dough is puffing up a bit, 1 to 2 minutes. With tongs, flip the cracker and cook until the second side is browned.

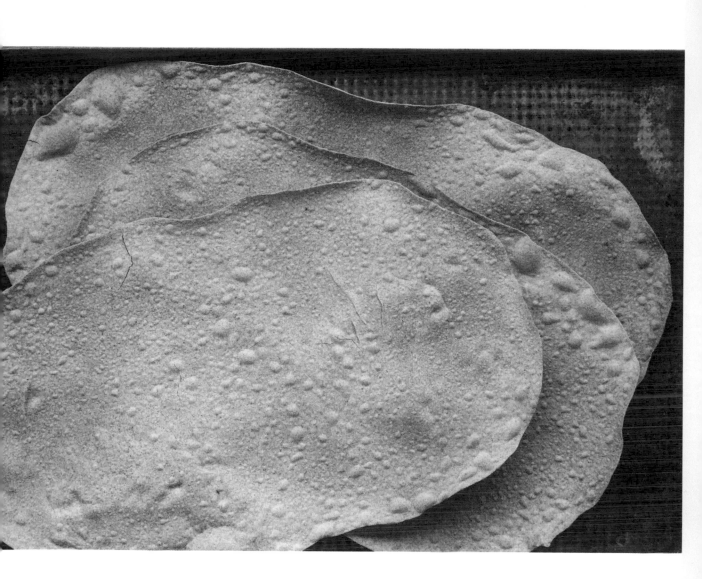

You want as even a browning as possible, but you'll likely get darker and lighter spots, which is okay. It's better to have a few burned spots than to have portions of the cracker that are too pale, because they will not be crisp. Remove the cracker from the oven and cool on a rack. The first side will always be the most attractive.

Put the baking sheet back in the oven while you roll out the next cracker. This explanation makes the process seem tricky and a hassle, but once you do it a couple of times, it becomes a lot of fun and you'll feel like a genius because the breads are so thin and crisp.

The crackers will stay crisp for a couple of days, either just on the counter or, if you're in a humid area, in an airtight container.

In the kitchen To transfer fragile doughs from work surface to baking pan, place your rolling pin on one edge of your dough round and carefully roll up the dough onto the pin. Position the pin so you're right over the hot baking sheet and quickly unroll onto it. Don't worry if you have a few tiny pleats.

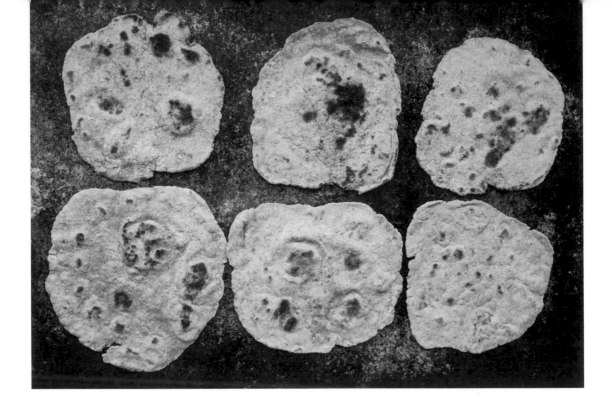

Slightly Tangy Flatbreads

This recipe is easy, quick, and perfect to make for a party—you can set your dinner table with vegetable dishes and sauces and then keep the flatbreads coming to the table hot off the griddle as everyone is enjoying the food. These are definitely better freshly cooked; if you need to reheat some, I would brush with olive oil and heat in a hot oven, to get them slightly crisp around the edges.

» Makes 6

1 cup (4.5 ounces by weight) unbleached all-purpose flour, plus more for dusting

1 cup (4.5 ounces by weight) whole wheat flour

2 teaspoons kosher salt

½ teaspoon sugar

½ teaspoon baking powder

1 cup plain whole-milk or low-fat yogurt (not Greek), plus more if needed

Put the all-purpose flour, whole wheat flour, salt, sugar, and baking powder in a large bowl and whisk to blend everything well. Make a well in the center of the bowl and add the yogurt. Mix the flour into the yogurt a little bit at a time, using your hands or a rubber spatula to blend. If the dough seems dry, add another small spoonful of yogurt.

When the flour is mostly all mixed with the yogurt, dump the dough onto a flour-dusted work surface and knead it gently until smooth, about 30 seconds. Cut it into 6 equal portions. Using a rolling pin and your hands, shape each portion to a nice round about ⅛ inch thick; don't worry if the shapes are not perfect.

Heat a dry cast-iron skillet or griddle until it is super hot. Add the flatbreads, one or two at a time, depending on the size of your pan, and cook until slightly puffy and lightly browned and freckled with some charred spots, about 1 minute on each side. It's better to overcook these than to undercook them, which would leave them doughy and heavy. Reduce the heat a touch if you find the breads are charring before the interiors are cooked; wipe out the inside of the pan between batches to remove any burned flour.

Let cool on a rack. These are best eaten within an hour or two of cooking.

Pecan Dough

This is a rich dough, meaning it has a high butter-to-flour ratio. That makes it a touch tricky to roll, as do the nuts, but the final crust is so delicious that it's worth the tiny bit of fuss. You can substitute any nut for the pecan, in the same amount. The dough freezes well, too, so make a double batch and keep one in the freezer; it will stay perfect for 3 months or longer. Let frozen dough thaw overnight in the fridge.

» Makes enough for one 9-inch single-crust pie

½ cup pecans

1⅔ cups (7.25 ounces by weight) unbleached all-purpose flour, plus more for dusting

¼ cup plus 1 tablespoon sugar

1 teaspoon kosher salt

4 ounces very cold unsalted butter, cut into 8 pieces

2 tablespoons very cold water

Put the pecans in a food processor and pulse until they are very fine and uniform, though not to the point of pecan butter. Add the flour, sugar, and salt and pulse a few times to blend. Add the butter and pulse again until the largest piece is the size of a small pea.

With the processor running, drizzle in the water and process until the mixture climbs up the sides of the processor. Remove the top and squeeze a big pinch of the dough to see whether it's still dry and crumbly or holds together and feels moist. If it is dry, pulse in a few more drops of water.

When the dough is the right consistency, dump it on a lightly floured counter and gather it into a ball. Push the dough away from you with the heel of your hand and then with a dough scraper or thin spatula, scrape it back into a ball. Repeat for a few strokes until the dough starts to come together. Don't overwork it; it's okay if it's still slightly crumbly. Shape it into a flat disk. Wrap in plastic and chill for about 30 minutes; if you chill it longer, leave at room temperature for a few minutes before rolling, to avoid cracking.

Store in the fridge for up to 2 days; freeze for up to 3 months.

Very Flaky Pastry Dough

I like this dough for savory pies and galettes; it's easy to work with yet still rich and buttery. Make a double batch and keep half in the freezer for up to 3 months.

» Makes enough for one 9-inch tart (or 8 hand pies; see page 338)

4 ounces unsalted butter, cut into ½-inch cubes

1½ cups (6.75 ounces by weight) unbleached all-purpose flour, plus more for dusting

½ teaspoon kosher salt

¼ cup ice water

Spread the butter cubes on a plate and freeze for about 15 minutes. They should be very cold but not rock hard.

MIXER METHOD: Combine the flour, salt, and butter in a stand mixer fitted with the paddle. Mix on low speed until the butter cubes are smashed up a bit and the chunks are about half their original size; don't worry if the chunks aren't uniform. With the mixer running, slowly pour about half the ice water into the flour and butter and mix just until the dough barely holds together; it will look quite shaggy. Take a big pinch and give it a squeeze. If it all holds together nicely and there's barely any loose flour in the bowl, no need for more water. If it feels dry and powdery, add more water a few drops at a time; depending on your flour, you may need to add a bit more than the ¼ cup.

HAND METHOD: Toss the flour, salt, and butter in a wide bowl and cut the butter into smaller pieces with a dough scraper (also called a bench scraper) or a table knife. Pinch and press the mixture with your fingers to encourage the butter to form flattened pieces. Gradually add about half the ice water as you toss the flour mixture with a fork to evenly distribute the liquid. Don't add all the liquid until you're sure you need it. Test by taking a big pinch and giving it a squeeze. If it all holds together nicely and there's barely any loose flour in the bowl, no need for more water. If it feels dry and powdery, add more water just a few drops at a time; depending on your flour, you may need to add a bit more than the ¼ cup.

FOR BOTH METHODS: Dump the dough onto a floured counter and shape it into a mound. Using the heel of your hand, press the mound to flatten a bit, pushing away from you slightly to smear the pieces of butter into the flour. With a dough scraper (bench scraper), scoop up an edge of the mound, fold it on top of itself, and continue pressing and smearing. You're basically kneading the dough to make it more workable but you're keeping larger layers of butter intact, which will make the dough very flaky. Continue 5 or 6 more rounds of pressing, smearing, and folding, until the dough no longer feels shaggy and is smooth but not sticky. If the dough is soft at this point, wrap in plastic and chill for 20 to 40 minutes. You can make the dough ahead and freeze it well wrapped for up to 3 months. Thaw overnight in the refrigerator before rolling.

Farro

You don't have to toast farro before you cook it, but I know that once you've tasted farro made with this toasting method, you'll never look back. This basic method calls for 3 to 5 minutes of toasting, but if you're patient and have some time, you can toast the farro even more deeply. Stir constantly and keep an eye on it; this will only intensify the flavor.

» Makes about 2 cups

Extra-virgin olive oil	1 cup farro
2 garlic cloves, smashed and peeled	4 cups water
	1 bay leaf
½ teaspoon dried chile flakes	2 teaspoons kosher salt

Put a nice glug of olive oil into a large skillet that has a lid and heat over medium heat. Add the smashed garlic and chile flakes and cook slowly to toast the garlic so it's beginning to get soft, fragrant, and nicely golden brown, about 3 minutes.

Add the farro and cook over medium heat, stirring more or less constantly so the grains toast evenly, for 3 to 5 minutes. They will darken slightly and become quite fragrant.

Add the water, bay leaf, and salt and bring to a boil. Cover, adjust the heat to a nice simmer, and cook until the farro is tender but not so much that it has "exploded" and popped fully open—it will be mushy if cooked that long. Depending on your farro, this could take 15 to 30 minutes or even a bit longer.

Drain the farro well. If you're using the farro warm, you're all set. If you want to use it cold, such as in a salad, dump it onto a baking sheet, toss with a tablespoon of olive oil, and spread it out to cool.

Freekeh

Freekeh is a form of wheat that is eaten usually as a whole grain, like a wheat berry, though some cuisines dry and crack it, more like bulgur. The cool thing about freekeh is that it's toasted by actually burning it. The traditional method of producing it is to harvest winter wheat while it's still slightly green or immature, and then burn the stalks in the field to burn off the chaff and release the grain within. You're left with a sweet and nutty grain with a sexy, subtle smoke flavor.

» Makes 3 cups

1 cup freekeh	1 bay leaf (optional)
Kosher salt	1 dried chile (optional)

Put the freekeh in a saucepan and add water to cover by about 2 inches. Bring to a boil and add 1 teaspoon salt. Add the bay leaf and chile (if using). Cover the pan and adjust the heat to a slow simmer.

Figuring out doneness requires a bit of patience, because different batches of grain cook at different rates. Start tasting around 20 minutes and keep tasting, adding a touch more salt if needed, until you have a chewy but not crunchy texture.

Drain in a sieve and either use the freekeh warm right away, or toss it with a small glug of olive oil, spread it on a baking sheet, and let it cool to room temperature.

Couscous

Couscous isn't a grain, but because its shape is sort of "grainy," it's often served as such. Couscous is really pasta—tiny little balls of dried flour and water (though traditional North African couscous is actually tiny grains, similar to cracked wheat). So-called Israeli or pearl couscous, with much bigger, peppercorn-size grains, is available in a lot of markets now.

FINE COUSCOUS: The best way to cook fine couscous is by absorption: Put dry couscous, an equal amount of boiling water (cup for cup), and ½ teaspoon kosher salt per cup of couscous into a bowl or saucepan. Cover and let it sit for 5 to 10 minutes so the couscous can absorb the liquid. Fluff it with a fork and season with more salt, if needed, black pepper, and a glug of olive oil or some butter.

LARGER COUSCOUS: Cook it like pasta by boiling it in generously salted water and then draining well, like a regular pasta noodle.

At the market A cool substitute for Israeli couscous is fregola, a Sardinian version that's toasted and full of flavor with a more rustic texture.

Batter for Fried Vegetables

This batter is quick to make and produces a very light coating, perfect for allowing vegetable colors and flavors to come through.

» Makes enough for about 1 pound vegetables

½ cup cornstarch

½ cup all-purpose flour

¼ teaspoon dried chile flakes

Kosher salt and freshly ground black pepper

About 1 cup sparkling water

Whisk together the cornstarch, flour, chile flakes, and a generous amount of salt and black pepper. Whisk in enough sparkling water to make a batter the consistency of thin pancake batter. Use the batter within an hour or two.

Soft-Cooked Eggs

Soft-cooked eggs are ideal for salads—the white is tender and the yolk is creamy and still slightly runny—perfect for coating other ingredients in the dish. While working on this book, we learned from friend and cookbook author Andrea Slonecker a brilliant way to cook the eggs so you get the best textural result and the eggs are easy to peel—the peeling part always being a challenge. Andrea surmises that the shock of the already boiling water helps separate the membrane from the shell.

» Makes as many as you want

Leave the eggs on the counter until they are at room temperature. Bring a pan of water to a boil and adjust the heat so the water is still boiling but not raucously. Gently lower the eggs into the water. Boil for 6 minutes. Transfer the eggs to a bowl of ice water. Leave until either just cool enough to handle, if you'd like to use them while still warm, or until cold.

Peel immediately if using right away, or leave in their shells in the refrigerator until you're ready to use, preferably within 1 day.

Smashing Garlic

I use a lot of garlic and I often call for a "garlic clove, smashed and peeled." To smash, put the garlic clove on the work surface and either with the flat side of your chef's knife, a mallet, or a heavy saucepan, give it a sharp blow. This will do three things: First, it will crush the papery skin that clings tightly to the clove, making it much easier to peel away. Second, it sets up the clove for maximum flavor release· When that smashed garlic gets toasted in some olive oil, the increased surface area of the garlic infuses the oil with more flavor. And third, if you're going to chop or mince the garlic, a smashed clove is much easier to chop through because it's flatter.

Toasting Garlic

You'll see in this book that I begin many recipes by toasting garlic in olive oil. With this step, I'm both infusing the oil with garlic flavor but also softening the garlic itself so that it will break up and integrate itself into the rest of the dish. The gentle toasting also mellows the flavor of the garlic. To toast garlic, pour a glug (about 2 tablespoons) of olive oil into your pan, add the smashed garlic, and cook slowly over medium heat until the garlic is very soft, fragrant and nicely golden brown—but not burnt—about 5 minutes.

Making Scallions Mild and Crisp

First of all, don't discard the green tops! Trim off just the top ½ inch or so. Also trim off the hairy root bit at the other end. If the outermost layer of scallion seems either dried out or slimy, peel it off. Cut the scallion crosswise and on a very sharp angle into thin slices. If being used in a salad, soak the scallions in ice water for 20 minutes, then drain well and pat dry. This tempers their bite a bit and makes them crisp and refreshing. For cooked recipes, don't use the ice water trick; just trim and cut according to the recipe.

HOW TO DRESS A SALAD

I am a fanatic at the restaurant about several things: perfectly cooked beans, al dente pasta, the storage of herbs, and dressing salads properly. This last one is about as important as it comes.

Salads have to be fresh and crisp with texture. The greens must taste like greens, and the whole salad should be colorful and beautiful. The statement I use most often is "there's no place to hide," meaning the greens, herbs, vinegar, and extra-virgin olive oil are all of equal importance.

I don't make many separate vinaigrettes at the restaurant; we use maybe three or four vinaigrettes that we make ahead, and even those get adjusted with every use. I have a theory that when you use the classic 3-to-1 ratio of oil to acid, you rely too much on that ratio and not enough on your tasting judgment.

That's why for most of the salads in this book, I tell you to add and taste, then add a little more, so that you don't overwhelm the ingredients with too much of any of the seasonings. You want a beautiful leaf of lettuce or an herb to taste exactly like itself . . . only better.

So here's how to put together a salad:

*   Put the lettuces and herbs in a nice big bowl—you'll need room to toss. Give the greens a careful pick-through; nobody wants a bad leaf in their salad.

*   Add some vinegar to the lettuce and with one hand toss it around to coat the leaves—do not drench the leaves! Taste. It should be both green and acidic.

*   Season the greens with salt and several cranks of black pepper. Taste it again. You should now taste the greens, the vinegar, and both the salt and the pepper. These seasonings should have flavor and almost a texture. (I always tell my cooks that at this point, the salad should taste good enough to serve without extra-virgin olive oil.)

*   Add the extra-virgin olive oil, thinking about what flavor it's going to add. Toss the greens around again with one hand so the oil coats everything evenly. Taste it one more time and then eat it right away. And please, eat salads with your hands.

In the field Seed farmer Frank Morton grew some of the original salad mixes, back in the '80s. He would unite mild lettuces with assertive greens such as spicy cresses or mustards, and brassicas such as kale, tatsoi, or mizuna, adding some aromatic notes from celery leaf, mint, parsley, and epazote. Like Morton, I aim for a crazy mix of flavors, colors, textures in my salads, and when I can, I use every part of the plant—leaves, shoots, petals.

Pickles: Six Seasons in a Jar

When I was a kid, the farmer down the road made a killer pickle-laden Bloody Mary mix. The grown-ups would drink the cocktails, while I fished out all the pickles and gorged on them. Whether that was the start of my pickle love affair or not, I continue to be a pickle fanatic. Now as a chef who fantasizes about being a farmer, I appreciate pickles not just for their tangy, crunchy goodness but also for their ability to stop time and capture the perfection of the season.

I want to give a nod to David Chang, for whom I worked at Momofuku in New York City. He showed me that really great pickles should not be too sharp. Low acid and always a touch of sweetness will allow you to taste the vegetable, not just the brine.

All my pickles are what are called refrigerator pickles. They are preserved and flavored by a brine, not by fermentation. The brine will keep them in good shape for quite a while, but they should stay refrigerated unless you actually process them, following good preserving practices, which you can find in the *Ball Blue Book Guide to Preserving*, among other sources.

I suggest you make a big batch of brine and then customize it according to the vegetables you're going to pickle at one time.

Basic Vegetable Pickle Brine

The brine will keep nicely in the fridge, so make a triple batch and be ready for sudden pickling urges.

» Makes enough for about 3 pints pickles (depending on their size and shape and the amount you stuff into the jar)

½ cup rice vinegar	5 tablespoons sugar
1 tablespoon white wine vinegar	1 tablespoon plus 1 teaspoon kosher salt
1½ cups hot water	

Put everything in a pot or big pitcher and stir until the sugar and salt have dissolved.

Using clean canning jars, fill with your vegetable in a way that shows off the beauty of it, pour over the brine until the vegetables are completely covered and the jar is full, and screw on the cap. Refrigerate for up to 2 months. Start tasting after the first day to see how the flavor and texture are developing. They are ready to eat as soon as you think they are.

Cold Brine

VEGETABLE	SEASONING	PREP NOTES
Beets	4 thyme sprigs, rinsed	Best with smaller spring beets. If using several colors, pickle each in its own jar to keep the colors from bleeding. Remove any greens, rinse beets, peel with a vegetable peeler. Cut the beets as thin as you can—potato chip thin. Layer with thyme sprigs.
Carrots	5 smashed garlic cloves, 2 dried chiles, 3 or 4 thyme sprigs, 1 tablespoon toasted coriander seeds; all seasonings rinsed	Best with slender springtime carrots. Remove tops, leaving ¼ inch of greens. Scrub but don't peel. With larger late-season carrots, peel and cut into two-bite sticks. Arrange standing up in the jar; tuck seasonings in between.
Cauliflower	5 smashed garlic cloves, 4 thyme sprigs; all seasonings rinsed	Break a head of cauliflower into uniform bite-size pieces. Layer with seasonings.
Celery	5 smashed garlic cloves, 2 dried chiles, 4 fresh thyme sprigs, 1 tablespoon toasted coriander seeds; all seasonings rinsed	Slice celery stalks crosswise into ¼-inch half-moons. Layer with seasonings.
Cherries	6 thyme sprigs, rinsed	Use ripe, dark sweet cherries, such as Bing, Brooks, or Lapins. Pit and pile into the jar, layering with thyme.
Cucumbers	None, basic brine only	Kirby cucumbers are ideal; lemon or other smaller varieties are fun as well. Cut into ¼-inch-thick slices.

Fennel	5 smashed garlic cloves, 2 dried chiles, 3 strips of orange zest, 2 rosemary sprigs; all seasonings rinsed	Use small baby fennel. Cut off the stalks, halve and slice the bulb lengthwise (preferably with a mandoline) through the core into thin slices, leaving the core intact. Layer with seasonings.
Radishes	None, basic brine only	Use bright red round radishes; the color stays better than other colors. Cut off the tops, leaving ¼ inch of greens, clean well.
Spring onions	None, basic brine only	Slice into rings ⅛ inch thick.
Turnips	5 smashed garlic cloves, 3 strips of orange zest, 1 tablespoon black peppercorns; all seasonings rinsed	Use early-season Japanese turnips. Remove tops, leaving ½ inch of greens. Scrub but don't peel, then cut into quarters lengthwise. With larger late-season turnips, peel and cut into wedges. Layer with seasonings.
Wax beans	5 smashed garlic cloves, 2 dried chiles, 2 rosemary sprigs; all seasonings rinsed	Wax beans are pretty, but use green beans if you like, or a mix. Trim the stem end, leave on the curly tip. Stand them up in the jar and tuck seasonings in between.
Zucchini and summer squashes	5 smashed garlic cloves, 2 dried chiles, 2 rosemary sprigs; all seasonings rinsed	Use small, firm, blemish-free squash. Slice from top to bottom into thin ribbons, preserving their shape (a mandoline will help). Stuff the ribbons of squash into the jar and tuck seasonings in between.

Hot Brine

On my lifelong pickle journey, I've learned that the following four vegetables need a little boost to get the best texture and flavor as a pickle. You'll make the exact same brine as for the other vegetables, but add a boiling step. Here's how: Pack the vegetables into the jar up to 1 inch below the top. Fill the jar with brine—this tells you how much brine you need. Then pour the measured brine back out of the jar and into a pan and bring to a boil. Add the seasonings to the jar and pour over the very hot brine. Let cool before refrigerating.

VEGETABLE	SEASONING	PREP NOTES
Asparagus	5 smashed garlic cloves, 2 dried chiles; all seasonings rinsed	Trim the asparagus spears so they fit standing up in the jar. Fill the jar, tuck in the seasonings, and add the hot brine as per above.
Brussels sprouts	5 smashed garlic cloves, 2 dried chiles, 1 tablespoon black peppercorns; all seasonings rinsed	Trim and halve the sprouts, pack into the jars, tuck in the seasonings, and add the hot brine as per above.
Fresh chiles	5 smashed garlic cloves, 3 or 4 thyme sprigs	Use a mix of flavors, shapes, and colors. Seed and derib the chiles. Cut large ones into smaller pieces, pack into the jars, tuck in the seasonings, and add the hot brine as per above.
Ramps	1 or 2 dried chiles	Trim the root end, clean well between all the greens. Stuff the whole ramps into the jar so they are all tangly, tuck in the seasonings, and add the hot brine as per above.

Season One

Spring

It sounds like a cliché, but I feel it every year—spring is miraculous. To watch as the dreary landscape, covered in frost, snow, and mud, transforms into this impossibly fresh and green new world is soul-stirring.

And spring comes just in time, right? Because as much as we love root vegetables and winter squash, after a few months, we crave tender things. Green things. Grassy, delicate vegetables that don't even need to be cooked, just plucked from the ground and enjoyed. They are never as sweet and delicious as when they first emerge from the newly warmed earth.

I'll eat raw peas by the handful or munch my way through asparagus stalks. When cooking for guests and friends, I do as little as possible to these early arrivals, usually nothing more than a light dressing with extra-virgin olive oil, some lemon or vinegar, salt, and pepper. Okay, and maybe some Parmigiano-Reggiano.

After a few weeks of reveling in pristine spring vegetables, I'm ready to bring in some heat and a few more ingredient partners. As the season progresses and the weather warms, some of the early vegetables become perhaps a touch more fibrous or starchy and therefore benefit from cooking and more creative treatments.

WARNING!
Do not touch. Use tongs
Stinging Nettles
$8.00/lb.

Recipes of Spring

Artichokes

Artichokes are huge and imposing, all prickly leaves, spiny buds (the artichokes themselves), and, when not harvested in time, gorgeous purple flowers. Hand in hand with that grandeur goes the fact that artichokes are a royal pain. Steamed whole and eaten leaf by leaf, an artichoke is simple to prepare, but if you want to incorporate the succulent flesh from the base and stem into another dish, be ready to do some work. The fact that fresh artichokes require effort is part of why I love them—I make it a spring ritual.

Two crops per year. Most of the artichokes sold in the United States are grown in California and are at their peak season from March through May, but locally grown examples may arrive later in the summer. Fall usually brings a second crop, and by then I'm usually ready for another challenge. The early spring artichokes are my favorites, however, because the slow grow through a cool winter makes the base and stem grow thick and meaty.

The big green globe artichoke is what most commercial farms grow, but local farms may offer some Italian varieties, usually tinged with purple or maroon, smaller, and with more open, upright leaves. I find that Italian artichokes, such as Violetta di Chiogga, have a deeper, sweeter flavor.

From tip to bottom. Artichoke terminology can be misleading. Technically the "heart" of the artichoke is the center portion, which includes the inedible choke. But the term "artichoke heart" has come to mean an artichoke that has been trimmed and had the choke removed. The cup-shaped base of the artichoke is all meat and is delicious simply dipped in melted butter (or one of my mayonnaises) or cut away from the leaves and cooked independently. Whatever you do, don't throw it away!

Baby artichokes are misnamed as well, not being babies at all but simply small artichokes that form lower down on the plant's stalk. They are more tender, however. All artichokes will keep in the fridge for up to a week loosely wrapped in a plastic bag, but be sure they are dry before wrapping, because they are prone to mold.

Prepping the heart. Start by pulling and snapping off the darker outer leaves until you reach the pale green-yellow tender inner leaves. Slice off the top inch or so—the tender lower leaves, the saucer-shaped base, and the stem are the edible portions of the artichoke.

Take a look at the stem—some artichokes have stems of several inches, others just have a stub of a stem. In any case, the stem itself is succulent and sweet, though the outside is fibrous. If the recipe has you leave the stem on, peel the outer layers with a paring knife or vegetable peeler.

Next, with a sharp paring knife, pare away any dark green or tough leaf ends from the bottom and sides of the artichoke base. You're sort of sculpting it into a smooth form. At this point, you will either halve the artichoke lengthwise or leave it whole—follow the recipe.

Pry open the tender leaves that remain and scoop out the hairy choke from the top of the base with a spoon, slice it away with a paring knife, or use a melon baller. Rub the base all over with some lemon juice. You're now ready to move to the next step in the recipe.

Raw Artichoke Salad with Herbs, Almonds, and Parmigiano

Don't even try this salad unless you have very early artichokes, the first ones to show up in the spring markets. As with all spring vegetables, the still-cold nights help the artichoke's sugars develop for the best flavor; and because they are smaller, young artichokes are less fibrous and more tender . . . but only if you slice them very fine.

» Serves 2

2 early-season artichokes

2 lemons, halved

Kosher salt and freshly ground black pepper

¼ teaspoon dried chile flakes

¼ cup lightly packed mint leaves

¼ cup lightly packed flat-leaf parsley leaves

¼ cup lightly packed chives cut into 2-inch lengths

¼ cup chive blossoms (if you can find them)

½ cup roughly chopped toasted almonds (see page 31)

15 to 20 shavings Parmigiano-Reggiano cheese (shaved with a vegetable peeler)

¼ cup extra-virgin olive oil

Pull and snap off the darker outer leaves of the artichokes until you reach the pale green-yellow tender inner leaves. Slice off the top third of the artichoke. Trim the very end of the stem and then peel the outer layers of the stem with a paring knife or vegetable peeler. (The outer layer of the stem is super fibrous but the inner, lighter heart is sweet and succulent.)

Slice the whole artichoke in half lengthwise (don't use a carbon-steel knife, or the artichoke will discolor) and rub the whole exterior with one of the lemon halves. Scoop out the hairy choke with a spoon, or slice it away with a paring knife. Squeeze some lemon juice into the choke space.

Place an artichoke half cut side down on the work surface and slice it lengthwise as thinly as you can. If you have a mandoline slicer, this is the perfect time to use it. Repeat with the other artichoke halves.

Put the sliced artichokes in a bowl. Squeeze in the juice of the remaining 3 lemon halves (try to retrieve and discard the seeds!) and add ½ teaspoon salt, lots of twists of black pepper, the chile flakes, mint, parsley, chives, chive blossoms (if using), almonds, and Parmigiano and toss. Taste and adjust the seasoning so the salad is lively and well balanced, then drizzle with the olive oil. Toss the salad again, taste, and serve.

Trimming the fibrous exterior to reveal the sweet center of the stem

Artichoke and Farro Salad with Salami and Herbs

I call this dish the "man snack," because the salami adds a meaty edge that makes it almost like an Italian hoagie. I wish I could find a bowl of it every time I open my fridge. You could use another grain such as freekeh in this salad, but farro is dense and chewy and doesn't absorb too much dressing. You end up tasting the grain as well as the other ingredients.

» Serves 4

2 cups cooked farro (see page 50)

Extra-virgin olive oil

3 ounces thinly sliced salami, cut into half- or quarter-moons

½ large red onion, very thinly sliced

White wine vinegar

Kosher salt and freshly ground black pepper

Dried chile flakes

4 poached artichoke quarters (see page 70)

½ cup lightly packed flat-leaf parsley leaves

½ cup lightly packed basil leaves

½ cup lightly packed mint leaves

¼ cup dried breadcrumbs (page 30)

Drain the farro well, dump it onto a baking sheet, toss with a small glug of olive oil, and spread it out to cool.

Pile the farro, salami, and onion into a bowl and season with ¼ cup vinegar. Taste and add salt, lots of twists of black pepper, and a few chile flakes. Add the artichokes, parsley, basil, and mint. Toss, taste again, and adjust with more salt, chile flakes, or vinegar. Finish by tossing with ¼ cup olive oil and sprinkling with the breadcrumbs.

In the field Good soil contributes to good flavor, of course, but Oregon farmer Anthony Boutard actually seasons his soil in the way I season the food in my kitchen. He recalls from childhood the bright flavor of the artichokes from Castroville, California, which he attributes to the Pacific winds that brought a trace of salt to the crops.

Grilled Artichokes with Artichoke-Parmigiano Dip

The dish is an example of something I love to do when I cook—doubling up to use the same ingredient in two ways. Here I grill some of the artichokes and then turn the others into the dip.

» Serves 4

3 lemons

6 medium early-season artichokes

4 garlic cloves, smashed and peeled

2 teaspoons dried chile flakes

2 tablespoons coriander seeds

3 tablespoons white wine vinegar

Kosher salt

1½ cups crème fraîche

3 or 4 dashes Tabasco sauce

¼ cup lightly packed finely sliced chives

¼ cup freshly grated Parmigiano-Reggiano cheese

Extra-virgin olive oil

¼ cup lightly packed roughly chopped flat-leaf parsley

Cut one of the lemons in half and cut one half into 4 wedges to serve with the artichokes. Using a rasp-style grater, zest the remaining 2 lemons and set the zest aside. Halve the zested lemons and set 2 halves aside for the dip; the remaining lemon halves are for the artichoke prep.

Trim all the artichokes and slice lengthwise into quarters (see page 66). Rub the exteriors with a lemon half. Scoop out the hairy center—the choke. Squeeze some lemon juice into the choke space.

POACH THE ARTICHOKES: Put 3 of the garlic cloves, the chile flakes, coriander seeds, and vinegar into a large pot (big enough to hold 2 of the trimmed artichokes). Add 2 quarts water and bring to a simmer. Once it's simmering, add 2 teaspoons salt. This is called a court bouillon, and it should taste well seasoned and like all of the ingredients in the pot. Take it off the heat and let it cool down.

Add 8 of the artichoke quarters to the court bouillon (reserve the remainder for grilling) and bring up to a simmer. Poach until they are fully tender, 10 to 15 minutes. You can check by poking the stem with the tip of a knife, like you would a potato.

Drain the artichokes well on a rack, and when they're cool enough to handle, blot with paper towels so they are quite dry.

MAKE THE DIP: Very finely chop the artichokes and place them in a large bowl. Add the crème fraîche, along with half the reserved lemon zest, the juice from 2 lemon halves, the Tabasco sauce, chives, Parmigiano, and salt to taste. Taste and adjust the seasoning so that it's savory and balanced, and then whisk in ¼ cup olive oil to make the dip rich and creamy. Taste again and add more salt, Tabasco, or lemon if you like.

GRILL THE ARTICHOKES: Heat a grill, a grill pan, or a heavy skillet over high heat. Add a slick of olive oil and the remaining garlic clove to flavor the oil (skip this if you're using an actual grill). Lay the remaining 16 artichoke quarters in the pan and grill on all sides until nicely browned and starting to crisp around the edges, about 10 minutes total. You may need to do this in batches or in two pans.

Transfer the grilled artichoke quarters to a platter, shower with the parsley, the rest of the lemon zest, and a drizzle of olive oil. Serve warm or at room temperature with the artichoke dip and lemon wedges for squeezing.

Trimming small artichokes to get to the heart

Asparagus

Once asparagus starts showing up at your farmers' market, you know winter is officially over. Hallelujah. And though you likely don't need much prodding to load up on those tender green stalks, keep in mind that asparagus really does have a short window of seasonality. While you may find imported asparagus in your grocery store year-round, local asparagus cannot be coaxed to grow beyond six weeks or so—all the more reason to cherish it.

Prep. Asparagus is an obliging vegetable that doesn't need much prep at all. The one thing you need to do is remove the lower portion of the stalk, which is usually very fibrous and no fun to eat. Some people like to bend the stalk and let it snap at the natural spot where it goes from fibrous to succulent. A quicker way to do that is to choose one stalk from the bunch, bend it until it snaps at that sweet spot, and then line up the rest of the stalks and simply cut them at about the same point.

Size doesn't matter. You should choose your asparagus by how crisp and juicy it is, not by how thin or thick. Thinner spears are not necessarily more tender or less fibrous than big fat spears, they are simply skinny. An asparagus plant will produce thin, medium, and thick spears at the same time; spear diameter doesn't relate to age. Whatever size you prefer, look for tightly closed tips and cut ends that don't look too dried out or woody. I cook with green and purple varieties; their flavors will be the same, so it's a matter of color. I love mixing purple and green in a salad of thinly sliced asparagus to get a jumble of colors on the plate. Store your asparagus in a loosely closed plastic bag in the refrigerator and use it pronto, especially if you're going to serve it raw.

Try them raw. When you're ready to cook with it . . . don't. Honestly, if you can get first-of-the-season asparagus, forgo cooking and serve it raw, very thinly sliced on an angle (see opposite). The juicy-crisp texture and sweet grassy flavor are spring turned into a mouthful, and you should experience it while you can. Once my initial crush on asparagus has faded a bit, I'll cook it a number of ways: pan-steaming, roasting, grilling, or incorporating into other dishes. The only wrong way to cook it is to overcook it. Mushy asparagus is a sin.

Raw Asparagus Salad with Breadcrumbs, Walnuts, and Mint

Make this dish before you do any cooked asparagus dishes, at the start of the season when you get pristine spears. At first glance, the dish looks kind of "meh," but once you taste it, the flavor and texture blow you away. Be sure to cut the asparagus very thin.

» Serves 4

⅓ cup dried breadcrumbs (page 30)

½ cup freshly grated Parmigiano-Reggiano cheese

½ cup finely chopped lightly toasted walnuts (see page 31)

1 teaspoon finely grated lemon zest

Kosher salt and freshly ground black pepper

Dried chile flakes

1 pound asparagus, tough ends trimmed

About ¼ cup fresh lemon juice

¼ cup lightly packed mint leaves

Extra-virgin olive oil

Put the breadcrumbs, Parmigiano, walnuts, and lemon zest in a large bowl. Add 1 teaspoon salt, a bunch of twists of black pepper, and ½ teaspoon chile flakes. Toss to combine everything.

Cut the asparagus on a sharp angle into very thin slices and add to the crumb mixture. Add ¼ cup lemon juice and toss some more. Taste and dial in the flavors by adding more salt, black pepper, chile flakes, or lemon juice.

When the flavors are bright and delicious, add the mint and ¼ cup olive oil and toss. Taste and adjust again, and serve.

Asparagus, Nettle, and Green Garlic Frittata

Nettles—also known as stinging nettles—need special handling, because they do indeed "sting." The wild-growing spring green is coated with tiny needlelike hairs, which can cause a very painful reaction if you touch them with your bare hands. I usually just grab them with tongs, but you can also wear gloves or slide a plastic bag over your hand when picking them up. Miraculously, however, once they are cooked, the sting is totally gone and what remains is a lovely green, almost spinachy—a beautiful partner to asparagus.

» *Serves 4*

2 tablespoons unsalted butter

3 stalks green garlic or spring onions, trimmed (including ½ inch off the green tops), thinly sliced

½ pound asparagus, tough ends trimmed, cut on a sharp angle into very thin slices

About 4 big handfuls nettles—but don't pick them up with your hands!

Kosher salt and freshly ground black pepper

6 eggs

¼ cup crumbled feta cheese

Heat the broiler.

Melt the butter in a 10-inch ovenproof skillet over medium heat. Add the green garlic and cook until it begins to soften, 1 to 2 minutes. Add the asparagus and sauté until it is crisp-tender, another 3 to 4 minutes.

Pile the nettles into the skillet—with tongs—and toss to wilt and tenderize, 2 to 3 minutes. Season everything with salt and pepper.

Beat the eggs with a fork or a whisk in a medium bowl until they are fully blended and just slightly foamy. Season with salt and pepper. Pour the eggs into the pan over the garlic, asparagus, and nettles, scraping all the egg out of the bowl with a rubber spatula.

Let the eggs cook without disturbing them for about 1 minute. Then with a silicone spatula or a table knife, gently lift the edges of the eggs, letting the liquid eggs pour over the edge and underneath. Let that set for another few seconds and then continue lifting and letting the eggs flow. This will create layers and make the frittata lighter.

When the eggs aren't super runny anymore but the top is still moist and undercooked, slide the pan under the broiler for a minute or two to lightly brown the top of the frittata.

Careful, the pan handle is hot now! Run the spatula or a small knife around the edge of the frittata and then flip the pan over onto a cutting board or cooling rack. Shake and tap to release the frittata. If a bit sticks to the pan and rips, don't worry, just piece it back together. Invert the frittata again so it's right side up. Scatter the feta over the top. Let the frittata cool until it's just warm, and serve in wedges.

MORE WAYS:

Turn leftover frittata into an open-faced sandwich: Spread some fresh goat cheese on a slice of good bread (walnut bread would be awesome), arrange a handful of arugula or other tender greens over the cheese, top with thin slices of cold frittata, and finish with a drizzle of olive oil.

Make a main-dish salad with cold frittata: Cut it into ¼-inch sticks, toss with some lemon juice, lemon zest, chile flakes, salt, black pepper, and plenty of olive oil. Let the frittata marinate for a few minutes, then toss with fresh greens and fresh herbs, such as mint and parsley, and a handful of grated sharp cheddar.

Create easy appetizers: Cut the room-temperature frittata into 1-inch squares. Spread some Whipped Ricotta (page 37) onto a serving plate and arrange the frittata squares on top. Add some toothpicks and you're set.

Asparagus, Garlic Chives, and Pea Shoots, with or without an Egg

This dish is a variant on the classic "mess o' greens"—a big tangle of asparagus and other early spring treats. I serve this as a main dish by topping it with a fried or poached egg; eggless, it makes a lovely bed for a piece of fish.

» Serves 2 or 3

Extra-virgin olive oil

1 bunch green garlic or spring onions, trimmed (including ½ inch off the green tops), thinly sliced

1 pound asparagus, tough ends trimmed

4 cups lightly packed pea shoots and tendrils

1 bunch garlic chives

Kosher salt and freshly ground black pepper

Juice of 1 lemon

Pecorino Romano cheese, for grating

2 or 3 eggs (optional)

2 tablespoons dried breadcrumbs (page 30; optional)

Pour a healthy glug of olive oil into a large skillet over medium-high heat. Add the green garlic and cook for about 30 seconds. Add the thicker spears of asparagus to the pan in a single layer. Cook until the asparagus are slightly tender, 2 to 3 minutes.

Add the thinner spears and cook, pulling out spears as they become tender. (If the green garlic starts to get too dark, scoop it out with a spoon.)

Once all the asparagus are cooked and out of the pan, drop in the pea shoots and splash in a bit of water to create some steam to wilt them.

Add the garlic chives and sauté, tossing frequently so everything wilts nicely, for 4 to 5 minutes, depending on how tough the pea shoots are. Return the asparagus to the pan, season generously with salt and pepper, and add another healthy glug of olive oil.

Cook until all is tender—but not mushy—another minute or two. Squeeze the lemon juice over everything, toss, taste, and adjust the seasoning.

Serve as is, with a shower of grated pecorino and breadcrumbs. Or set aside the greens in a warm place while you gently fry the eggs in olive oil. Season them with salt and pepper and slide an egg onto each portion of greens. Serve right away.

In the kitchen Use baby mustard greens instead of pea shoots, or toss in a handful of sliced sugar snaps or English peas.

Grilled Asparagus with Fava Beans and Walnuts

I think walnuts and asparagus taste similar—both are slightly bitter—so I love to work them together in a dish. For the topping, you'll be making a wettish, textural salsa with favas, breadcrumbs, walnuts, cheese, lemon, and olive oil. If favas aren't available, just skip them.

» Serves 4

2 pounds fava beans in their pods

1½ pounds asparagus, tough ends trimmed

About 5 tablespoons fresh lemon juice

Kosher salt and freshly ground black pepper

½ cup dried breadcrumbs (page 30)

½ cup chopped lightly toasted walnuts (see page 31)

½ cup finely grated Parmigiano-Reggiano cheese

Extra-virgin olive oil

Shell, blanch, and peel the fava beans (see page 90).

Heat a grill or grill pan to medium-high and grill the asparagus (with no oil) until it's nicely charred and slightly tender, 4 to 6 minutes, depending on the thickness.

Transfer the asparagus to a wide bowl or a platter, drizzle with 4 tablespoons of the lemon juice, season generously with salt and pepper, and toss gently to coat without breaking up the spears.

Toss the peeled favas in a bowl with the breadcrumbs, walnuts, Parmigiano, and another tablespoon or so of lemon juice. Season generously with salt and pepper. Taste and adjust the seasoning until the fava-walnut mixture is highly seasoned and delicious. Add ¼ cup olive oil and toss again.

Pile the fava mixture onto the asparagus and gently toss everything together. Taste a bite of asparagus and favas and adjust with more lemon, salt, pepper, or olive oil as needed. Serve at room temperature.

Vignole

This is my straightforward interpretation of a classic Roman springtime dish, in which a handful of spring vegetables are gently stewed together until they have lost their bright green color . . . but not their green flavor. Asparagus and fava beans are typical, and I like to add whatever else looks good at that time—English peas, sugar snaps, spring onions.

Vignole is fantastic the second day because all those flavors have had a chance to develop. And it's great with some short pasta, such as ditalini, or some farro stirred in. Don't forget the grilled bread on the side and a drizzle of olive oil.

» Serves 4 to 6

½ pound spring onions, trimmed (including 1 inch off the green tops), bulbs quartered or cut even smaller if they are big

3 ounces thinly sliced prosciutto

2 pounds fava beans in their pods

Extra-virgin olive oil

3 garlic cloves, smashed and peeled

Kosher salt and freshly ground black pepper

½ pound sugar snap peas, cut into ½-inch pieces (about 2 cups)

½ pound asparagus, tough ends trimmed, stalks cut on an angle into ½-inch slices, tips left whole

½ head escarole or other sturdy and tasty green, root end trimmed, cut crosswise into 1-inch pieces, washed really well

¼ cup lightly packed mint leaves

½ cup lightly packed roughly chopped flat-leaf parsley

Finely grated zest and juice of ½ lemon

Freshly grated Parmigiano-Reggiano cheese, for serving

Cut the spring onions into 1½-inch lengths (you want to have a bit more than 2 cups).

Stack the prosciutto slices, roll them up into a cylinder, and slice crosswise into thin strips. Then cut across the coils of the strips so that you're chopping the prosciutto into small bits. (This process is easier if you chill the prosciutto in the freezer for a few minutes first.) You want around ¾ cup.

Shell, blanch, and peel the fava beans (see page 90).

Heat ¼ cup olive oil in a large Dutch oven or other big heavy-bottomed pot over medium heat. Add the garlic, onions, and prosciutto. Reduce the heat, season lightly with salt and pepper, and cook until the onions are soft and fragrant but not browning at all, 12 to 15 minutes.

Add the fava beans, snap peas, asparagus, escarole, and 1 cup water. Cover and cook at a simmer until the vegetables are very soft and the flavors are all blending together, 15 to 25 minutes. You want the consistency to be slightly brothy, and though most of the liquid will come from the vegetable juices, add a bit more water if need be.

Add the mint, parsley, lemon zest, and lemon juice. Taste and adjust the seasoning so the stew is rich and savory. Drizzle on a bit more olive oil.

Serve on its own or over pasta. Finish individual plates with more olive oil and pass the Parmigiano at the table.

English Peas

English peas—the type of pea grown for the pearl-shaped seeds on the inside rather than for the pods—are absolutely one of spring's treasures. Even if you find peas later in the summer, they will not compare to first-of-the-season peas, which are sweet and crunchy yet tender, with no starchiness at all. This is the time to shuck a bowl of peas and eat them totally raw, maybe dressed in a bit of olive oil and lemon juice, but nothing else to interfere with their youthful appeal.

Curvy is beautiful. Look for pods that show the contours of the peas inside, so you know they're fully developed, and of course pick ones that are super green and not dried out. The peas will stay freshest in their pods, so only shuck them when you're ready to eat them.

Briefly boil. If you don't serve them raw, serve them as close to raw as you can—just dunk them briefly in boiling water or add them late in the process of your recipe, so they keep their lovely green sweetness. The more mature and starchy the pea, the longer you should cook it.

> **In the field** When you grow your own peas, you get to harvest the delicate and tasty tendrils, also called pea shoots. Snap peas and English peas produce these curling strands, which can be clipped from the plant and used like a fresh green, eaten raw or lightly wilted.

English Pea Toast

A perfect showcase for the early-season peas, this toast can be an appetizer, a first course, or a light main course. A layer of fresh sheep's cheese, sweet and mild, would be so nice with the peas, but I also use my go-to cheese topping, Whipped Ricotta (page 37).

» Serves 4 as an appetizer

1½ to 2 pounds English peas in their pods, shelled (1½ to 2 cups peas)

3 red spring onions or scallions, trimmed (including ½ inch off the green tops), thinly sliced on a sharp angle, soaked in ice water for 20 minutes, and drained well (see page 53)

1 lemon, halved

Kosher salt and freshly ground black pepper

1 small handful mint leaves

Extra-virgin olive oil

Four ½-inch-thick slices country bread

1 cup fresh sheep cheese, fromage blanc, mild goat cheese, or Whipped Ricotta (page 37)

Parmigiano-Reggiano cheese, for grating

Put the shelled peas and onions in a bowl, squeeze on the juice from half the lemon, and season generously with salt and pepper. Add the mint, taste and adjust with more lemon, salt, or pepper, and then add ¼ cup olive oil.

Grill, broil, or toast the bread on both sides. Spread the fresh cheese onto each toast and arrange on plates. Tumble the peas onto each toast, pressing lightly so that most of the peas stick to the cheese. Finish with a nice shower of grated Parmigiano and a thin ribbon of olive oil.

English Pea and Pickled Carrot Salsa Verde

Though I'm calling this a *salsa verde*, which usually refers to a sauce or condiment, I like to serve it as an actual side dish or as the bed for a grilled pork chop, chicken breast, or a piece of fish. Don't limit yourself to pickled carrots—any good pickled vegetable will do, and the more types, the merrier.

» Serves 2 to 4

2 pounds English peas in their pods, shelled (2 cups peas)

Kosher salt and freshly ground black pepper

1 small bunch flat-leaf parsley

1 small handful mint leaves, cut into fine shreds

3 scallions, trimmed (including ½ inch off the green tops), thinly sliced on a sharp angle, soaked in ice water for 20 minutes, and drained well (see page 53)

1 cup thinly sliced pickled carrots, store-bought or homemade (page 58)

1 lemon

2 tablespoons capers, rinsed, drained, and chopped

Extra-virgin olive oil

Bring a pot of water to a boil and add salt until it tastes like the sea. Drop in the shelled peas and boil for just 30 seconds (or closer to a minute if the peas are more mature). Drain and immediately run under cold water or dunk into a bowl of ice water to stop the cooking. Drain and dry.

Separate the stems from the parsley leaves. Trim off the dried end bits of half the parsley stems (compost the others or use in another dish) and very finely slice the stems crosswise, the way you would chives. Chop the parsley leaves medium fine.

Put the parsley stems and leaves and the mint into a small bowl. Add the scallions, pickled carrots, and peas. Grate the lemon zest into the bowl. Add the capers and season generously with pepper. Pour over ½ cup olive oil and toss together.

When you're ready to serve, halve the lemon, squeeze about 2 tablespoons lemon juice over the mixture, and season with salt. Taste and adjust the seasoning with more lemon, oil, salt, or pepper.

In the kitchen Equip yourself with a rasp-style grater (Microplane is one brand). All your grating tasks will become so much easier, and the final results will be fine and fluffy.

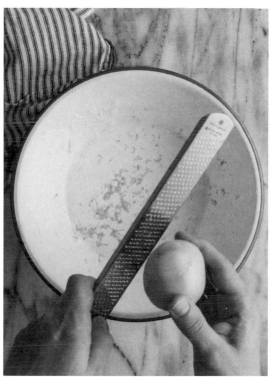

English Peas with Prosciutto and New Potatoes

When you have truly young, creamy potatoes and sweet, tender peas, this supersimple side dish is close to perfect. You can swap pancetta for the prosciutto or leave out the meat altogether to make it vegetarian.

» Serves 3 or 4

½ pound new potatoes, scrubbed and cut into ½-inch dice

Kosher salt and freshly ground black pepper

Extra-virgin olive oil

½ small onion, finely chopped

3 ounces prosciutto, chopped

2 pounds English peas in their pods, shelled (2 cups peas)

1 small handful fresh mint leaves

Put the diced potatoes in a medium pot, add water to cover by 1 inch, and add 1 tablespoon salt. Bring to a boil and simmer gently until the potatoes are just tender, 10 to 12 minutes. Drain.

Meanwhile, heat a small glug of olive oil in a large skillet over medium heat. Add the onion and prosciutto and a bit of salt. Sauté until the onion is soft and fragrant, but not browned, and the prosciutto has rendered some fat and is getting crisp around the edges, 5 to 6 minutes.

Add the shelled peas and potatoes and season generously with salt and lots of pepper. Add a couple of tablespoons of water to steam-cook the peas until they are tender and all the flavors have married, another 3 to 4 minutes.

Toss in the mint, taste and adjust the salt and pepper, and finish with a nice drizzle of olive oil. Serve warm.

MORE WAYS:

Create a crusty hash: Once the peas and potatoes are tender, drizzle with a bit of cream and a handful of grated Parmigiano, increase the heat, and crush the peas and potatoes with a spatula so the mixture flattens out and sticks together. Cook over medium-high heat, turning several times, until the surface is nicely browned and crisp, about 10 minutes. Serve the hash with a fried egg or on its own.

Make a springtime pasta: Make the recipe and boil some pasta such as penne or ditalini. Reserve some pasta water and toss the pea-potato mixture with the cooked pasta, a knob of butter, a handful of grated pecorino, and enough pasta water to make the consistency nice and creamy.

Make a spring medley: Cook small-diced carrots and young turnips with some chopped scallions along with the onion. Finish with mixed herbs—parsley, tarragon, dill, and mint.

Pasta Carbonara with English Peas

Adding peas to a carbonara is by no means classically Italian, though the combination of black pepper, pancetta, and peas is. I barely cook the peas—a quick blanching in the pasta cooking water right before you pull the pasta is all it takes. Instead of (or in addition to) the peas, you could use asparagus or thinly sliced sugar snap peas.

» Serves 2

Kosher salt and freshly ground black pepper

3 ounces pancetta, cut into small dice

Extra-virgin olive oil

8 ounces dried fettuccine, linguine, or spaghetti

1 pound English peas in their pods, shelled (1 cup peas)

3 scallions, trimmed (including ½ inch off the green tops), thinly sliced on an angle

1 small handful pea tendrils (optional)

1 egg, whipped well with a fork in a little bowl

½ cup freshly grated Parmigiano-Reggiano cheese

½ cup freshly grated Pecorino Romano cheese

Bring a large pot of water to a boil and add salt until it tastes like the sea.

Put the pancetta and a small glug of olive oil in a skillet or Dutch oven that's large enough to hold all the pasta. Cook until the pancetta is lightly browned but still slightly chewy, 9 to 12 minutes (or less if you're using thinly sliced pancetta). Season the pancetta very generously with pepper. Take the skillet off the heat, but don't drain anything—you'll use that fat!

When the water is at a boil, add the pasta and cook according to the package directions until almost al dente. When the pasta is almost ready, add the shelled peas to the pasta pot.

Put the skillet back over medium heat and reheat the pancetta gently.

With a ladle or a measuring cup, scoop out about 1 cup of the pasta cooking water. Drain the pasta and peas. Whisk a couple of tablespoons of the pasta water into the fat and pancetta in the skillet, to make the bacon fat lighter and creamier by emulsifying it with the water. Pull the pan off the heat.

Whisk some of that warm fat into the beaten egg to temper it (meaning to gently warm up the egg so that it doesn't scramble when you add it to the hot skillet), then whisk the egg into the skillet.

Dump the pasta, peas, scallions, and pea tendrils (if using) into the skillet. Add both the cheeses and toss everything quickly and thoroughly to blend. Add a few more small splashes of the pasta water and keep tossing until the noodles are cloaked in a creamy sauce. Taste and adjust the seasoning with more salt or black pepper as needed. Serve right away. This dish does not wait.

Couscous with English Peas, Apricots, and Lamb Meatballs

The ingredients list looks long, but the meatballs are very easy to assemble. To make ahead: The night before, prep all the vegetables, herbs, and dried fruit, and cook the couscous and the meatballs. When it's time to fix dinner, bring the couscous up to room temperature, toss in the goods, and gently reheat the meatballs in a low oven, covered. Ideally, your peas will be so fresh and young that they need no cooking, but if they taste starchy, blanch them in boiling salted water for about 1 minute.

» Serves 4

YOGURT SAUCE

1 cup plain whole-milk or low-fat yogurt (not Greek)

3 scallions, trimmed (including ½ inch off the green tops), finely sliced on a sharp angle, soaked in ice water for 20 minutes, and drained well (see page 53)

¼ cup chopped mint leaves

1 small garlic clove, minced

¼ teaspoon dried chile flakes

Kosher salt and freshly ground black pepper

COUSCOUS

8 dried apricots, cut into bits

¼ cup white wine vinegar or red wine vinegar

¼ cup warm water

1 cup couscous

Juice of ½ lemon

Extra-virgin olive oil

Kosher salt and freshly ground black pepper

3 large scallions, trimmed (including ½ inch off the green tops), sliced on a sharp angle, soaked in ice water for 20 minutes, and drained well

½ cup lightly packed mint leaves

2 pounds English peas in their pods, shelled (2 cups peas)

½ cup roughly chopped toasted almonds (see page 31)

MEATBALLS

1 pound ground lamb

3 scallions, trimmed (including ½ inch off the green tops), finely chopped

¼ cup lightly packed chopped mint leaves

1 teaspoon ground cumin

1½ teaspoons kosher salt

⅛ teaspoon cayenne pepper

1 tablespoon dry white wine

¼ cup soft fresh breadcrumbs

Extra-virgin olive oil

1 egg

FOR THE YOGURT SAUCE: Stir together the yogurt, scallions, mint, garlic, chile flakes, and salt and black pepper to taste in a small bowl. Taste and adjust the chile flakes, salt, and black pepper. Let the sauce rest for at least 30 minutes so the flavors can develop.

FOR THE COUSCOUS: Put the apricots in a small bowl with the vinegar and water. Soak until they are plumped, at least 30 minutes, then drain thoroughly.

Hydrate and fluff the couscous (see page 51). Add the lemon juice and ¼ cup olive oil, and season generously with salt and pepper. Toss thoroughly and let cool to room temperature.

Add the apricots, scallions, mint, shelled peas, and almonds. Toss lightly, taste for seasoning, and add more salt, pepper, lemon, or olive oil. Set aside.

FOR THE MEATBALLS: Heat the oven to 450°F.

Break the ground lamb into smallish chunks and put in a large bowl. Sprinkle the scallions, mint, cumin, salt, cayenne, wine, and breadcrumbs over the meat. Gently work the ingredients to blend them, by pushing and folding with your fingers. You want to be as gentle as possible in order to not make tough, compact meatballs. Once the ingredients are mostly blended, take a small spoonful of the mixture and fry it in a small skillet or pot. Taste the cooked sample for seasoning, then add more of whatever is needed, especially salt. You want the meatballs to be quite savory and highly seasoned.

Once you've adjusted the seasoning, whisk a small glug of olive oil and the egg together, pour it over the meat, and work it in using the same gentle method.

Divide the meat into 4 piles, then divide each pile into 4, and shape each piece into a nice ball (to make a total of 16 meatballs). Arrange all the meatballs on a rimmed baking sheet (to catch any fat or juices during cooking).

Bake the meatballs until they are no longer pink in the center, 8 to 10 minutes (test one by gently prying it apart . . . you can just press it back together to serve).

To serve, divide the couscous among 4 large shallow bowls. Top each portion with 4 meatballs and a nice drizzle of yogurt sauce. Pass more sauce at the table.

Fava Beans

Fava beans are hugely popular in the Mediterranean and parts of the Middle East, but not as well known in the United States. They are a spring vegetable that demands a bit of work, and what seems like a lot of fava pods yields very little by the time you're done. But their bright green color, buttery texture, and sweet nutty flavor make it worth it. Favas paired with some young pecorino, a touch of mint, and of course olive oil is the best spring combo ever.

30 seconds, then immediately drain. Rinse well with very cold water to stop the cooking. Cut a small slit in the whitish membrane of each bean with the tip of a paring knife or your thumbnail, then gently squeeze out the two halves of the bright green fava. You are now ready for action.

Once prepped, they're cooked. As with English peas, minimal cooking is key. When you've blanched and peeled them, they're fully cooked, so add them to dishes late in the process. If you're really lucky, you may find fava leaves early in the season, which can be used like any tender greens, or baby favas, which are immature enough to eat whole, pod and all.

Pleasantly plump. But mostly what you'll find, and what I like best, are the long shiny pods full of beans. Aim for ones that are thick enough to indicate plump beans inside but not so thick and big that the beans will be overly mature and heading for starchiness. Don't worry about a few brown spots or scraggly brown leaves and stems—that happens quickly on favas and doesn't mean the beans are over the hill.

Shelling, blanching, and peeling. Favas come in large, puffy pods that are lined with a spongy layer. Inside the pods are large, flat beans, each in its own tough skin. Start by splitting open the fava pods and popping out the beans. To peel the membranes off, you have to blanch them: Bring a pot of water to a boil, salt it generously, and drop in the fava beans. Cook for about

Make room. Store them in the fridge in plastic until you're ready to shuck and cook. It can be hard to know how many pounds of pods you need, so a good rule of thumb is that 2 pounds of pods will yield about 1 cup of shelled and peeled fava beans.

Smashed Fava Beans, Pecorino, and Mint on Toast

This is a loose pesto of fava beans and mint, with plenty of olive oil. Use it as a pasta sauce or as a dip for vegetables, spoon it over crushed boiled new potatoes, or spread some on toasted country bread, as I do here. If you have a mortar and pestle, use it, though a food processor will work fine, as long as you don't overprocess.

» Serves 4 as an appetizer or light lunch

2½ pounds fava beans in their pods

2 stalks green garlic or scallions, trimmed (including ½ inch off the green tops), roughly chopped

Kosher salt and freshly ground black pepper

½ cup lightly packed fresh mint leaves

Extra-virgin olive oil

Freshly grated Pecorino Romano cheese

About 1 tablespoon fresh lemon juice

Four ½-inch-thick slices country bread

Shell, blanch, and peel the favas as previously described.

Put the green garlic and a pinch of salt into a food processor and pulse a few times. Add half the mint leaves and pulse a few more times so the garlic is fairly fine. Add the peeled favas and 2 tablespoons olive oil and pulse again. Your goal is to bash up the favas but not completely puree them. You may need to scrape down the sides of the processor bowl between pulses.

Scrape the mixture into a bowl, season with some pepper, and stir in ¼ cup grated pecorino and 1 tablespoon lemon juice. Taste and adjust the flavor with more salt, pepper, or lemon juice, and adjust the consistency with olive oil so that it is loose and luscious.

Brush the bread on one side with olive oil and grill or broil until crisp. Arrange on plates, top with the fava mixture and the rest of the mint leaves (torn if they're big), and finish with a nice shower of grated pecorino and another drizzle of oil.

Fava, Farro, Pecorino, and Salami Salad

The pairing of favas and pecorino is a typical springtime dish in Rome—often you'll see them speared on toothpicks as a snack. Here I'm tossing it all together with chewy farro and cubed salami to make a hearty but still springlike salad.

» Serves 4 to 6

2½ pounds fava beans in their pods

2 cups cooked and cooled farro (see page 50)

¼ pound salami, cut into ¼-inch-thick slices and then into ¼-inch dice

4 ounces pecorino fresco, cut into ¼-inch-thick slices and then into ¼-inch dice

½ bunch scallions, trimmed (including ½ inch off the green tops), thinly sliced on an angle, soaked in ice water for 20 minutes, and drained well (see page 53)

Red wine vinegar

¼ teaspoon dried chile flakes

Kosher salt and freshly ground black pepper

½ cup loosely packed flat-leaf parsley leaves

¼ cup loosely packed mint leaves

Extra-virgin olive oil

Shell, blanch, and peel the favas (see page 90).

Put the farro, favas, salami, pecorino, and scallions in a large bowl. Add ¼ cup vinegar, the chile flakes, 1 teaspoon salt, and lots of twists of black pepper, and toss. Let the salad sit for about 5 minutes so the vinegar soaks into the farro.

Add the parsley and mint and toss. Taste and adjust the seasoning. Drizzle on a glug of olive oil, toss, and taste again—adjust as needed. Serve at room temperature.

At the market I love to eat vegetables at every stage of their development, and fava beans give me that opportunity—with their leaves! They're not easy to find—ask around at your farmers' market, or try growing favas yourself. The leaves are beautiful pale blue-green, smooth-edged, pointed ovals about two inches long. Their flavor, best when young and tender, is a cross between the actual fava bean and a mild lettuce. Add them to salads or give them a whirl in a skillet with some olive oil.

Fava and Pistachio Pesto on Pasta

Yes, shelling and blanching the fresh fava beans is time consuming, but the rest of this dish is simple to prepare, balancing out the work you do up front. Once you get this recipe down, you'll be able to make it again without even looking at the recipe. You can use almost any noodle you want, short or long.

» Serves 4

2 pounds fava beans in their pods

1½ cups lightly packed basil leaves

4 garlic cloves, smashed and peeled

1 cup lightly packed flat-leaf parsley leaves

½ cup pistachios, lightly toasted (see page 31)

Kosher salt and freshly ground black pepper

Extra-virgin olive oil

¼ teaspoon dried chile flakes

1 pound dried pasta, such as spaghetti or fettuccine

1½ cups freshly grated Parmigiano-Reggiano cheese

1 tablespoon unsalted butter

¼ cup lightly packed mint leaves

Shell, blanch, and peel the favas (see page 90). Don't drain the favas, however; scoop them out so that you can use the boiling water for the following steps.

Set a bowl of ice water on the counter. Drop the basil leaves into the pot of boiling water and immediately scoop them out and plunge them into the ice water. This quick blanching helps to set the green color.

Drop 2 of the garlic cloves into the boiling water and blanch them for about 1 minute. Drain and drop the garlic into the ice water, too.

Pull out the basil and garlic and blot everything dry with paper towels. Put the basil, blanched garlic, parsley, pistachios, half the favas, and ½ teaspoon salt in a food processor. Pulse to make a coarse puree, occasionally stopping to scrape down the sides. With the motor running, drizzle in ½ cup olive oil.

Heat ¼ cup olive oil in a large skillet over medium heat. Add the remaining 2 garlic cloves and the chile flakes. Cook the garlic, stirring constantly, until lightly toasty and broken up into bits, 3 to 5 minutes. The garlic should not become dark brown. Pull the pan off the heat while you cook the pasta.

Bring a large pot of water to a boil and add salt until it tastes like the sea. Add the pasta and cook until al dente (usually 1 or 2 minutes short of the time listed on the package). With a ladle or a measuring cup, scoop out about a cup of the pasta cooking water, then drain the pasta.

Put the pasta pot back over medium heat, scrape the pesto from the processor into the pot, and cook for a few seconds. Add about ½ cup of the pasta water, the pasta, Parmigiano, the rest of the fava beans, and the butter. Toss to blend everything. Taste and adjust the seasoning with more salt, black pepper, chile flakes, or cheese; adjust the texture with more pasta water if needed to make the sauce creamy.

Pile into pasta bowls and top with the mint and a final drizzle of olive oil.

Fava Beans, Cilantro, New Potatoes, and Baked Eggs

Here I give the favas a more robust treatment, teaming them up with plenty of garlic, tomatoes, spices, and fragrant cilantro to make a vegetable stew. You can serve the stew alone or on toast, but I like to crack a few eggs into it and bake it in the oven. Keep the yolks runny so they can enrich the spicy stew.

» Serves 4

½ pound new potatoes, scrubbed and cut into quarters

Kosher salt

3 pounds fava beans in their pods

Extra-virgin olive oil

2 bunches scallions, trimmed (including ½ inch off the green tops), sliced into ¼-inch rounds

4 garlic cloves, sliced

1 tablespoon smoked paprika

1½ teaspoons ground cumin

Dried chile flakes

Freshly ground black pepper

One 28-ounce can diced tomatoes, with their juices

1 small bunch cilantro, roughly chopped (stems and leaves)

1 cup lightly packed flat-leaf parsley leaves, roughly chopped

4 eggs

Slightly Tangy Flatbreads (page 48; optional), for serving

Put the potatoes in a medium pot, add water to cover by 1 inch, and add 1 tablespoon salt. Bring to a boil and simmer gently until the potatoes are just tender, 12 to 14 minutes. Drain.

Shell, blanch, and peel the favas (see page 90).

Pour a healthy glug of olive oil into a 10-inch ovenproof skillet or sauté pan and heat over medium heat. Add the scallions, garlic, and a pinch of salt and sauté until soft and fragrant but not browned, about 5 minutes. Add the smoked paprika, cumin, 1 teaspoon chile flakes, and several twists of black pepper and cook for another 30 seconds or so. Add the tomatoes and juices, adjust the heat to a nice simmer, and cook, stirring and scraping occasionally, until the tomatoes are thicker and concentrated, about 10 minutes.

Add most of the cilantro and parsley (save a bit to sprinkle over the top), the favas (reserve a small handful for garnish), and the potatoes. Simmer for another 5 minutes, crushing the potatoes a bit so they soak up the sauce. Taste and adjust with more salt, cumin, smoked paprika, or chile flakes so the sauce is quite zippy.

Heat the oven to 400°F.

Crack an egg into a small bowl, scoop away a bit of sauce in one quadrant of the skillet to make a well for the egg, and slip the egg into the well. Repeat with the other eggs.

Put the skillet in the oven and bake until the eggs are done to your liking, 10 to 15 minutes—the ideal is just until the whites are cooked but the yolks are still runny.

Top with the reserved cilantro and parsley and the reserved favas, and serve right from the skillet, with the flatbreads, if you like.

Lettuces and Early Greens

At this early point in the season, all leafy things are sweet and tender, and perfect for delicate treatment. My preference with perfect spring greens is to mix them up and dress them lightly with beautiful oil and vinegar, and if I have a handful of edible flower petals, I'll add them as well.

Shop early. If you're buying at a farmers' market or harvesting your own, get your greens early in the morning while the air is still cool. They wilt easily in the warmth of midday. (Grocery stores tend to keep their greens perked up by spritzing them frequently . . . annoying, but effective.) Keep them as cool as possible once you get them home. I'll often loosely wrap my greens in paper towels or a clean kitchen towel and then stuff them into a plastic bag, a method that seems to keep the greens happy for a couple of days at least. The good thing is that all but the wiltiest greens can be revived with a soak in cold water and a spin dry.

And shop early in the season as well, especially if you live in a hot climate. Lettuce becomes bitter in high heat, so even when a head might look glorious and green, its flavor may be too strong; I always taste a leaf before I buy.

Wash your greens. To wash greens, fill a large bowl with cold water (you can use the base of your salad spinner), add the greens, swish them around a bit, and let them soak for a few minutes. Then lift the greens out of the water; don't pour into a strainer or you'll be pouring all the dirt back onto the greens. Repeat until no more grit comes off. Check the central ribs of the lettuce leaves to be sure—grit likes to hide there. A nice cold soak will also crisp up the greens. If you're going to cook the greens, you can leave a few drops of water clinging to them. For salad greens, spin the leaves until they're completely dry—this is important!

Mix and match textures. I find the biggest differences among lettuce varieties is in their colors and textures, more so than in the flavors, so build a salad mix with lots of contrast. For crunch, try any of the romaines, including the adorable Little Gem. For a softer, floppier lettuce, buttercrunch is wonderful—tender yet with some crunch at the root end. Iceberg (which deserves more respect than it gets) adds crispness and succulence. I am not a fan of any of the loose-leaf varieties, especially oakleaf lettuces. I find them way too eager to wilt.

Add a bitter bite. With more assertive bites and slightly tougher leaves, young greens such as kales and mustards will give you the flavor punch you want. As these greens mature during the season, I like to briefly wilt them in a sauté pan with some garlic, olive oil, and olives. They still have the taste of spring, but with the new dimension that heat brings.

"Herbed" Butter with Warm Bread

This is one of my favorite things to have on the table during the spring and summer. It's impossible to write a precise recipe for this, so use this as a guide to set you up for success.

Bread and butter all by itself is one of the perfect things in life. Good butter—grass-fed, real butter, the yellow, almost cheeselike butter—is popping up at farmers' markets in small batches and is even showing up on supermarket shelves. Butter has gotten a bad rap, but finally the nutrition world is realizing that it's actually quite good for us. One of the healthiest, most brilliant people I know—Eliot Coleman of Four Season Farm in Maine—thinks it's the perfect food. He eats it almost like peanut butter, spread on the bread so thickly that he can see his teeth marks after he takes a bite.

Once you have found some good butter to celebrate, gather the herbs, edible flowers, shoots, baby greens . . . just mix it up. The end result will be stunning and will tell a story—every bite is unique.

HERE'S HOW YOU DO IT: Smear the butter flat on a cutting board or plate, season generously with flaky salt, several cranks of black pepper, and a sprinkle of chile flakes. Then just start layering on the greens and herbs, some grated citrus zest if you have it, toss on some chopped pickles or capers, and keep adding. Place on the table with a nice warm country loaf to rip into and let the good times begin. I've never put this on a table without it prompting a lot of conversation and happy faces.

Little Gems with Lemon Cream, Spring Onion, Radish, and Mint

Little Gems are a mini romaine type of lettuce—compact little heads with crisp cores and tender green leaves. Because of their size, a half head makes a perfect portion, or you can separate the slightly ruffled leaves and toss them to make a loose salad.

» Serves 4

4 small or 2 large heads Little Gem lettuce, cores cut out, leaves washed and dried well in a salad spinner

1 small bunch spring onions or scallions, trimmed (including ½ inch off the green tops), very thinly sliced on an angle, soaked in ice water for 20 minutes, and drained well (see page 53)

About ½ bunch radishes, scrubbed, tops trimmed off, thinly sliced, soaked in ice water for 20 minutes, and drained well

1 small handful fresh mint leaves

⅓ cup Lemon Cream (page 41)

Kosher salt and freshly ground black pepper

¼ cup dried breadcrumbs (page 30)

2 tablespoons salted roasted sunflower seeds

Put the lettuce, spring onions, radishes, and mint in a large bowl. Add the lemon cream and toss well (your clean hands are the best tool for this) to distribute. Season with salt and lots of pepper, toss again, taste, and adjust with more dressing or salt and pepper.

Toss in the breadcrumbs and sunflower seeds and serve right away.

Butter Lettuce with New Potatoes, Eggs, and Pancetta Vinaigrette

Here's the salad you'll want to make on that first warm spring day, when you realize that lunch on the patio is once again a possibility. The salad is light and springlike, yet the potatoes, eggs, and pancetta dressing make it substantial enough to be a whole meal.

» Serves 4

Kosher salt and freshly ground black pepper

½ pound new potatoes, scrubbed and halved, or quartered if larger than a walnut

About ½ cup Pancetta Vinaigrette (page 39)

1 tablespoon grainy Dijon mustard

1 large head butter lettuce, leaves separated, washed, and dried well in a salad spinner

2 Soft-Cooked Eggs (page 52)

1 small handful flat-leaf parsley leaves

½ cup pickled onions, store-bought or homemade (page 59; optional)

½ lemon

Fill a large pot with cold water and add salt until it tastes like the sea. Add the potatoes and bring to a boil. Reduce the heat to a gentle simmer and cook until tender, 15 to 20 minutes. Because they are new potatoes, this will happen fast, so check often so they don't overcook. Once cooked, drain the potatoes and let them cool slightly.

Warm ⅓ cup of the pancetta vinaigrette in a saucepan and stir in the mustard. Add the potatoes and shake to coat. Set the potatoes aside.

Put the lettuce leaves in a large bowl. Pull the eggs into pieces and add to the lettuce, along with the parsley and pickled onions (if using). Toss, squeeze over the lemon half, season lightly with salt and pepper, and toss again.

Add the potatoes and another 2 tablespoons of the vinaigrette. Toss gently, taste, and add more vinaigrette if you like.

Serve while the potatoes are slightly warm.

Bitter Greens Salad with Melted Cheese

Baking a salad might make you nervous, but a quick moment in the oven will only wilt the greens slightly and yet melt the cheese so that it cloaks the greens nicely.

» *Serves 6*

3 tablespoons red wine vinegar

Extra-virgin olive oil

Kosher salt and freshly ground pepper

1 large head radicchio (¾ pound), cored and coarsely shredded

5 ounces arugula

¼ pound Crucolo, provolone, Taleggio, or Fontina cheese, grated

½ cup roughly chopped lightly toasted hazelnuts (see page 31)

Saba or balsamic vinegar, for drizzling

Heat the broiler to high.

Whisk the red wine vinegar with ¼ cup olive oil in a large bowl and season generously with salt and pepper. Add the radicchio and arugula and toss to coat them nicely. Taste and adjust the seasoning.

Pile the salad on ovenproof plates or an ovenproof platter and top with the cheese. Broil the salad just until the cheese is melted, about 1 minute. Sprinkle the toasted hazelnuts on top and finish with a drizzle of saba. Serve right away.

Sautéed Greens with Olives (Misticanza)

The key to this dish is to cook it quickly at high heat so that you can taste each green in your mix. Too much cooking and you create one big mono flavor. Treat this recipe as a base for improvising; you can take it in so many directions—dress it with a touch of Spicy Fish-Sauce Sauce (page 43) or Citrus Vinaigrette (page 39) or use a soy sauce dressing.

» Serves 4

Extra-virgin olive oil

4 garlic cloves, thinly sliced

¼ teaspoon dried chile flakes

10 cups lightly packed torn mixed greens (such as kale, turnip greens, beet greens, escarole, and hearty lettuces)

Kosher salt and freshly ground black pepper

¼ cup black olives, such as Kalamata, pitted and halved

About 2 tablespoons fresh lemon juice

Heat a glug of olive oil in a large skillet over medium heat. Add the garlic and cook, stirring often, until just beginning to brown, about 2 minutes—don't let it burn! Add the chile flakes and cook, stirring, until fragrant, about 1 minute.

Add the greens a handful at a time, tossing until wilted between additions (if you can, start with the tougher greens such as kale or escarole). Season generously with salt and black pepper and cook until all the greens are wilted and softened, about 3 minutes more after your last addition.

Add the olives and 2 tablespoons lemon juice and toss to combine. Taste and adjust the seasoning with more chile flakes, salt, or lemon juice. Finish with a nice drizzle of olive oil.

Onion Family (*Early Season*)

Unlike mature onions that are cured for longer storage (see page 352), early alliums (the name for the onion family) are all very juicy, sweet, and perishable, whether slender green onions, young shallots, bulbous young Walla Wallas, or the forest-foraged wild ramps that I love so much. With these early-season onions, you get not only the bulb but also the fresh greens—a bonus! I use both the whites and the greens, as I do with scallions (which are available year-round). The whites will generally be mild and sweet, while the greens have a stronger oniony bite.

Use them up. Don't buy them if you don't have plans to use them within several days. If your onions feel a touch slimy when you retrieve them from the fridge, you can simply peel off their outer layer.

Cheap tricks. When serving scallions raw, as in salads, I like to use my "ice water trick" (see page 53) to mellow any bite and crisp them up. When cooking, remember that all onions are full of sugar, so they take kindly to high-heat methods such as grilling. But that same sugar content puts them at risk for burning, so be vigilant.

At the market Scallions = green onions. The names are interchangeable. But *spring* onions are a different thing altogether, though they can look like bulbous scallions. Spring onions are the young versions of onions that will eventually grow into mature, round onions. Look for young spring Walla Wallas or Vidalias for a real treat.

Agrodolce Ramps on Grilled Bread

Ramps are kind of a cult vegetable. They're only available foraged, so they have that wildness mystique, and their season is about as short-lived as a crocus. Not to mention that they're one of the first spring edibles, so they truly are celebratory. Their oniony-garlicky bite can be strong, so I always serve them cooked.

» Serves 4 as an appetizer

Extra-virgin olive oil

1 bunch ramps, ends trimmed, bulbs finely sliced, leaves cut across into 2-inch ribbons

¼ teaspoon dried chile flakes

2 tablespoons raisins, plumped in warm water for 15 minutes, drained

1 tablespoon pine nuts, lightly toasted (see page 31)

Kosher salt and freshly ground black pepper

1½ tablespoons red wine vinegar

Four ½-inch-thick slices country bread

½ recipe Whipped Ricotta (page 37)

Pour a healthy glug of olive oil into a small skillet over medium-high heat. Add the sliced ramp bulbs and chile flakes, and cook until the ramps are soft and fragrant, but not browned, about 2 minutes.

Add the ramp leaves, raisins, and pine nuts, season with salt and black pepper, and cook until all is soft and fragrant, another minute or so. Add the vinegar and toss everything around to deglaze the pan. Cook for about a minute to heat everything through and finish with a drizzle of olive oil. Taste and adjust the salt, pepper, vinegar, and chile levels.

Grill or toast the bread, spread a nice thick layer of whipped ricotta on each piece, and top with the ramps and their juices. Serve warm.

Leeks with Anchovy and Soft-Boiled Eggs

Leeks deserve a spot in the limelight for their impressive sweetness. Here they're roasted until golden brown and balanced out with a healthy amount—this dish can take a lot—of anchovies. Smoked trout would also work well here in place of the anchovies.

» Serves 2 as a main dish, 4 as a first course

Extra-virgin olive oil

Kosher salt and freshly ground black pepper

1¾ pounds leeks (about 3 large), trimmed, halved lengthwise, cleaned well, and cut crosswise into about 4-inch lengths

6 anchovy fillets

About 3 tablespoons fresh lemon juice

2 to 4 Soft-Cooked Eggs (page 52); number of eggs depends on whether this is a main or first course

2 tablespoons dried breadcrumbs (page 30)

Heat the oven to 425°F.

Drizzle a rimmed baking sheet with a glug of olive oil and season with salt and pepper. Arrange the leeks, cut side down, on top. Scoot the leeks around so the cut sides get oiled. Drizzle another 2 tablespoons oil over the top and season with salt and pepper.

Roast the leeks until the undersides are browning nicely and the leeks are getting steamy and soft, 15 to 20 minutes. Stir them around a bit to prevent them from burning, keeping them in a nice cluster toward the center of the baking sheet, and roast until the leeks are very soft and slightly melted, with some browned crunchy pieces around the edges, 15 to 20 minutes longer.

Mash the anchovies with 3 tablespoons lemon juice in a small bowl. Stir in 3 or 4 tablespoons olive oil. Pile the leeks into a bowl, pour the dressing on top, and toss gently. Taste and add more lemon, salt, or pepper as needed.

Arrange the leeks on a platter, gently break the eggs into chunks and distribute over the top, and finish with a sprinkling of the breadcrumbs.

Charred Scallion Salsa Verde

Scallions are underdogs, and I would like to be their champion. Maybe people take them for granted because they're available in the grocery store year-round, unlike other spring onions. But for me, scallions are my go-to allium. They're sweet but not too sugary, and they are so easy to handle. Here I cook the hell out of them to develop deeply sweet flavors, then I fold them into a classic Italian *salsa verde*.

» Makes about 2 cups

1 bunch flat-leaf parsley, thick stems trimmed off and reserved, leaves chopped medium fine

Extra-virgin olive oil

2 bunches scallions, trimmed (including ½ inch off the green tops)

Kosher salt and freshly ground black pepper

1 lemon

2 tablespoons capers, rinsed, drained, and chopped

Measure out half the parsley stems (compost the others or save for another use), trim off the dried end bits of the stems, and very finely slice them crosswise, as you would chives. Combine the parsley stems and leaves in a small bowl and pour on ½ cup olive oil.

Heat a glug of olive oil in a heavy-bottomed skillet over high heat. Add the scallions in a single layer (cook them in batches if necessary), season with salt and pepper, and weight with another heavy pan (make sure the bottom is clean!) so the scallions are pressed down. Cook until they are charred, fragrant, and limp, 3 to 5 minutes. When the scallions are cool enough to handle, cut them into 1-inch chunks and fold into the parsley mixture.

With a rasp-style grater, zest the lemon into the bowl. Add the capers and season generously with pepper. When you're ready to serve, halve the lemon and squeeze over about 2 tablespoons lemon juice, toss, and season with salt.

> **In the kitchen** Many recipes direct you to only use the white and light green parts of a scallion. But that's crazy—all the greens are flavorful and should not be wasted. Just trim off about ½ inch from the top, and of course trim off the hairy roots.

Onions Three Ways, with 'Nduja on Grilled Bread

I love using one ingredient in different ways to compound the flavor. Here I rub the bread with Onion Number One (actually garlic, but it's in the allium family) and then top the toasts with Onions Two and Three: roasted onions and caramelized whole scallions. If you can find young, tender garlic scapes, add a few along with the scallions.

» Serves 4

½ pound young torpedo onions or shallots, ends trimmed and skins removed

Kosher salt and freshly ground black pepper

Extra-virgin olive oil

2 bunches slender spring onions or scallions, trimmed (including ½ inch off the green tops)

Four ½-inch-thick slices country bread

2 garlic cloves, halved

4 ounces 'nduja, slightly soft at room temperature

Heat the oven to 300°F.

Arrange the torpedo onions on a baking sheet and roast until they are very soft and collapsed, 30 minutes to 1 hour, depending on the size and type of onion. Let them cool, then roughly cut into halves or quarters. Season with salt and pepper.

Meanwhile, heat a slick of olive oil in a large skillet over medium heat, and arrange the scallions in a single layer in the pan. Season with salt and pepper. Put another pan that's slightly smaller than the skillet right on top of the scallions to press them (be sure the bottom of that pan is clean!). Cook until they are soft and slightly caramelized, 8 to 10 minutes. Let them cool and drain on a paper towel.

Toast the bread under the broiler (or in a toaster) until the edges are nicely browned. Rub the cut garlic over the surface of all the toasts, then drizzle or brush one side with some olive oil.

Spread a nice layer of 'nduja over each toast and top with the soft onion and caramelized scallions. Season with another pinch of salt and a drizzle of olive oil. Serve right away.

At the market *'Nduja* is a Calabrian-style salami with an incredible spreadable texture that delivers all the salty, tangy, spicy flavors of a classic firm salami. It isn't easy to find, but it's crazy good and worth seeking out.

Radishes

Radishes have become rather glamorous in recent years, moving from being just one of the usual suspects on a vegetable platter to an ingredient with status. This renewed affection has, thankfully, spurred growers to expand their offerings from your basic round red radish to a crazy multitude of shapes and colors—varieties such as slender, pink-and-white ombré-ed French breakfast radishes; austere all-white, long Icicle radishes; dramatic Spanish black radishes; and the mix of gem-toned round radishes sold as Easter Egg. And I'm not even talking about the many varieties of Asian daikon-type radishes.

Variety is the spice. Radish flavors vary only in their level of spiciness, which is mostly determined by how long the radish has been growing; the longer it takes to mature, the spicier the flavor, which is why I like to work with farmers who harvest as soon as the radish has reached its proper size. All young radishes should share a dense crunchiness; those that were left in the soil for a long time will become woody and pithy.

Use the tops. Because radishes grow quite fast, their greens are generally in great shape when they get to the market. Be sure to cut them off when you get home, then wash, dry, and store them as you would salad greens. The radishes themselves store nicely in the fridge up to a week or so, but as with everything, their quality fades over time, so use them soon.

Crudités are just the beginning. The classic spring appetizer is ice-cold radishes with a chunk of good butter and a pile of sea salt on the side. Smear, dip, crunch . . . delicious. But I think of radishes as way more than a simple crudité. I like to use them raw in many shapes (chunks, slices, chopped), and I also love to cook radishes, which opens up a whole new world.

Radishes with Tonnato, Sunflower Seeds, and Lemon

This salad is like an inside-out tuna salad, with the radishes as the centerpiece and tonnato, a smooth creamy tuna mayo, as the binder. It makes a beautiful simple supper on a warm spring night or a great side dish to a grilled veal chop. It's best not to assemble this salad until close to serving time, as the radishes are prone to weeping a bit.

» Serves 2 as a main dish, 4 as a side

½ recipe Tonnato (page 45)

Juice of ½ lemon

2 bunches radishes, greens trimmed off and reserved for another dish, radishes halved or quartered

1 small handful mint leaves

Kosher salt and freshly ground black pepper

¼ cup sunflower seeds, lightly toasted

1 small handful sunflower sprouts (optional)

Put the tonnato in a large bowl, squeeze in a couple of tablespoons of lemon juice, and stir to mix. Add the radishes and toss to coat them.

Add the mint and season well with salt and pepper. Taste and adjust with more salt, pepper, or lemon juice.

Add half the sunflower seeds and sprouts (if using). Toss, then top with the remaining seeds and sprouts. Serve soon.

Grilled Radishes with Dates, Apples, and Radish Tops

When you cook a radish, it loses much of its spicy heat and becomes quite friendly. The cooked radishes also develop a texture similar to the apples in this dish. If you have radishes with nice-looking tops, incorporate them into the dish, as you would with turnips, beets, and carrots. Some grated extra-sharp cheddar would also be nice in this dish.

» *Serves 4*

1 bunch radishes, with their tops if they're nice and fresh

Extra-virgin olive oil

Kosher salt and freshly ground black pepper

Dried chile flakes

Red wine vinegar or white wine vinegar

4 ounces pitted dates, cut into small bits

1 apple, halved, cored, and thinly sliced

½ small red onion, thinly sliced

½ cup lightly packed flat-leaf parsley leaves

½ cup roughly chopped toasted almonds (see page 31)

If you're using the greens, cut them from the bunch of radishes and wash well in cool water, as you would salad greens. Once they're hiding no more grit, spin them dry in a salad spinner.

Heat a slick of olive oil in a skillet over medium-high heat and when it's hot, add the greens. Toss with tongs until the greens are slightly wilted. Season with salt, black pepper, and a few chile flakes and cook for another few seconds, until the greens are tender.

When the greens are cool enough to handle (but still warm), roughly chop them, then pile them into a bowl. Douse with a couple of teaspoons of vinegar and toss to blend. Taste and adjust the salt, black pepper, chile flakes, and vinegar. When the flavors are bright and balanced, toss with a small glug of olive oil. Set aside.

Prepare a charcoal grill, heat a gas grill to high, or heat the oven to 450°F.

Scrub the radishes. Grill or roast the whole radishes—with no oil—until they are slightly soft when you squeeze them, 12 to 15 minutes depending on their size (slightly longer if you're roasting them). Turn them a few times during grilling. Let the radishes cool, then cut them in half.

Toss the halved radishes in a large bowl with the dates, apple, onion, marinated radish tops, and parsley. Add ¼ cup vinegar, 1 teaspoon salt, lots of twists of black pepper, and ½ teaspoon chile flakes and toss again. Taste and adjust the seasoning. Add ¼ cup olive oil and the almonds, toss again, taste again, and make any final adjustments in the seasoning.

Roasted Radishes with Brown Butter, Chile, and Honey

Raw radishes and fresh butter are a classic pairing, but here we cook the two together until toasty and nutty. A splash of vinegar, a pinch of chile, and a drizzle of honey create a delicious tension that makes this dish unexpectedly satisfying.

» Serves 4

Extra-virgin olive oil

2 bunches radishes, with their tops if they're nice and fresh, radishes halved lengthwise if large

Kosher salt and freshly ground black pepper

Dried chile flakes

2 tablespoons unsalted butter

2 tablespoons red wine vinegar

2 tablespoons honey

Heat the oven to 375°F.

If you're using the greens, cut them from the bunch of radishes and wash well in cool water, as you would salad greens. Once they're hiding no more grit, spin them dry in a salad spinner.

Put a small slick of olive oil in a large ovenproof skillet and heat over medium-high heat. Arrange the radishes cut side down and cook until lightly browned, about 3 minutes. Transfer to the oven and roast until the radishes are nicely browned and starting to get tender, about 10 minutes.

Add the radish greens and roast until the radishes are fully tender and the greens have wilted, another 5 minutes.

Take the skillet from the oven and set over low heat on the stove (careful, the handle is hot!). Season nicely with salt, black pepper, and ½ teaspoon chile flakes. Add the butter and cook until the butter has melted and is starting to get golden brown and nutty smelling, 2 to 3 minutes.

Add the vinegar to the skillet and gently fold everything to combine. Drizzle on the honey and fold again. Taste and adjust the seasoning with more salt, black pepper, chile flakes, vinegar, or honey. Serve warm.

In the kitchen Radishes look cheerful and friendly, but they can deliver quite a bite, especially later in the season or during very hot weather. Tame the pepperiness by peeling them—most of the spice is in the outer layer—or by cooking. Sautéing or roasting will mellow their kick.

Sugar
Snap
Peas

Sugar snaps may be the most aptly named vegetable in the garden. When freshly picked in spring, they are indeed sugary and they have a juicy, snappy crunch to them. These are peas that are grown for the pod itself, though you'll find little underdeveloped peas inside. Everything is edible except for the stem end and the fibrous string along one side, which is easy to pull off like a zipper. The string of really young snap peas won't be developed enough to bother removing.

Taste for sweetness. I don't distinguish much between varieties of sugar snaps—they're all about the same to me. But that doesn't mean they're all equal. Always take a bite of a couple of sugar snaps before you buy them. You want to feel that snappy texture, almost like a crisp apple, and you want an upfront sweetness, with just a hint of greenness following. Sugar snaps that have stayed too long on the vine, or that have been harvested too far in advance, will be fibrous and starchy, and not worth playing with.

Keep them loosely wrapped in plastic in the fridge, and try to eat them within a day of purchase—their sugars will quickly fade to starch.

Use whole or sliced. I like to serve snap peas whole—they're a natural two-bite size—but I also love to play with their shapes, cutting them into nuggets or slicing them so fine they're almost shredded. Even thinly cut their crunch remains, creating an appealing texture in your dish.

Sugar Snap Peas with Pickled Cherries and Peanuts

Cherries appear in late spring or early summer, so you may be lucky enough to have both snap peas and cherries in season together. If not, look for pickled cherries in specialty grocery stores.

» Serves 4

1 pound sugar snap peas, strings pulled off, peas cut in half on an angle

1 generous cup drained pickled cherries (page 58)

1 cup redskin (Spanish) peanuts

1 bunch scallions, trimmed (including ½ inch off the green tops), thinly sliced on a sharp angle, soaked in ice water for 20 minutes, and drained well (see page 53)

¼ cup pickling juice (from the cherries)

1 small handful basil leaves

1 teaspoon dried chile flakes

Kosher salt and freshly ground black pepper

Extra-virgin olive oil

Toss together the snap peas, cherries, peanuts, scallions, pickling juice, and basil in a large bowl. Add the chile flakes and season generously with salt and black pepper, especially the pepper. Taste and adjust until the salad is fully vibrant, then add ¼ cup olive oil and toss again.

Taste and adjust the seasoning so the salad is zippy but balanced. Serve lightly chilled.

Sugar Snap Peas with Mustard Seeds and Tarragon

The spices give this dish a vaguely Indian feel, though the tarragon brings us right back to western Europe. I keep all the seasonings in check here because what I really want to taste are the delicately sweet snap peas.

» Serves 4

1 tablespoon yellow mustard seeds

½ teaspoon cumin seeds

Extra-virgin olive oil

1 pound sugar snap peas, strings pulled off

Kosher salt and freshly ground black pepper

2 tablespoons unsalted butter

1 teaspoon finely grated lemon zest

½ lemon

¼ cup lightly packed tarragon leaves

½ cup lightly packed flat-leaf parsley leaves

Put the mustard seeds and cumin seeds in a small skillet over medium heat and toast until the spices become fragrant, shaking the pan so nothing burns, about 4 minutes. Be careful because the mustard seeds might pop. Pour them onto a plate to cool.

Heat a small glug of olive oil in a large skillet over medium-high heat. Add the snap peas, season lightly with salt and pepper, and sauté for a minute or two.

Add ¼ cup water to the pan and quickly cover it. Steam the snap peas for a minute or so, then uncover. The peas should be approaching crisp-tender. Once the water has evaporated, add the butter and the toasted seeds and cook for another minute.

Remove the pan from the heat, add the lemon zest, a big squeeze of lemon juice, the tarragon, and parsley. Taste and adjust the seasoning with more salt, pepper, or lemon juice. Serve warm.

Sugar Snap Pea and New Potato Salad with Crumbled Egg and Sardines

When you're making this salad, you might think that it's too liquidy at first. But all that delicious sauce will get absorbed into the potatoes as the salad sits, and as you mash things together on your plate.

» Serves 4

½ pound new potatoes, scrubbed but not peeled (unless the skin is really tough)

Kosher salt and freshly ground black pepper

2 lemons

½ pound sugar snap peas, strings pulled off, thinly sliced on an angle

1 bunch scallions, trimmed (including ½ inch off the green tops), sliced on a sharp angle, soaked in ice water for 20 minutes, and drained well (see page 53)

6 boneless canned sardines, drained and broken into pieces

2 teaspoons dried chile flakes

Extra-virgin olive oil

4 Soft-Cooked Eggs (page 52)

1 handful mint leaves

Fill a large pot with cold water and add salt until it tastes like the sea. Add the potatoes and bring to a boil. Reduce the heat to a gentle simmer and cook until tender, about 15 minutes (since they are new potatoes, this will happen fast, so check often so they don't overcook). Drain the potatoes and let them cool.

Using a rasp-style grater, zest both lemons into a bowl large enough to hold the whole salad. Cut the lemons in half and squeeze in the juice (try to retrieve and discard the seeds). Add the potatoes, sugar snaps, scallions, sardines, and 1 teaspoon of the chile flakes.

Season with 1 teaspoon salt and many twists of black pepper. Toss gently to mix everything, then let marinate for 10 minutes. Add ½ cup olive oil and toss again. Taste and adjust the seasoning.

Break up the eggs by pulling them apart into quarters and dropping them into the bowl. Add the mint. Mix gently, taste again, and adjust the seasoning if necessary. Serve at room temperature. If you make this ahead and need to refrigerate it, be sure to let it warm up a touch before serving.

Pasta alla Gricia with Slivered Sugar Snap Peas

Pasta alla gricia is a very simple Roman pasta dish consisting of guanciale (cured pork jowl) and pecorino. As I do with many traditional Italian dishes, I use the classic as a springboard for improvisation. Here I add very thinly sliced snap peas, which creates an amazing texture as well as adds a fresh green note to the otherwise quite rich pasta. And I use my Cacio e Pepe Butter as a perfect shortcut, once again demonstrating that a well-stocked larder means delicious food in minutes.

» Serves 4

Kosher salt and freshly ground black pepper

3 ounces guanciale or pancetta, diced or chopped

Extra-virgin olive oil

8 ounces spaghetti, fettuccine, or tagliatelle

1 pound sugar snap peas, strings pulled off, peas very thinly sliced on a sharp angle (so they're almost shredded)

6 tablespoons Cacio e Pepe Butter (page 34)

Pecorino Romano cheese, for grating

Bring a large pot of water to a boil and add salt until it tastes like the sea.

Put the guanciale and 2 teaspoons olive oil into a skillet or Dutch oven that's large enough to hold all the pasta. Cook until it's lightly crisped and most of the fat has rendered out, 9 to 12 minutes. Take the skillet off the heat and spoon off the fat except for about 1 tablespoon.

When the water is boiling, add the pasta and cook according to the package directions until almost al dente. When the pasta is almost ready, add the snap peas to the pasta pot.

Put the skillet back over medium heat to reheat the guanciale gently. With a ladle or a measuring cup, scoop out about ½ cup of the pasta cooking water. Drain the pasta and snap peas and add them to the skillet along with the cacio e pepe butter. Toss well to incorporate, adding a few drops of the pasta water in order to make a cloaking, creamy sauce. Taste and adjust with more salt or pepper, though you probably won't need any.

Transfer to serving bowls and top with grated pecorino. Serve right away.

Very thinly sliced peas can be easily distributed into the pasta strands.

Crispy Sugar Snap Peas with Tonnato and Lemon

Sure, crudités are great, but sometimes I like to go beyond raw . . . way beyond, in this case. Once you get over any intimidation about deep-frying, this is a quick snack to make, and a lovely offering for friends who drop by for a glass of wine or a Negroni.

» Serves 4 to 6 as an appetizer

Vegetable or olive oil, for deep-frying

½ cup cornstarch

½ cup all-purpose flour

1 cup sparkling water

Kosher salt and freshly ground black pepper

Dried chile flakes

1 pound sugar snap peas, strings pulled off

Parmigiano-Reggiano cheese, for grating

Fresh mint leaves, for garnish

4 big lemon wedges

Tonnato (page 45)

Arrange a double layer of paper towels on a tray or baking sheet and set it near your stove. Pour 2 inches of oil (vegetable oil or a mix of olive and vegetable) into a saucepan, making sure there are at least 3 inches of headroom (the oil may bubble up a bit during cooking, and you don't want any spillovers—dangerous!).

Slowly bring the oil up to 375°F on a thermometer. (Alternatively, fry a small piece of bread: When it takes 60 seconds to get nicely crisp and brown, but not burnt, your oil is just about right.)

As the oil is heating, whisk the cornstarch and flour together in a bowl. Whisk in enough sparkling water to make a thin batter. Season with some salt and black pepper and ¼ teaspoon chile flakes.

When the oil is ready, dip the snap peas into the batter, let the excess drip off, and carefully immerse them in the hot oil. Take care to not add too many at once because that will cause the oil temperature to drop and the peas will get greasy. (To make things go faster, you can use a wire mesh spoon, called a spider, to add a bunch of the peas to the batter, tapping to encourage the excess batter to drip off.) Fry until the coating is puffed and very light golden (these will not get deeply colored). Transfer to the paper towels to drain.

Once all the snap peas are fried, turn off the heat under the oil and arrange the peas in a serving bowl. Shower with the Parmigiano, mint, and a pinch of chile flakes and serve right away with lemon wedges and a bowl of tonnato for dipping.

Season Two

Early Summer

The seasons don't ever divide themselves neatly. Spring flows into early summer in fits and starts. A week of T-shirt weather may be followed by a string of cool gray days, challenging our optimism about summer's arrival.

But such weather ambivalence is great in the garden and on the farm. It offers enough sun to give vegetables traction to start growing in earnest but keeps growth in check with still-cool nights. The soil itself is warming, too, encouraging roots and tubers to develop into harvestable sizes.

Not only is early summer a seesaw between warm and cool weather, it's also when you'll find vegetables in both young and mature stages. For example, you may encounter tender new carrots as well as more developed ones that overwintered from last fall. Those months in the cold developed their sugars and made their texture more dense and firm. I'll treat the true young carrots, beets, and turnips with a lighter hand than the mature ones.

Recipes of Early Summer

Beets (*Early Season*)

When early beets come into season, my cooking instantly gets more colorful. Between the magentas, marigolds, oranges, and those amazing pink-and-white bull's-eye-patterned Chioggia varieties, beets bring artistry to my dishes just by showing up. (For mature beets, see page 279.)

A bonus bunch. A freshly dug bunch of beets comes with a bonus—leafy greens, which are like tender, mild Swiss chard (they're actually from the same family). This early in the summer season, I choose my beets by how good the greens look. The beets themselves will be smaller than later in the summer—often only about the size of golf balls. Farmers usually bunch together beets of the same size, which makes prep and cooking easy. I sometimes see bunches of very tiny beets that are sold for their green tops only. I prefer to wait until each end of the beet has something for me to eat.

I cut off the beet tops as soon as I get to the kitchen and refrigerate them in a separate plastic bag, in the same way that I'd store salad greens. The beets themselves are good keepers, so provided they're loosely wrapped in plastic and kept cold, they'll be good for a few weeks.

Eat raw. When you do get a fresh young beet, eat it soon and don't bother cooking it. Crunchy and juicy, a young beet hasn't yet developed the full measure of pronounced minerality and earthiness of a mature beet. That earthiness, which some people say tastes like dirt, does actually come from dirt, though not directly. Certain microbes in the soil produce an organic compound called geosmin, which gives beets their distinct character.

Test before peeling. I decide whether to peel a young beet by biting into a slice. If I detect a big difference in the texture of the skin versus the texture of the interior, then I'll go ahead and peel the beet with a vegetable peeler or paring knife.

For cooked beets, I'll usually leave on the skins during cooking and then simply rub them off with my fingers or scrape them off with a knife.

Aim for al dente. Though I mostly eat them raw, when I do cook young beets I steam or roast them—and I have been known to grill them. But for any method, the trick is to cook them until just barely tender. You don't want the texture to be at all mushy. They should be a perfect al dente—soft, but with a memory of recent crunchiness.

At the market If you're lucky enough to get a bunch of root vegetables that still have their greens attached—and the greens are in pristine condition—you get a two-for-one bonus. The greens can be enjoyed on their own, as you would any cooking green, or integrated into the dish with the roots themselves.

Beet Slaw with Pistachios and Raisins

The pistachio butter underneath the slaw is like an Asian peanut sauce, bringing a much fuller nut flavor than the pistachios could offer alone. As you eat the dish, the juices from the slaw dissolve into the pistachio butter and make a crazy good sort of vinaigrette.

» Serves 4

2 garlic cloves, smashed and peeled

½ cup golden raisins

2 tablespoons white wine vinegar

1¼ pounds beets, peeled; use a mix of colors if you can

2 tablespoons fresh lemon juice

½ cup lightly packed flat-leaf parsley leaves

¼ cup lightly packed mint leaves

½ teaspoon dried chile flakes

Kosher salt and freshly ground black pepper

Extra-virgin olive oil

Pistachio Butter (page 37)

Combine the garlic, raisins, and vinegar in a large bowl and let sit for 1 hour.

Grate the beets on the large holes of a box grater or cut into fine julienne. Yes, your hands will get stained, but the color fades quickly.

Remove the garlic from the raisins and discard. Add the beets, lemon juice, most of the parsley and mint (save the rest for finishing), and chile flakes. Season with 1½ teaspoons salt and lots of black pepper and toss. Let it sit for about 5 minutes and then taste—the slaw should be tart, spicy, peppery, and sweet. Adjust the seasoning, if necessary, then add ¼ cup olive oil. Toss and taste again.

To serve, spread a layer of pistachio butter onto each plate and top with the slaw. Finish with the reserved fresh herbs and a drizzle of olive oil.

Roasted Beets, Avocado, and Sunflower Seeds

The pepperoncini and sunflower seeds make this like a "salad bar" salad, though the similarity stops there. I always use beet tops, in the same way I like to use radish tops (provided they're in good shape). I give them a quick sauté and a brief marination, then toss them into the dish.

» Serves 4

1 pound beets, ideally with pristine greens attached

Kosher salt and freshly ground black pepper

Extra-virgin olive oil

3 tablespoons red wine vinegar

¼ cup salted roasted sunflower seeds

½ cup lightly packed roughly chopped flat-leaf parsley leaves

4 scallions, trimmed (including ½ inch off the green tops), sliced on a sharp angle, soaked in ice water for 20 minutes, and drained well (see page 53)

½ cup lightly packed seeded, chopped pickled peppers, such as pepperoncini

2 firm-ripe avocados

Heat the oven to 375°F.

Trim the tops and bottoms off the beets. Wash the greens and spin dry in a salad spinner. Rinse and scrub the beets to remove any mud or grit. Cut up any larger beets so that they are all about the same size.

Put the beets in a baking dish that's large enough to accommodate all of them in a single layer. Season with salt, then pour ¼ cup water into the dish. Cover tightly with foil and steam-roast until the beets are tender when pierced with a knife. Depending on the size, density, and age of the beets, this could take between 30 minutes and 1 hour.

Meanwhile, if you have beet greens to cook, heat a medium skillet over medium heat. Add a glug of olive oil, add the beet greens, and toss them until they are wilted and a bit stewed, about 5 minutes. Set aside until cool, then chop through them a few times.

When the beets are tender, let them cool until you can handle them, then rub or pare away the skins. Cut into ½-inch wedges or chunks and pile into a bowl. Add the greens.

While the beets are still warm, sprinkle with the vinegar, ½ teaspoon salt, and many twists of black pepper. Toss to distribute the seasonings and let the beets absorb the vinegar for a few minutes. Add a healthy glug of olive oil and toss again. Let the beets sit at room temperature until you're ready to serve.

To assemble for serving, add the sunflower seeds, parsley, scallions, and pickled peppers and toss gently. Peel the avocados and cut them into neat chunks that are about the same size as the beet wedges, and add them to the beets, too. Toss thoroughly but very gently, so you don't mash the avocado too much. Taste and adjust with more salt, black pepper, vinegar, or oil. Serve right away.

In the kitchen Always dress cooked roots and potatoes while they're still warm. The acidic ingredients will be absorbed more deeply, making your final dish nicely bright.

Carrots (*Early Season*)

May I correct the record here? Those stubby orange nubs in plastic bags labeled "baby carrots" have nothing to do with an early-season, truly young, freshly dug carrot. A real baby carrot is delicately sweet with a touch of herbal flavor, with a clean snap to the texture that you'll never get in a mature carrot, even if it is shaved down to a nugget.

Buy the roots, get the greens. Young carrots usually come with their big spray of green tops intact. (The smaller the carrot, the more tender the tops.) When you buy carrots at the farmers' market, the vendor usually asks whether you'd like them removed. Say no, and bring yours home. While carrot tops are not as versatile as the tops of other roots (such as beets or radishes) because their frilly leaves are slightly tough, fibrous, and a tad bitter, they are indeed edible and extremely nutritious. Wash and dry them as you would herbs or salad greens and then make a puree, pesto, or *salsa verde* from them.

Pick them small. My ideal early carrot is about six inches long—young enough to be delicate and sweet, but large enough to have developed some depth of flavor. We grew Napolis at the farm in Maine, which are a perfect all-around carrot, and

I adore the multicolored carrot varieties (different seed companies have different names for these). Also look for tiny, round Thumbelinas. They are super sweet and sort of adorable.

No rush. Store the carrots in the fridge in plastic, separate from the greens. Other than wanting to enjoy them, there's no great hurry to use a carrot, since they keep well. (Explore the virtues of mature carrots on page 290.)

Start with raw. Raw is definitely the first way to go when carrot season arrives. Once you've had your fill munching out of hand, look to raw carrot salads. Nothing is prettier than a carrot slaw made from purple, orange, yellow, and white carrots. Carrots make terrific pickles to serve on a pickle plate and to incorporate into other dishes, and pan-roasted or grilled carrots are a treat this time of the season.

Carrots, Dates, and Olives with Crème Fraîche and Frico

This is a perfect salad in which to use the rainbow carrots that show up at the market in early summer, but it works equally well in the dead of winter with storage carrots. For a party, make a dramatic presentation by plating individual salads and arranging one large frico over each. And of course the salad is fantastic frico-less if you don't have time for garnish making.

» *Serves 4*

1 pound carrots, trimmed and peeled

Extra-virgin olive oil

½ teaspoon dried chile flakes

Kosher salt and freshly ground black pepper

⅓ cup roughly chopped pitted Niçoise or other nice black olives

⅓ cup roughly chopped pitted Castelvetrano or other nice green olives

4 Medjool dates, pitted and very roughly chopped

3 tablespoons white wine vinegar

½ cup lightly packed roughly chopped flat-leaf parsley

1 cup crème fraîche

Frico (page 31)

If the carrots are large, split them lengthwise; if slender, leave them whole. Cut them on a sharp angle so you have long, angled, ¼-inch-thick pieces of carrot.

Put the carrots in a medium saucepan or skillet, add a glug of olive oil and ½ cup water, and season with the chile flakes, 1 teaspoon salt, and many twists of black pepper. Cook at a lively simmer, uncovered, until the carrots are just crisp-tender, 5 to 7 minutes—they should still have definite crunch.

Cool the carrots slightly, drain off any liquid, and pile into a bowl. Add the olives and dates. Pour in the vinegar and toss. Taste and adjust with salt, black pepper, chile flakes, or vinegar until the flavor is super vibrant. Add the parsley and toss again. Drizzle with a glug of olive oil and toss again.

Divide the crème fraîche among 4 plates or a platter and spread it around in a nice schmear. Pile the carrot salad on top, leaving some cream visible. If you're serving with the fricos, lay them on top, either whole or broken into shards.

A sharp angle creates more surface area for the carrots to absorb the seasoning.

Grilled Carrots, Steak, and Red Onion with Spicy Fish-Sauce Sauce

This dish came to be while I was working on the farm and grilling out one summer night. Somehow a carrot ended up on the grill, and from that point on, every vegetable became fair game for the flame! Be sure you don't coat your carrots with oil before you grill them; grilled oil just tastes like chemicals to me. Note that you can absolutely leave the steak out of this dish and it will be just as good.

» Serves 2

¾ pound steak that's good on the grill (skirt, tri-tip, rib-eye, or other cut that you like)

Kosher salt and freshly ground black pepper

½ pound carrots, trimmed and peeled, left whole if very slender or split lengthwise if larger

1 large red onion (about 12 ounces), ends trimmed, peeled, and cut into fat slices

About ¼ cup Spicy Fish-Sauce Sauce (page 43)

2 cups lightly packed mixed fresh herbs (such as flat-leaf parsley, mint, chives, dill, chervil, basil, even baby arugula)

3 big lime wedges

Extra-virgin olive oil

Season the steak with 1 teaspoon salt and several twists of pepper. Set aside.

Heat a gas grill to medium.

Arrange the carrots and onion slices on the grill and cook, turning frequently, until they are starting to soften and brown a bit (the carrots should be about as soft as a cooked beet, and the onions should be quite tender and juicy), about 15 minutes.

Increase the heat to medium-high, blot any moisture off the steak, and add it to the grill. Cook to rare to medium-rare, 3 to 5 minutes per side, depending on how thick it is. Don't overcook it! As you're cooking the steak, make sure the carrots and onions are not charring too much—a few dark edges will be nice, however.

Take everything off the grill. Let the steak rest as you cut the carrots on an angle into long slices and cut the onion rings in half—it's okay if they fall apart at this point.

After the steak has rested for at least 5 minutes, cut it across the grain, and at an angle to the cutting board, into thin strips. Pile the steak, onions, and carrots into a large bowl and pour on ¼ cup of the spicy fish-sauce sauce and any steak juices that have accumulated. Toss, taste, and add more sauce if you need for the flavors to be bright and delicious.

Gently toss the fresh herbs in a small bowl with the juice from one lime wedge, a bit of salt and pepper, and a small drizzle of olive oil. Gently fold the fresh herb salad into the steak salad. Serve with a lime wedge and more sauce on the side.

In the kitchen Don't oil your vegetables before you grill them, because the oil burns and tastes acrid. Instead, grill them "dry" to get a lovely char, and then dress with oil afterward.

Pan-Roasted Carrots with Carrot-Top Salsa Verde, Avocado, and Seared Squid

Carrot tops are full of flavor and nutrients, so make the carrot-top *salsa verde* and serve it with simple roasted carrots or as a condiment to grilled meats and fish. You can also grill the carrots for this recipe.

» *Serves 4*

1 bunch young carrots with very fresh greens (about 1 pound total)

½ cup lightly packed roughly chopped flat-leaf parsley leaves

½ cup lightly packed mint leaves

2 scallions, trimmed (including ½ inch off the green tops), finely chopped

¼ cup capers, rinsed, drained, and roughly chopped

1 teaspoon finely grated lemon zest plus the zest of 1 lemon

Kosher salt and freshly ground black pepper

Hot sauce, such as Sriracha

Extra-virgin olive oil

6 ounces cleaned squid, rinsed, tubes sliced crosswise into ½-inch rings, tentacles halved if large

1 firm-ripe avocado, peeled, pitted, cut into chunks, and coated in lemon juice to prevent browning

6 medium pickled peppers, such as pepperoncini, cored and sliced into rings

1 tablespoon pickling liquid from the peppers

2 tablespoons fresh lemon juice

¼ cup roasted salted pistachios, roughly chopped

Cut the green tops from the carrots (see Note), leaving a tiny bit of green visible on the carrots. Cut off and discard the thicker part of the stems, keeping the feathery tops. Rinse and spin dry, as you would salad greens. Roughly chop the greens and measure out about 1 cup lightly packed. If the carrots need peeling, peel them, but if they are nice and tender, just scrub a bit and rinse thoroughly.

Put the carrot tops, parsley, mint, scallions, capers, and 1 teaspoon of the lemon zest into a bowl. Add ¼ teaspoon salt, a dozen twists of black pepper, and a few drops of the hot sauce and toss. Taste and adjust with salt, pepper, or hot sauce. Stir in ½ cup olive oil. Taste again and adjust so that the salsa verde is bright and bracing.

Heat a large cast-iron or other heavy skillet over medium heat. Lay the carrots in the skillet (cut in half, if needed, to fit) and cook until you hear a bit of a sizzle, about 5 minutes.

Add a small glug of olive oil and roll the carrots around a bit. Cook, rolling so that all sides get cooked, until the carrots are getting lightly browned and tender, about 30 minutes—you should be able to smash them a bit.

Let the carrots cool slightly and pile into a large bowl.

Toss the squid with a small glug of olive oil, ½ teaspoon salt, and about 20 twists of black pepper. Heat the skillet used for the carrots until it's very hot. Add the squid and sear, shaking and tossing so the squid cooks quickly, about 3 minutes. Add the squid to the carrots. Add ½ cup of the carrot top salsa verde to the carrots and squid, toss to coat, and let sit for a few minutes to marinate slightly.

Add the avocado slices, another ½ cup salsa verde, the pepperoncini and the pickling liquid, and the lemon juice and very gently fold together. Taste and adjust with more salt, black pepper, hot sauce, or lemon juice. Drizzle with olive oil and fold again. Arrange on plates, sprinkle with pistachios, finish with another thread of olive oil and a sprinkling of lemon zest, and serve while the squid is still slightly warm.

Note: If your carrots don't have greens or the greens look tired, skip them and use double the amount of parsley and mint in the salsa verde.

Lamb Ragu with Carrots and Green Garlic

Here the carrots don't stand out on their own but rather melt and merge into a sweet and mellow foundation for the ragu. If you can't find green garlic, you can use regular head garlic (if you do, you'll only need 5 or 6 cloves because it's so much more pungent).

» Serves 4

Extra-virgin olive oil

6 ounces green garlic, sliced into ¼-inch-thick pieces (about 1½ cups)

1 pound carrots (12 smallish), ends trimmed, peeled, cut into ¼-inch dice (about 2½ cups)

Kosher salt and freshly ground black pepper

2 pounds ground lamb

½ cup dry, unoaked white wine

½ cup water

1 teaspoon dried chile flakes

A generous sprig thyme

2 tablespoons unsalted butter

½ cup freshly grated Parmigiano-Reggiano cheese, plus more for serving

½ cup freshly grated Pecorino Romano cheese, plus more for serving

8 ounces short dried pasta, such as orecchiette, penne, or ditalini

Heat a glug of olive oil in a large skillet or Dutch oven over medium-high heat. Add the green garlic and carrots and season with 1 teaspoon salt and lots of twists of black pepper. As soon as the vegetables begin to sizzle, reduce the heat to medium-low. Keep cooking until they are soft and fragrant, but not browned at all, about 10 minutes.

Add the lamb, breaking up any big chunks, and cook until it's no longer pink, 5 to 10 minutes; take care not to actually brown the lamb or get really crusty bits.

Add the wine, water, chile flakes, 2 teaspoons salt, and the thyme. Cover the pan and cook at a gentle simmer until the flavors have married nicely, the liquid is brothy and flavorful, and the vegetables are fully tender, 35 to 45 minutes. Check on the ragu during cooking to be sure it's not drying out; if so, add a bit more water. You want the final texture to be loose and slightly brothy, but not watery.

Stir in the butter and the cheeses, and add a few more twists of black pepper. Taste and adjust the flavors with more salt, black pepper, chile flakes, or cheese.

Bring a large pot of water to a boil and add salt until it tastes like the sea. Add the pasta and cook according to the package directions until al dente. With a ladle or a measuring cup, scoop out about ½ cup of the cooking water, then drain the pasta and add it to the ragu. Simmer together for another minute or two to fully cook the pasta and infuse it with the sauce flavors, adding a few spoonfuls of the cooking water if the sauce is getting dry.

Pile everything into shallow bowls. Drizzle with a bit of olive oil and serve. Pass more cheese at the table.

At the market Look for green garlic at farmers' markets. It resembles a slightly chubby scallion, and is actually the garlic plant at the stage before it has formed a head with individual cloves. The flavor is sweet and mild.

Celery

In my world of vegetables, celery is the undisputed flavor king. But an unfamiliar king, as most of us associate it only with the healthy snack forced on us as kids. Not even many chefs treat celery with the respect I think it deserves; it can totally stand on its own.

Shop the farmers' market. The first step toward celery appreciation is to shop for it at the farmers' market. Local, in-season celery will always be less fibrous and sweeter than grocery store celery, and the flavor is bright and assertive. Celery is a super-thirsty vegetable, however, and needs a lot of attention from the grower, which is why you don't see it too frequently at farmers' markets. If not consistently and adequately watered, celery gets very tough and stringy. Look for heads with tightly clustered, dense stalks—the whole bunch should feel heavy for its size. And don't be surprised if you start to see celery beyond the classic pale green. Heirloom varieties are appearing, with stalks ranging from deep purple to magenta, looking a lot like rhubarb.

Keep them together. Keep the celery in a plastic bag in the fridge, with all the stalks still attached, until you're ready to use it. If you encounter a bunch that is very stringy, you can simply peel off the fibrous outer layer with a vegetable peeler.

In the kitchen The very tender, pale yellow leafy stalks in the center of a bunch of celery are the prize. You can save them and add them to a salad, or munch on the stalks on their own as you're cooking and use the leaves like herbs— anything to treasure their delicate crunch and distinctive celery flavor.

Celery Salad with Dates, Almonds, and Parmigiano

This is one of my favorite dishes. It's so simple, but the combination of ingredients creates a wonderful, intriguing aroma. Try to use really good olive oil for this salad.

» Serves 4

8 celery stalks
(leaves separated and
reserved), tough fibers
peeled off, sliced on an
angle into ¼-inch-thick
pieces

4 Medjool dates, pitted
and roughly chopped

½ cup roughly chopped
toasted almonds
(see page 31)

3 tablespoons fresh
lemon juice

¼ teaspoon dried
chile flakes

Kosher salt and freshly
ground black pepper

2 ounces Parmigiano-
Reggiano cheese,
shaved into shards with
a vegetable peeler

Extra-virgin olive oil

Put the celery in a bowl of ice water and soak for about 20 minutes to heighten the crispness. Drain and pat dry, then pile into a medium bowl.

Add the celery leaves, dates, almonds, lemon juice, and chile flakes and toss together. Season generously with salt and black pepper. Taste and adjust the seasoning. Add the Parmigiano and ¼ cup olive oil and toss gently. Taste again and adjust the seasoning so you have a lovely salty, tart, sweet balance. Serve cool.

Celery Puntarelle-Style

The inspiration here is classic Roman *puntarelle alla romana*—made with puntarelle, a late-fall/early-winter bitter green that is just starting to make its way to America, and plenty of garlic and anchovies. If you can find salt-packed anchovies (page 26), this would be a good recipe to use them in. They take more work to prepare than the oil-packed anchovies, but their texture and flavor are really meaty and delicious.

» Serves 2

½ pound celery, preferably including some inner stalks and leaves

6 anchovy fillets, minced

2 garlic cloves, minced

½ cup freshly grated Parmigiano-Reggiano cheese, plus more for serving

Extra-virgin olive oil

Juice of ½ lemon

Kosher salt and freshly ground black pepper

1 cup torn croutons (page 29)

Cut the celery stalks on a sharp angle into thin slices, keeping any leafy parts whole. Put everything in a bowl of ice water and soak for at least 20 minutes; this will make the celery very crisp. Drain and spin dry in a salad spinner.

Meanwhile, put the anchovies, garlic, Parmigiano, and a drizzle of olive oil in a medium bowl and mash thoroughly to make a paste. Squeeze in the lemon juice and add several twists of pepper.

Add the celery and celery leaves and toss thoroughly to get everything coated with the dressing. Taste and add a bit of salt and adjust with more lemon, Parmigiano, or pepper; the salad wants to be very bright. Add the croutons and toss again. Finish with a nice shower of more cheese and a drizzle of olive oil. Serve right away.

Slice celery on a sharp angle to maximize crunch but minimize any stringiness.

Celery, Sausage, Provolone, Olives, and Pickled Peppers

Think of this salad like an Italian hoagie, but without the roll. It will be just fine without sausage if you want to make a vegetarian version, and of course feel free to improvise with other pickled vegetables, capers, even some croutons. The salad gets better as it sits, so it's a great contribution to a potluck dinner.

» Serves 4 to 6

½ head celery, wide stalks halved lengthwise, cut crosswise into ½-inch chunks

½ pound fresh garlic sausage, cooked, cooled, and cut on an angle into ¼-inch-thick slices

½ pound provolone cheese, cut into ½-inch dice

1 cup roughly chopped pickled peppers, such as pepperoncini

½ cup pitted Kalamata olives

½ small red onion, thinly sliced

1 teaspoon fresh thyme leaves

Kosher salt and freshly ground black pepper

¼ cup red wine vinegar

Extra-virgin olive oil

Put the celery in a bowl of ice water and soak for about 20 minutes to heighten the crispness. Drain and pat dry, then pile into a bowl.

Add the sausage, provolone, pickled peppers, olives, onion, and thyme. Toss to mix, then season with a bit of salt and lots of black pepper. Add the vinegar and toss. Let the salad sit for about 5 minutes and then toss again. Taste and adjust the vinegar, salt, and black pepper. When it's as good as a hoagie, drizzle on a healthy amount of olive oil, toss again, and serve.

In the field When you grow celery, you can control the color and delicacy of its flavor by using a method called blanching. As the bunches get closer to harvest time, cover the lower stalks with a sleeve or piece of cardboard. This keeps the sun off them, reducing the production of chlorophyll. The trade-off for more delicacy is less nutrition, however.

Celery, Apple, and Peanut Salad

I learned to appreciate celery when I worked at Four Season Farm, and now I always have a celery salad on my menu. Good, fresh, in-season celery is dense and juicy with flavor, unlike the dry, stringy stuff you find at supermarkets.

» Serves 4

4 large celery stalks (about ½ pound), tough fibers peeled off, sliced on an angle into ¼-inch-thick pieces

3 or 4 scallions, trimmed (including ½ inch off the green tops), sliced on a sharp angle

1 large medium-hot fresh chile, such as Anaheim or poblano (or several smaller chiles), seeded, deribbed, and cut into thin julienne strips (about ½ cup)

2 medium apples (a crisp variety, such as Braeburn, Ashmead's Kernel, or Fuji), halved, cored, and sliced into thin wedges

2 tablespoons fresh lemon juice

Kosher salt and freshly ground black pepper

½ cup roasted peanuts, roughly chopped

1 small handful flat-leaf parsley leaves

Extra-virgin olive oil

Put the celery and scallions in a large bowl of ice water to soak for about 20 minutes—this will make them crisp and will temper the bite of the scallions. Drain and blot them dry with paper towels, and put them in a large bowl.

Add the chile, apples, and lemon juice and toss to distribute. Season with ½ teaspoon salt and many twists of black pepper and toss again. Taste and adjust with more lemon, salt, or black pepper to make the flavor very vibrant.

Add the peanuts and parsley and a healthy glug of olive oil. Toss well, taste, and give the salad a final seasoning adjustment. Serve cold.

In the kitchen To tame the heat of your chiles, don't simply remove the seeds—slice away the whitish ribs inside the chile, which is where most of the capsaicin resides.

Cream of Celery Soup

This soup is so simple and pure in flavor that I often serve it unadorned. Make a simple topping with a few torn croutons, a grating of Parmigiano, or a swirl of extra-virgin olive oil, or go all the way with the unexpected sweet and nutty topping.

» Serves 4

2 tablespoons unsalted butter

1 head celery, cut into 1-inch pieces, leafy tops chopped and reserved

1 small onion, diced

Kosher salt and freshly ground black pepper

6 cups vegetable stock or water

½ cup roughly chopped lightly toasted walnuts (see page 31)

½ cup raisins, plumped in warm water for 15 minutes, drained

1 teaspoon celery seed

Extra-virgin olive oil

1 cup heavy cream

Put the butter, celery, and onion in a large pot over medium heat. Season lightly with salt and pepper and cook the vegetables slowly until they have begun to soften and release their juices, about 8 minutes. Don't let the vegetables brown at all.

Add the stock, adjust the heat to a simmer, and cook until the celery and onion are completely tender, about 30 minutes. Let the soup cool a bit, then process in a blender to make a smooth puree. You may need to do this in batches.

Meanwhile, toss together the reserved chopped celery leaves, walnuts, raisins, and celery seed in a bowl and moisten with a few drops of olive oil.

Return the puree to the pot, add the cream, and bring everything to a low simmer. Cook for about 5 minutes to soften the raw cream flavor. Taste and adjust the salt and pepper. Divide into serving bowls and top with the walnut-raisin mixture.

MORE WAYS:

Add a rich topping: Make some Brown Butter (page 36), gently heat some toasted pine nuts and raisins in the butter, season with a touch of chile flakes, and spoon onto each portion of soup.

Make a delicate seafood stew: Poach shrimp, scallops, and chunks of halibut or cod in the broth for the last 5 minutes. Scoop them out with a slotted spoon, finish the soup as directed in the recipe, and then return the seafood to the pot to heat up just before serving.

Texturize it: Fold in diced raw celery at the last minute and top with a big handful of torn croutons (page 29).

Braising celery transforms its crunchy raw texture (*left*) into dense silkiness with a mellow flavor.

Celery Gratin

A few aromatics and a finish of cheese turn a bunch of celery into a mellow, deeply flavored side dish—the beauty of simplicity. This dish is also gorgeous with a slice of rare roast beef.

» Serves 4

1 head celery, trimmed, stalks separated

1 tablespoon white wine vinegar

4 sprigs thyme

3 or 4 garlic cloves

1 bay leaf

¼ teaspoon dried chile flakes

Kosher salt and freshly ground black pepper

½ cup extra-virgin olive oil

1 cup freshly grated Parmigiano-Reggiano cheese

2 tablespoons unsalted butter, cut into bits

Heat the oven to 375°F.

Rinse the stalks to be sure there is no grit on the inner surfaces. If your celery seems stringy, peel off the outer layer of the larger stalks with a vegetable peeler.

Arrange the celery in a 9 x 13-inch baking dish so that it's more or less in an even layer; it's fine if things are slightly crowded. Add ½ cup water and the vinegar and pop in the thyme sprigs, garlic, and bay leaf. Sprinkle with the chile flakes, 1 teaspoon salt, and generous twists of black pepper. Pour the olive oil over everything.

Cover the dish with foil and bake until the celery is quite tender, 25 to 35 minutes. Remove the foil (careful, the steam is hot), sprinkle the Parmigiano over the top, and distribute the butter over the surface.

Return the dish to the oven, uncovered this time, and bake until the cheese is melty and there are just a few juices bubbling around the celery, another 15 to 20 minutes. Let cool for at least 15 minutes and then serve, spooning over any juices remaining in the dish.

Braised Celery and Radicchio Salad with Perfect Roast Chicken

This salad is extra delicious thanks to the addition of the lemony chicken juices from the roasting pan. Never let the flavors on the bottom of a roasting pan go to waste! Be sure to let the celery cool before slicing and incorporating into the salad.

» *Serves 4*

CHICKEN

One 3- to 4-pound chicken

½ lemon, very thinly sliced

3 or 4 big sprigs each thyme and rosemary

Kosher salt and freshly ground black pepper

3 tablespoons unsalted butter, at room temperature

SALAD

1 cup braised celery (see sidebar), cooled and cut on an angle into ½-inch-thick slices

½ medium head radicchio, cut into ½-inch-wide ribbons

1 large handful flat-leaf parsley leaves

¼ red onion, thinly sliced

1 lemon, halved

Kosher salt and freshly cracked black pepper

1 to 2 cups torn croutons (page 29)

½ cup freshly grated Parmigiano-Reggiano cheese

Extra-virgin olive oil

FOR THE CHICKEN: Heat the oven to 400°F.

With a pair of kitchen scissors or a sharp knife, cut along each side of the chicken's backbone to cut it out completely. Flip the chicken over breast side up and push down with the heel of your hand on the breastbone to allow the chicken to lie flat, like you're cracking open a hard-back book.

Arrange the lemon slices on a rimmed baking sheet or a roasting pan to cover the area that the chicken will be positioned on. Top with the herbs. Season both sides of the chicken generously with salt and pepper and lay the chicken skin side up on top of the flavorings. Smear the butter on the surface.

Roast the chicken until the flesh on the thickest part of the thigh is very tender when poked with a knife, the juices don't come out pink, and/or the temperature of the thigh registers 170°F. This should take 40 to 50 minutes.

When the chicken is done, transfer it to a platter or tray to cool. Carefully pour the chicken fat from the pan (reserve it for cooking potatoes later). Pluck off the lemon and herbs. Discard the herbs, but if the lemon slices are tasty, you can chop them and add to the salad. Add a few spoonfuls of water to the pan and scrape and stir to dissolve the cooked-on juices.

FOR THE SALAD: Put the celery, radicchio, parsley, and onion (and roasted lemon, if using) into a big bowl and toss. Pour on the deglazed chicken roasting juices and squeeze the juice from half the lemon and toss again. Taste and season with pepper and salt if needed—the celery and chicken juices will already be salty, so you might not need much.

Add the croutons and grated Parmigiano and toss again. Taste again, adjust the seasoning, and finish with a drizzle of olive oil.

Cut the chicken into pieces and arrange on a platter. Serve the salad on the same platter or on another one. Serve on the warm side of room temperature.

Braised Celery Having some simply braised celery on hand allows you to add a flavor punch to so many salads, soups, pastas, and more. Separate the stalks and arrange in a shallow baking dish. Add about ¼ cup dry white wine, ½ cup extra-virgin olive oil, a big pinch of salt, a few smashed garlic cloves, a pinch of dried chile flakes, and some thyme sprigs. Cover with foil and bake at 375°F until the celery is silky and tender.

Fennel

Fennel is a love-it or hate-it vegetable because of its mild licorice flavor. I'm in the love-it camp, as is much of the Mediterranean, where it's used in plenty of dishes—especially with seafood.

Choosing by feel. You won't be treated to many varieties of fennel in the market, so just select the bulbs that look young and tightly compacted, and avoid anything that feels leathery or fibrous on the surface.

Three in one. In the grocery store, you'll often get just the trimmed bulb, but at the farmers' market, you'll get the bulb with the stalks and fronds still attached, and each part has a use. The stalks are flavorful but quite tough and fibrous, so you can either pickle them or toss them into a stock. If the fronds are attached, I'll snip them off and use as I would fresh dill or other tender herb. Unless we're talking about wild fennel, whose licorice flavor is potent, fennel fronds aren't intensely flavored, but they can add an herbal note to a salad or *salsa verde*. And of course the bulb is where most of the action is.

Trim. To get a fennel bulb ready for cooking, cut off the stalks and trim the bulb to remove the toughest part of the core; if the feathery fronds look nice, trim them off to use as you would an herb. If the fennel isn't in its prime, the outer layer may be stringy. If so, peel off a thin outer layer using a vegetable peeler. You can now continue with your recipe, either slicing the whole bulb or halving it and going from there.

Fennel, raw and cooked. Fennel is fibrous, so slice it very thinly when eating it raw. I use shaved raw fennel in loads of salads, but I do love to cook with it as well. Cooked fennel gets tender when allowed to completely soften, though its delicate flavor notes can fade. I usually amp up the flavor with herbs, salty olives, and of course plenty of good olive oil.

Maximize the crunch. When serving fennel raw, I like to use the same ice water trick I use with scallions. Soak the slices in ice water for about 20 minutes, then drain and pat dry.

Shaving fennel: Halve the bulb lengthwise, keeping the core intact. Use a mandoline to create wafer-thin slices, ideal for raw dishes.

Chilled Seafood Salad with Fennel, Radish, Basil, and Crème Fraîche

When you get to the seafood counter, choose whatever looks pristine and delicious—crab, white-fleshed fish, shrimp, smoked trout, and poached or grilled scallops are some of my favorites. If you'd like to keep it vegetarian, you can add some sliced, salted cucumbers, some boiled new potatoes, or both. The key is to have all the ingredients refreshingly cold.

» Serves 6

2 fennel bulbs (about 2 pounds total, untrimmed weight), stalks and fronds trimmed off, bulbs trimmed

1 bunch radishes, with their green tops if pristine

Extra virgin olive oil

Kosher salt and freshly ground black pepper

1 lemon, halved

2 teaspoons finely grated lemon zest

½ teaspoon dried chile flakes

½ cup crème fraîche

½ cup lightly packed mixed fresh herbs (aim for three of these four: chives, tarragon, parsley, dill)

¼ cup capers, rinsed and drained

About ¾ pound cooked seafood, preferably a mix of white-fleshed fish, shellfish, squid

If the fennel looks fibrous, peel off a thin outer layer using a vegetable peeler. Use a mandoline to thinly slice the bulbs lengthwise through the core. If you don't have a mandoline, use a very sharp knife and slice as thin as you can.

Soak the fennel slices in a bowl of ice water for about 20 minutes. This will crisp them nicely.

If the radish tops look fresh and pristine, cut them off. (If they are scraggly or yellowed, skip the greens altogether.) Wash them in a few changes of cool water until there's no more grit, then spin or pat them dry.

Heat a glug of olive oil in a small skillet over medium-high heat and add the greens. Season nicely with salt and sauté until they're tender, 3 to 4 minutes. Give them a squeeze of lemon juice. Chop them roughly and then chill in the fridge while you finish the salad.

Scrub the radishes, trim the tops and bottoms, and very thinly slice them.

Drain the fennel slices and dry them well with paper towels or a clean kitchen towel. Pile them into a large bowl with the radishes, radish greens (if using), more lemon juice, the lemon zest, chile flakes, and a generous seasoning of salt and black pepper and toss well. Add the crème fraîche, herbs, and capers and toss again. Taste and adjust with more salt, black pepper, chile flakes, or lemon juice until the salad is lovely and bright.

Add the seafood and carefully fold everything together so you don't break up the seafood too much. Spread the salad on a platter and drizzle with a bit of olive oil. Serve cold.

Roasted Fennel with Apples, Taleggio Cheese, and Almonds

I created this dish by accident while working on the farm. I was making dinner and realized I didn't have enough fennel for the dish I had planned to make. But I had apples, and so in they went. It has been a go-to recipe ever since, and in retrospect, it would have not been as good with just fennel. That's what good cooking is about: adapting, trusting your instincts, and being willing to fail.

» Serves 6

Extra-virgin olive oil

½ pound fennel sausage (or ½ pound mild Italian sausage plus ½ teaspoon fennel seeds), bulk or with casings removed

2 garlic cloves, smashed and peeled

½ teaspoon dried chile flakes

1½ pounds fennel (2 medium bulbs), stalks and root end trimmed, cut lengthwise into eighths

1 large apple (8 ounces), such as Braeburn or Fuji, peeled, cored, and thinly sliced

½ cup almonds, toasted (page 31)

1 teaspoon fresh thyme leaves

6 ounces Taleggio cheese, rind trimmed off and torn into little bits (this cheese is too soft to actually grate)

Kosher salt and freshly ground black pepper

½ cup dried breadcrumbs (page 30)

1 tablespoon unsalted butter

Heat the oven to 375°F.

Heat a large skillet over medium-high heat, add 1 teaspoon olive oil, then add the sausage (if using the mild Italian, add the fennel seeds, too). Cook until it's no longer pink, about 5 minutes, breaking it up with your tongs or a spoon so it's in pieces about the size of popcorn. Scoop it out of the pan and set aside.

Reduce the heat to medium-low, add 1 tablespoon oil and the smashed garlic, and cook slowly to toast the garlic so it's very soft, fragrant, and nicely golden brown—but not burnt—about 5 minutes. Add the chile flakes and toast for another few seconds, then add the sliced fennel. Pour ⅓ cup water into the pan and cover it, adjusting the heat so the fennel steams and simmers. Check the fennel every few minutes, adding a bit more water when the first amount has evaporated.

Continue cooking like this until the fennel is about three-quarters of the way cooked through and is getting tender but not super soft, about 10 minutes. If there's any remaining water when the fennel is cooked, increase the heat to evaporate it quickly.

Return the sausage to the pan and add the apples, almonds, thyme, and half the Taleggio. Toss and then season generously with salt and black pepper.

Pile this into a 2- to 3-quart baking dish, top with the remaining cheese and the breadcrumbs, and dot with the butter. Bake until the ingredients are hot all the way through and the cheese is melting and starting to sizzle, 30 to 35 minutes.

Let the casserole rest for about 5 minutes and then serve hot.

Fennel Two Ways with Mussels and Couscous

I love the anise-licorice flavor of fennel, and the fennel seed in the finocchiona (fennel salami) adds even more of that flavor—an example of how using one ingredient in two different ways in the same dish brings complexity. This dish is good for entertaining because it's fun to eat with your hands—use an empty mussel shell to scoop up the couscous and all the goodness of the mussel liquor, chiles, and citrus. You can also make it without the couscous and serve some grilled bread to dip into the sauce.

» Serves 4

Kosher salt

1 cup Israeli couscous or fregola

Extra-virgin olive oil

2 garlic cloves, smashed and peeled

1 pound fennel (1 large bulb), stalks trimmed off, bulb halved, cored, and cut into ¼-inch slices

½ teaspoon dried chile flakes

1 pound mussels, scrubbed and debearded

¼ pound unsliced finocchiona, casings cut away, halved lengthwise, and cut into ¼-inch half-moon slices (if you buy presliced salami, cut into halves or quarters)

½ cup dry, unoaked white wine

1 cup lightly packed flat-leaf parsley leaves

1 teaspoon finely grated orange or tangerine zest

½ cup fresh orange or tangerine juice

2 tablespoons unsalted butter

Bring a medium saucepan of water to a boil and add salt until it tastes like the sea. Add the couscous and boil until barely al dente, about a minute shy of the package directions. Drain well and toss in a bit of olive oil. Set aside.

Pour ¼ cup olive oil into a large skillet or Dutch oven, heat over medium heat, add the garlic, and cook until the garlic is very soft, fragrant, and nicely golden brown—but not burnt—about 5 minutes.

Scoop out the garlic and set it aside so it doesn't burn. Add the fennel, season with ½ teaspoon salt, and cook over medium heat until it is tender, but not mushy, 12 to 15 minutes.

Increase the heat to medium-high and add the chile flakes, mussels, and finocchiona. Return the toasted garlic to the pan, pour in the wine, cover the pan, and cook, shaking the pan now and then, until the mussels have all opened, about 5 minutes. If some are not yet open, give it another couple of minutes, but at that point, discard any unopened mussels.

Add the parsley, orange zest, orange juice, and butter and shake to incorporate. Taste and add more salt or chile flakes if you like. Fold in the couscous, cover the pan, and remove from the heat. Let the couscous warm up for a minute or two. Uncover, tumble everything around to fluff and distribute the couscous, drizzle with olive oil, and serve right away.

Potatoes (*Early Season*)

Everyone has eaten a potato, but not everyone has eaten a truly new potato, freshly dug from the soil just days—or even hours—before serving. Once you do, your life is forever changed, because a new potato is everything good about a potato but more delicate, sweeter, and refined.

Size doesn't matter. Early-season new potatoes are usually small because they haven't had much time to grow, but smaller isn't necessarily better. A lemon-size potato could be every bit as creamy and tender as a walnut-size one. Aim to pick potatoes of similar size, though, which will make prepping and cooking easier. (See page 362 for mature potatoes.)

You'll see red, blue, yellow, and white varieties as new potatoes, and while I find white potatoes generally denser and creamier, all potatoes are good at this early-summer stage. New blues can be intensely sweet and densely creamy. A couple of my favorites that do well in the Pacific Northwest, where I live, are red Rose Golds, white Carolas, and yellow German Butterballs.

Don't be fooled into thinking a fingerling potato is a new potato. Even when fully mature, fingerlings are very small, and usually long and thin, hence the name. A tiny fingerling can be as old as a big storage potato, with none of the finesse of a new potato.

Don't touch that peeler. One of the beauties of a new potato is its undeveloped skin. That means no peeling, folks. In fact, never peel a new potato, unless there's a bad spot. Simply rinse them, and if the skins seem at all tough, just scrub them a bit or scrape them with the back of a knife.

Keep it dark and cool. Store your new potatoes in a loosely closed paper bag—no plastic, please—in a cupboard or other darkish place. If your house is very hot or humid, it's fine to store new potatoes in the refrigerator. However, don't put late-season potatoes in the refrigerator, because the cold converts the potato's starches into sugar. A new potato isn't very starchy to begin with, so the flavor won't change radically, but older potatoes can become oddly sweet and they will darken too much when cooking because of the high sugar content.

Cook simply, but do cook. Potatoes are one of the few vegetables that I don't suggest you eat raw. They aren't toxic, but they're not too tasty and they can give you indigestion. But simple cooking methods are best for these early-season potatoes—think boiling, steaming, and pan-roasting—and delicately flavor with fresh herbs.

> **In the kitchen** To make your potato salads deeply flavorful, season the potatoes while they are still warm so that they will absorb the dressing through to the center.

Smashed New Potatoes with Lemon and Lots of Olive Oil

This side dish is so perfect on its own that I hesitate to suggest any additions, but if you must, a handful of freshly picked herbs—especially chives and dill—is fantastic.

» Serves 4

Kosher salt

1½ pounds new potatoes, rinsed and just lightly scrubbed if they need it

Freshly ground black pepper

1 lemon, halved

Extra-virgin olive oil

Put the potatoes in a pot and add cold water to cover by 2 inches. Add salt until the water tastes like the sea. Bring to a gentle boil and boil the potatoes until they are very tender, 15 to 20 minutes.

With a ladle or a measuring cup, scoop out about ½ cup of the cooking water and drain the potatoes well. Put them back in the pot and crush them using a potato masher or a big fork or a wooden spoon. Squeeze on the lemon juice, season with ½ teaspoon salt and many twists of pepper, and add ¼ cup olive oil. Sprinkle on a tablespoon or so of the cooking water and crush a few more times and then taste. Adjust with more lemon, salt, pepper, or olive oil until the flavor is irresistible. Add a bit more cooking water if you like in order to make the texture chunky but a bit creamy.

MORE WAYS:

Make amazing hash browns: Shape the potatoes into little pucks, dip the top and bottom in breadcrumbs, and shallow-fry in a blend of oil and butter until browned and crisp.

Load it up for a gutsy version: Right before final seasoning, fold in chopped pitted olives, capers, and chopped scallions.

Add some California: Smash a diced avocado into the potatoes as you smash them.

In the kitchen Do-ahead restaurant trick: You can boil the potatoes until very tender, then drain and set aside. Just before serving, dunk in boiling water until heated through, then continue with your recipe.

Potato and Roasted Cauliflower Salad with Olives, Feta, and Arugula

Think potato salad with a fifty-fifty ratio of potato to cauliflower—it's lighter and less starchy, but every bit as satisfying. Served with some whipped feta and a handful of arugula tossed in, the salad is wonderful by itself and even more amazing with roasted or grilled chicken. I also like it on top of grilled flatbread.

» *Serves 4 to 6*

1 pound new potatoes, rinsed and just lightly scrubbed if they need it

Kosher salt and freshly ground black pepper

Juice of 1 lemon

Extra-virgin olive oil

1 pound cauliflower, cut or broken into florets (no bigger than about 1½ inches)

⅓ cup chopped pitted olives (a mix of black and green is nice)

¼ small red onion, thinly sliced

¼ cup roughly chopped seeded pickled peppers, such as pepperoncini, or pickled peppers in oil

1 teaspoon fresh thyme leaves (lemon thyme would be amazing!)

½ teaspoon dried chile flakes

3 ounces feta cheese

1 handful arugula leaves, chopped

Put the potatoes in a large pot of cold water and add salt until it tastes like the sea. Bring to a boil, reduce the heat to a gentle simmer, and cook until tender, 20 to 25 minutes. Once the potatoes are cooked, drain them and return to the pot.

Smash the potatoes with a fork to crush them and create lots of crevices, add 2 tablespoons of the lemon juice and a healthy glug of olive oil, season with salt and black pepper, and toss gently. Let them cool.

Heat the oven to 375°F.

Put the cauliflower in a bowl, add ¼ cup olive oil and ½ teaspoon salt, toss to coat all the florets, and spread them over a rimmed baking sheet. Roast until tender and nicely browned around the edges, 20 to 30 minutes. Add the cauliflower to the smashed potatoes.

Add the olives, onion, pickled peppers, thyme, and chile flakes to the potatoes and cauliflower. Toss gently, season with more salt and black pepper and some olive oil and a bit more lemon, and toss again.

Put the feta in a food processor and pulse until creamy. With the motor running, drizzle in 3 tablespoons olive oil.

Add the feta to the salad and fold gently. Add the chopped arugula and fold again. Taste and do your final seasoning adjustment to make this irresistible.

Serve slightly warm or at room temperature, with a final squeeze of lemon over everything.

In the kitchen Almost all vegetable salads are best when served cool (but not ice cold) or at room temperature. The textures will be looser and the flavors will blossom.

Pan-Roasted New Potatoes with Butters

I like to pan-roast new potatoes, especially a little later in the season, when they are less pristine than in the early weeks. Pan-roasting gives you textural contrast—a crisp roasted surface and a creamy interior. Start them on the stovetop to ensure a rich, even browning and then finish them in the oven—a hands-off method that produces even cooking. To serve these without the flavored butters, toss them in olive oil and some fresh herbs such as rosemary and thyme before roasting.

» Serves 4

Extra-virgin olive oil

Kosher salt and freshly ground black pepper

1½ pounds new potatoes, halved or quartered if necessary to make all the potato pieces about the same size

Alla Diavola Butter (page 33), Green Garlic Butter (page 34), or Pickled Vegetable Butter (page 35), or all three

Heat the oven to 400°F.

Heat a heavy skillet over medium-high heat, add a glug of olive oil, and sprinkle the surface of the skillet with salt and pepper. Working in batches if necessary, arrange the potatoes cut side down in a single layer and season the tops with a bit more salt and pepper. (Or you could do this in two skillets.)

Cook the potatoes until the cut faces are nicely browned, regulating the heat so they don't get too browned too fast—you may need to swap positions in the pan so the potatoes brown evenly. You want this step to take 6 to 8 minutes.

If your pan is ovenproof, transfer the whole skillet to the oven. If not, or if you have too many potatoes for one pan, transfer the potatoes to a rimmed baking sheet or roasting pan, cut side down, and roast until they are completely tender when poked with a knife, 12 to 18 minutes.

Pile the potatoes into a serving bowl and serve with the compound butter(s) on the side for diners to "custom mash" at the table.

Clockwise, from top left: Green garlic, pickled vegetable, and alla diavola butters

Turnips (*Early Season*)

The turnips we see in early summer are mostly Japanese varieties, often named Hakurei or Tokyo turnips. These small, smooth, white turnips (also called salad turnips) are wonderful to cook with and just as wonderful not to cook with—they are amazing raw. To me, a young Japanese turnip is like a better radish, with a more reliably crisp and almost juicy texture. Unlike beets, these early-season turnips aren't simply a young version of the turnip you'll see in fall and winter. When Japanese turnips mature too far, their flavor deteriorates, becoming bitter and overly spicy. The succulent texture of that young specimen becomes simply watery and fibrous. If confronted with an old Japanese turnip, I'll add it to a gang of other vegetables to be roasted, so that excess water and bitter flavor can be cooked away. (Learn about true late-season turnips on page 370.)

Use both greens and roots soon. Like all early season root vegetables, early-summer turnips come with a beautiful crown of greens, which is always my first consideration when choosing a bunch. Pick the turnips with the most pristine greens and look for bunches with roots the same size—that makes prepping and even cooking easier.

When you get them home, cut off the greens and take care of them as you would salad greens. The turnip roots store fairly well in the refrigerator, though not nearly as long as their mature cousins. Try to use them within 3 days, especially if you want to show off their snowy white hue, which will discolor after a few days.

Crisp in ice water. Salad turnips are only mildly spicy and have little of the mustardy notes of mature turnips, which means they are delicious raw. And with their small size and very white flesh, they look beautiful in salads. I never peel these turnips. I just give them a quick rinse and trim the green stem ends to a tidy ¼ inch, or cut them off entirely. I usually give thinly sliced raw turnips a 20-minute soak in ice water to enhance their crispness.

If you cook, keep it quick. These young turnips make incredible pickles, which look gorgeous in the pickle jar or on a pickle plate. They are also amenable to pan-steaming and even roasting, and because of their high water content will cook quickly. However, they're not high in starch, so they can be less than satisfying when mashed.

Turnip Salad with Yogurt, Herbs, and Poppy Seeds

The large amount of poppy seeds in this dish adds an amazing floral quality, plus plenty of crunch. You could swap crème fraîche for the yogurt, if you're feeling luxurious, and if you have some chervil, add that to the mix of herbs. Make sure you drain the turnips super well and serve the dish right away; otherwise, things may get a bit soggy.

» *Serves 4*

1 bunch Japanese turnips, with their tops if they're nice and fresh, trimmed so there's just a nice ¼ inch of green stems left

1 lemon, halved

½ teaspoon dried chile flakes

Kosher salt and freshly ground black pepper

½ cup plain whole-milk or low-fat yogurt (not Greek)

About 1 cup lightly packed mixed herbs: mint leaves, flat-leaf parsley leaves, and chives cut in 2-inch lengths

4 scallions, trimmed (including ½ inch off the green tops), sliced on a sharp angle, soaked in ice water for 20 minutes, and drained well (see page 53)

Extra-virgin olive oil

¼ cup poppy seeds

Slice the turnips lengthwise as thin as you can. If you have a mandoline, use it; otherwise make sure your knife is sharp and just go slowly. Soak the slices in ice water for 15 to 20 minutes, then drain very well.

Rinse, dry, and roughly chop the turnip greens (if they're not in great shape, give them a quick sauté in a small amount of olive oil). Put the turnips in a bowl and squeeze in about half the lemon. Add the chile flakes, ½ teaspoon salt, and many twists of black pepper and toss to blend. Add the yogurt and toss again. Taste and adjust the seasoning so they are quite bright. Add the herbs, scallions, and ¼ cup olive oil and toss again. Taste and adjust the seasoning.

Scatter half the poppy seeds on the bottom of a platter or individual serving plates, top with the turnip salad, and finish with the rest of the poppy seeds. Serve right away.

In the kitchen Japanese turnips are crisp and refreshing because of their high water content. The downside is that they can weep moisture into your dish, so serve right after assembly.

Sautéed Turnips with Prunes and Radicchio

Most people would not consider prunes an exciting ingredient, but when cooked, the plush texture and deep toffee sweetness of a prune can really bring some sex appeal to a dish.

» *Serves 4*

8 pitted prunes, quartered

2 tablespoons balsamic vinegar

Extra-virgin olive oil

2 garlic cloves, smashed and peeled

¼ teaspoon dried chile flakes

1 bunch Japanese turnips, greens cut off and reserved, trimmed and halved

Kosher salt and freshly ground black pepper

Small head radicchio, cut into 1-inch ribbons (soak in ice water for 20 minutes to reduce bitterness, then drain well)

Put the prunes in a small bowl and add 1 tablespoon of the vinegar. Add warm water just to cover the prunes. Let them soak for 20 minutes to soften and plump.

Heat a glug of olive oil in a large skillet over medium heat. Add the garlic and cook gently until it's nicely golden brown, very fragrant, and soft, about 5 minutes—do not burn the garlic! Add the chile flakes and then arrange the turnips in the pan, cut sides down. Season with salt and black pepper and cook until the turnips are starting to brown lightly on the cut side, 4 to 5 minutes. Flip the turnips over and add the prunes and a few spoonfuls of their soaking liquid.

Cover the pan and steam the turnips until they are tender when pierced with a knife, adding a few more splashes of the soaking liquid as you cook them. You want there to be just enough water to continually create steam but not so much water that the turnips are boiling.

When the turnips are just about tender, add the greens and the drained radicchio. Increase the heat to high and finish cooking with the cover off, tossing and stirring to wilt the greens and mix everything together.

Remove from the heat and season with salt, black pepper, and the remaining 1 tablespoon vinegar. Taste, adjust the seasoning, and finish with a drizzle of olive oil. Serve warm.

In the field Precise timing for peak seasons varies between weather, regions, and overall climate changes. Anthony and Carol Boutard of Ayers Creek Farm in Oregon see weather as an oscillating continuum rather than a series of distinct seasons. Farmers face great challenges with weather patterns that are becoming more erratic and unpredictable.

Midsummer

Midsummer isn't a fixed block of weeks on the calendar; it's a state of mind. This phase shows up at different points in different parts of the country. When it does arrive, it brings an assurance that yes, indeed, summer is actually here. No more cold snaps. You can relax now.

Once I'm past the initial postwinter joy of eating anything fresh and green, I get more expansive in my cooking. In these warmer weeks I can choose from a wide range of vegetables. Joining those ever-faithful brassicas, such as cauliflower and broccoli, are so-juicy-they-quench-your-thirst cucumbers; string beans in yellow, green, and purple; and summer squash in its youth—slender, taut, and delicious. (Which is the only stage in which to eat squash. Once it's bigger than a small hot dog bun, the flesh will be seedy and watery.)

Many of these early-summer vegetables will continue through the golden days of autumn. But they are ripe and ready to enjoy now, in big platters of colorful salads, weeknight pastas, and pickles and preserves.

Recipes of Midsummer

Broccoli

Broccoli belongs to the large multimember brassica clan, which includes kale, collards, and Brussels sprouts, among many others. But even in the narrower scope of the broccolis, there's quite a bit of variety, from the chubby florets and fat stems of common broccoli, to slender, sweet Broccolini, to gangly sprouting broccoli, which often has a purple hue. Sprouting broccoli doesn't form a big dense head, but rather is all sweet stems and shoots with just small loose florets at the tip. One foot in the broccoli family and one in the turnip clan, the more robust broccoli rabe (see page 185), with lots of leaves and only a few florets, is aggressively bitter-sweet. I like to tame its bitterness with salt and fat—anchovies or fish sauce and of course lots of extra-virgin olive oil.

New kid. I am pleased to see a leafy broccoli rabe relative called Spigarello making its way to farmers' markets and onto restaurant menus. I came across it in southern Italy and it blew my mind. It looks like broccoli rabe—pretty much all leaf and no florets, with slim, tender stems—but the flavor is pure broccoli. It cooks quickly, so you can toss it into dishes at the last minute. (Before I discovered Spigarello, when I was working at Four Season Farm, I would use just the leaves of the regular broccoli plants to make pesto or to add to pastas and stews.)

Green, with blue notes. With any variety of broccoli, you want to look for a deep green color, bordering on blue-green, sometimes purple. Stay away from anything yellowed. The florets should be tight little clusters, not opened-out buds, which indicate age. Check the ends of the stalks and avoid those that are significantly dried out.

Storage is easy. Store the broccoli in a plastic bag in the fridge. The broccoli family isn't especially perishable, but do use it within a couple of days of purchase for the sweetest flavor.

Stop throwing away the stems! For starters, buy whole heads of broccoli (not broccoli crowns), because the juiciest, sweetest part of broccoli is the stem. Start by trimming away any leaves (I like to cook with those, too, so save them unless they are very large and mature) and then shave off the outer layer of the stem, removing any hard bits or fibrous layers. Slice the stem into thin or thick "coins," depending on your recipe. Break the head apart gently and cut away individual florets, following the natural branching of the vegetable to yield long-stemmed florets.

Wet heat for pasta, fire for excitement. I grew up eating broccoli mostly steamed or boiled. This is still how I prepare it when I'm using it in a pasta dish. But my go-to method for broccoli and its kin is high heat: either roasting or grilling. For roasting, I toss the broccoli in some olive oil and seasoning first. But for grilling, I just throw it naked on the grill—no oil until after it's cooked—because when oil hits the intense heat of a grill, it creates an unpleasant chemical flavor. Grilled broccoli, with a deep char and almost burnt caramelization, and seasoned with a bit of extra-virgin olive oil and lemon juice, is addictive . . . the potato chip of green vegetables.

Smashed Broccoli and Potatoes with Parmigiano and Lemon

This dish delivers the same comfort factor as classic mashed potatoes, but with more complexity and nutrition. Don't be timid with the lemon and olive oil—they're what makes the dish.

» Serves 4 to 6

Kosher salt and freshly ground black pepper

2 pounds potatoes (Yukon Golds or other medium-starch potatoes work well), peeled and halved

¾ pound broccoli, dried ends trimmed and stems peeled, cut into chunks and small florets

1 cup freshly grated Parmigiano-Reggiano cheese

Juice of 1 lemon

Extra-virgin olive oil

Fill a large pot with water and add salt until it tastes like the sea. Add the potatoes, bring to a boil, and cook until the potatoes are quite tender but not fully tender, about 15 minutes from when the water starts to boil.

Add the broccoli and keep boiling until both are fully tender, another 6 to 8 minutes. Drain thoroughly and return to the pot.

Mash the vegetables with a potato masher or big spoon until the vegetables are crushed but still chunky. Add the Parmigiano, followed by the lemon juice, and then season generously with salt and pepper. Mash a bit more and fold to blend everything. Taste and adjust the salt, pepper, and lemon. Finish with a good dose of olive oil—start with ¼ cup and add more to taste.

Serve right away, though you can make these ahead and reheat them gently in a covered dish in the oven or in a pan on the stovetop with a little bit of water to loosen them.

Pan-Steamed Broccoli with Sesame Seeds, Parmigiano, and Lemon

Pan-steaming in just a small amount of water keeps the vegetable from getting waterlogged—plus, it's so much easier than setting up a proper steamer basket.

» Serves 4

1 lemon

Extra-virgin olive oil

2 garlic cloves, smashed and peeled

¼ teaspoon dried chile flakes

1½ pounds broccoli, stems trimmed and peeled, then cut lengthwise into long-stemmed florets the full length of the stems (aim for even sizes)

Kosher salt and freshly ground black pepper

¼ cup sesame seeds, lightly toasted (see page 31)

½ cup freshly grated Parmigiano-Reggiano cheese

Grate the zest from the lemon into a large bowl. Halve the lemon and squeeze the juice into the bowl (fish out and discard the seeds) and set aside.

Heat a nice glug of olive oil in a large skillet that has a lid over medium heat. Add the garlic and cook slowly to toast the garlic so it's very soft, fragrant, and nicely golden brown—but not burnt—about 5 minutes. Add the chile flakes and arrange the broccoli in an even layer—it's okay if the pan is crowded. Season with ½ teaspoon salt.

Increase the heat to medium-high and add a nice big splash of water, about ¼ cup (enough water to create steam, but not so much that the broccoli sits in water and gets soggy), and put the lid on right away. Steam the broccoli until it's tender, adding more water a few times. The whole process should take about 10 minutes.

When the broccoli is cooked, transfer it to the bowl where the lemon is waiting. Add the sesame seeds and lots of twists of black pepper and toss gently. Taste, adding more salt, chile flakes, or black pepper as needed. Add ¼ cup olive oil, toss again, and then shower with the Parmigiano. Serve warm or at room temperature.

MORE WAYS:

Transform this into a main dish: Add some diced fresh chile—hot or mild, as you like—to cook along with the garlic. Just before you add the broccoli, increase the heat and add 1-inch chunks of boneless chicken breast or chicken thighs, let them cook for a minute, then add the broccoli and continue with the recipe.

Make a medley: Use a mix of vegetables in addition to the broccoli: carrot coins, cauliflower florets, chunks of summer squash.

Take the flavors to a deeper place: Use broccoli rabe instead of broccoli. Increase the amount of garlic and chile flakes. Add a few chopped anchovy fillets to the oil along with the chile flakes. Omit the sesame seeds, and add nice black olives and capers and a big handful of chopped flat-leaf parsley to finish.

Rigatoni with Broccoli and Sausage

There are two cooking tricks in this recipe. First, tossing the florets into the pasta pot for the last couple of minutes of cooking: It's efficient, but it also integrates the broccoli into the pasta sauce, as all the florets break up when you drain and toss the pasta. The second trick is shaping the sausage into patties instead of crumbling the sausage into the pan and browning it. You get a deep, browned crust on both sides of the sausage patty, but the interior stays moist. When I finish the dish, I break up the patty, producing crunchy bits, soft bits, tender bits—you get a lot of texture and flavor without overcooking the sausage. The hot pasta water added to the dish finishes off any of the undercooked bits of sausage.

» *Serves 4*

3 to 4 garlic cloves, very thinly sliced

Extra-virgin olive oil

1 pound sweet or hot Italian sausage, bulk or casings removed

Kosher salt and freshly ground black pepper

8 ounces rigatoni

1 pound broccoli, stems trimmed and peeled, stems sliced crosswise into ¼-inch coins, and tops cut into florets

¼ teaspoon dried chile flakes

½ cup Whipped Ricotta (page 37)

About 1 cup freshly grated Parmigiano-Reggiano

¼ cup dried breadcrumbs (page 30; optional)

Put the garlic in a small bowl and pour over enough olive oil to cover. Shape the sausage into 4 balls, then flatten them like a hamburger patty.

Bring a large pot of water to a boil and add salt until it tastes like the sea. Add the pasta and cook to just shy of al dente according to the package directions.

Meanwhile, heat a small glug of olive oil in a large skillet over medium heat. Add the sausage patties and cook until nicely browned on one side, about 4 minutes.

Add the broccoli coins and the sliced garlic, including the oil, to the skillet. Flip the sausage patties and keep cooking until the sausage is just about fully cooked (it's okay if it's a touch pink in the center, because it will continue to cook a bit), another 4 minutes or so. Break up the sausage with a spoon into bite-size chunks. Add the chile flakes and cook for 30 seconds or so. With a ladle or a measuring cup, scoop out about ¼ cup of the pasta cooking water, add it to the pan to stop the cooking of everything, and slide the pan from the heat.

About 3 minutes before the pasta should be al dente (according to the package directions), add the broccoli florets and cook all together until the pasta is ready. Scoop out another cup of pasta cooking water, drain the pasta and broccoli, and add to the skillet.

Return the skillet to the heat. Add ¼ cup or so of the pasta water, the whipped ricotta, and half the Parmigiano. Season generously with salt and black pepper. Shake the pan to combine the ingredients, put back over medium heat, and cook for a couple of minutes to warm everything through and make a nice saucy consistency.

Serve with more Parmigiano and top with the breadcrumbs (if using).

"Chinese" Beef and Broccoli

There's nothing Chinese about this dish, other than that it reminds me of the takeout treat of my youth. The vinaigrette (which lasts in the fridge for weeks) is good on just about anything, including pork, sausages, and lots and lots of vegetables, so I'm pretty sure you'll be keeping a batch on hand. Once you've made the vinaigrette, putting this dish together takes literally 15 minutes.

» Serves 2

¾ pound tender steak, such as rib-eye or filet mignon

Kosher salt and freshly ground black pepper

1 pound broccoli, stems trimmed and peeled, stems sliced crosswise into ⅛-inch coins, and tops cut into florets

About ⅓ cup Caper-Raisin Vinaigrette (page 39)

1 cup dried breadcrumbs (page 30)

Season the steak heavily with salt and pepper. Let it sit for at least 10 minutes and up to 1 hour.

Heat a heavy medium skillet over high heat. Blot off any moisture from the surface of the steak, add it to the skillet, reduce the heat to medium, and cook until the first side is nicely browned and the steak looks about one-third done.

Flip the steak and cook until rare or medium-rare. The timing depends totally on the thickness and texture of your steak; a 1-inch filet mignon will take about 10 minutes total to get to medium-rare. Transfer to a plate to rest and tent with foil. Don't wipe out the skillet.

Pile the broccoli florets and coins into the still-hot skillet, increase the heat to high, add ½ cup water, cover, and steam for 3 to 4 minutes. Uncover and cook until the broccoli is tender and the water has evaporated, another 3 to 4 minutes, depending on the size of your florets.

Remove the pan from the heat, add ⅓ cup vinaigrette, and toss to combine. Taste and adjust with more vinaigrette, salt, or pepper.

Slice the steak across the grain. Arrange the broccoli on a plate or platter, top with the steak and any accumulated juices, sprinkle the breadcrumbs over everything, and serve right away.

In the kitchen Don't worry so much about serving your steaks hot—focus instead on serving them juicy and tender by letting them rest for a good 5 to 10 minutes. The bigger the cut, the longer the rest.

Charred Broccoli with Tonnato, Pecorino, Lemon, and Chiles

Chips and dip, but with fresh vegetables instead of potato chips! Most charred vegetables are delicious, but broccoli takes to charring especially well because the tips of the florets char at a different rate than the dense stem, which creates layers of crispy and juicy textures.

» Serves 4

1½ pounds broccoli, stems trimmed and peeled, cut into long florets

1 lemon, halved, and one of the halves cut into 4 wedges

Dried chile flakes

Kosher salt and freshly ground black pepper

Extra-virgin olive oil

A nice chunk of aged Pecorino Romano, for grating

2 tablespoons dried breadcrumbs (page 30)

Tonnato (page 45; optional)

Heat the broiler.

Spread all the broccoli on a rimmed baking sheet and broil—with no oil—until it is slightly softened and nicely charred on most surfaces, turning once, 5 to 7 minutes. You can also do this on a grill, but you'll need a grill basket.

Pile the broccoli into a bowl and squeeze the half lemon all over it. Season with ½ teaspoon chile flakes and generous amounts of salt and black pepper. Add ¼ cup olive oil and toss. Taste and adjust the seasoning until it's delicious.

Arrange the broccoli on a serving platter, grate a nice shower of pecorino over the top, sprinkle on the breadcrumbs, if using, and serve with the lemon wedges. Set out the tonnato as a dip.

Broccoli Rabe, Mozzarella, Anchovy, and Spicy Tomato

This easy-to-put-together casserole is a bit like eggplant Parmesan, but way lighter and more nutritious. If you want to make the dish fully vegetarian, leave out the anchovy.

» Serves 4

½ pound fresh mozzarella cheese

Extra-virgin olive oil

2 garlic cloves, smashed and peeled

5 or 6 anchovy fillets

Dried chile flakes

1 pound broccoli rabe, dried ends trimmed, chopped 2 or 3 times to shorten the stalks

Kosher salt and freshly ground black pepper

One 14-ounce can whole peeled tomatoes, drained and roughly chopped

2 tablespoons grated Parmigiano-Reggiano cheese

Slice the mozzarella into ¼-inch rounds and arrange on paper towels. Cover with more towels and then set a heavy pan or baking sheet on top to apply moderate pressure. This will remove some of the moisture in the cheese and help it brown nicely. Leave to drain until you're ready to assemble the dish.

Heat a nice glug of olive oil in a large skillet over medium heat. Add the garlic and cook slowly to toast the garlic so it's very soft, fragrant, and nicely golden brown—but not burnt—about 5 minutes. When toasted, smash the garlic cloves with a wooden spoon, add the anchovy, and let it dissolve into the oil. Add ¼ teaspoon chile flakes.

Add the broccoli rabe, season lightly with salt and black pepper, and toss around in the pan so it's coated with the seasoning. Cook over medium heat until the leaves are wilted and the stems are starting to soften a bit, 6 to 8 minutes.

Add the tomatoes and shake the pan so the tomatoes settle around the broccoli rabe. Cook until the broccoli rabe is fully tender and the tomatoes are reduced, 10 to 12 minutes more. The tomatoes should be thick and almost pasty, not saucy-liquidy. If it's not thick enough, you can take out the broccoli rabe, transfer it to the baking dish you'll use, and cook the tomatoes for another couple of minutes, stirring and scraping the pan.

Heat the broiler. Arrange the broccoli rabe and sauce in a baking dish large enough to accommodate it all in more or less a single layer.

Arrange the drained mozzarella on top, drizzle with some olive oil, and broil until the cheese is browned and the casserole is bubbling slightly, about 10 minutes.

Let cool for a couple of minutes, sprinkle with the Parmigiano, drizzle with a bit more olive oil, and serve hot, so the cheese is melty.

In the kitchen To prevent fresh mozzarella from getting rubbery when you cook it, press out as much liquid as possible before cooking. Arrange slices between several layers of paper towels and press with a heavy weight, such as a frying pan.

Cauliflower

When you imagine a cauliflower, you probably picture it white, but these days the vegetable comes in multiple colors, from snowy white to orange to green . . . even vivid purple. And while I'm pretty sure you couldn't tell any difference in flavor if you tasted them all blindfolded, the colors are fantastic to play with when creating a dish. Cauliflower is wonderful raw, though be sure to season it well. But it's totally versatile and loves to be roasted, fried, steamed, pickled, or grilled.

Weight and wait. When selecting your cauliflower, look for very tight, heavy, and brightly colored heads. A cauliflower's size does not affect the flavor. Avoid any heads that are speckled with dark mold, which means they're old or have been stored poorly. Cauliflower will keep happily in the refrigerator for several days—longer than many vegetables—but don't make it wait for you for more than four or five days.

Getting inside the head. The whole head can be eaten—florets (called "curds"), center stem, and tender leaves. The leaves have usually been cut off before the cauliflower ever reaches the supermarket, but farmers' market cauliflower will still be cradled by pale celadon leaves that are succulent and crisp. Slice them thin and add to your dish, raw or cooked. Cauliflower can be vexing because the head is dense and not easy to break apart with your hands. Start by cutting away any leaves, and if they're tender, reserve them to add to your dish. With a sharp, stiff paring knife, cut out the central stem, reserving it to use in your dish as well. The stem of a cauliflower doesn't need to be peeled, like broccoli does; just cut away the very end if it's dried. Now you can maneuver your knife to the interior, where you'll cut away individual florets, following the natural branching of the vegetable to yield long-stemmed florets. Cut pieces of the stem into coins or chunks.

Raw "Couscous" Cauliflower with Almonds, Dried Cherries, and Sumac

In this dish, I crumble the raw cauliflower so that it has the look and texture of couscous—it's easy and unexpected and makes you think of cauliflower in a whole new way. If you can't find dried tart cherries, use golden raisins or even chopped dried apricots; the idea is to have a sweet-tart and chewy element as contrast to the granular vegetable. And be sure to dress and season this salad generously. Underdressed, it risks being dry.

» *Serves 4 to 6*

3 ounces dried tart cherries, roughly chopped (about ½ cup)

⅓ cup red wine vinegar

¾ pound cauliflower or Romanesco

3 scallions, trimmed (including ½ inch off the green tops), sliced on a sharp angle, soaked in ice water for 20 minutes, and drained well (see page 53)

2 teaspoons ground sumac

½ teaspoon dried chile flakes

Kosher salt and freshly ground black pepper

Extra-virgin olive oil

1 cup almonds, toasted (see page 31), half very roughly chopped and half more finely chopped

½ cup roughly chopped flat-leaf parsley leaves

½ cup mint leaves

Put the dried cherries and vinegar in a small bowl and leave to plump for at least 30 minutes.

If the cauliflower still has outer leaves and they look fresh, chop them. Cut the stem from the cauliflower and cut the head into small florets. Chop the stem into small chunks.

Add some of the stem chunks to a food processor; don't fill beyond halfway. Pulse to chop the stems finely, scraping down the sides a couple of times, and then dump into a large bowl. Finish processing the stems this way, and then do the same with the florets. The goal is to create dry, crumbly cauliflower bits that resemble couscous.

Add the scallions to the bowl with the cauliflower. Add the cherries and soaking vinegar and toss to mix well. Season with the sumac, chile flakes, 2 teaspoons salt, and generous twists of black pepper. Taste and adjust the salt, chile flakes, and vinegar until the cauliflower is highly seasoned and well balanced. Now add ¼ cup olive oil, all the almonds, the parsley, and mint and toss well. Taste again and add more seasonings and oil if you like. Serve cool or at room temperature.

Roasted Cauliflower, Plums, Sesame Seeds, and Yogurt

In my book, it's impossible to add too many sesame seeds, so pour 'em on. You want the plums to be bright and juicy, so choose something like a Santa Rosa or even one of the pluot varieties. Italian prune plums are not right for this dish, because they are drier and generally less acidic. The salad is best at room temperature, which allows the flavors to blossom.

» Serves 4

1 large head cauliflower (1¾ to 2 pounds)

Extra-virgin olive oil

Kosher salt and freshly ground black pepper

¾ pound plums (3 medium), pitted and cut into small chunks

Juice of 1 lemon

½ teaspoon dried chile flakes

½ cup plain whole-milk yogurt (not Greek)

¼ cup sesame seeds, toasted (see page 31)

3 scallions, trimmed (including ½ inch off the green tops), sliced on a sharp angle, soaked in ice water for 20 minutes, and drained well (see page 53)

1 cup lightly packed flat-leaf parsley leaves

½ cup mint leaves

Heat the oven to 425°F.

If the cauliflower still has outer leaves and they look fresh, chop them. Cut the center stem from the cauliflower and cut the head into florets. If there are big pieces of stem without florets, cut them into chunks. Toss the cauliflower with a glug of olive oil, 1 teaspoon salt, and many twists of black pepper.

Spread the cauliflower out on a rimmed baking sheet and roast until tender and nicely browned around the edges, 15 to 20 minutes. Let cool to room temperature and then pile into a large bowl.

Add the plums, half the lemon juice, chile flakes, ½ teaspoon salt, and lots of twists of black pepper. Toss to distribute the seasonings. Add ¼ cup olive oil and the yogurt and toss again. Taste and adjust the seasoning, adding more salt, black pepper, chile flakes, or lemon juice as you like.

Top with the sesame seeds, scallions, parsley, and mint, and serve at cool room temperature.

Cauliflower Ragu

I think of this dish as one of my sleeper recipes—it's not super sexy on paper, but it is surprisingly delicious and crowd-pleasing. Part of the appeal comes from adding the cauliflower in two batches—the first addition becomes meltingly tender and breaks down through the long cooking. The second addition holds on to a bit of its fresh texture and flavor, forming a flavor "chord." Another key is to finish cooking the pasta in the ragu, so that it soaks up some of the sauce. And be sure to season this well!

» Serves 4

1 large head cauliflower or Romanesco (1½ to 1¾ pounds)	1 big sprig rosemary
Extra-virgin olive oil	Kosher salt and freshly ground black pepper
3 garlic cloves, smashed and peeled	12 ounces fusilli or other spiral- or tube-shaped pasta
¼ teaspoon dried chile flakes	1 tablespoon fresh lemon juice
1 medium yellow onion, diced	3 tablespoons unsalted butter
½ cup dry, unoaked white wine	1 cup freshly grated Parmigiano-Reggiano cheese
1½ cups water	

If the cauliflower still has outer leaves and they look fresh, chop them. Cut the center stem from the cauliflower and cut the head into small florets. Chop the stem into small chunks.

Heat ¼ cup olive oil, the garlic, and the chile flakes in a large deep skillet or Dutch oven over medium-high heat. Add about two-thirds of the cauliflower florets and chopped stems (you'll add the last third in a bit) and the onion. Add the wine, 1 cup of the water, rosemary sprig, 1 teaspoon salt, and several generous twists of black pepper. Tumble everything together.

Cover the pan and adjust the heat so the mixture simmers nicely. Cook until the cauliflower is fairly tender, about 25 minutes, stirring and smashing with a wooden spoon or spatula a few times as you cook.

Add the rest of the cauliflower and the remaining ½ cup water and cook until the second batch of cauliflower is very tender, though it will have more tooth to it than the first batch, which should be quite sloppy by now. This second cooking should take another 20 minutes or so. The ragu at this stage should be loose but not watery, so if it seems dry or tight, add a few more spoonfuls of water.

Meanwhile, bring a large pot of water to a boil and add salt until it tastes like the sea. Add the pasta and cook until 2 minutes shy of al dente (according to the package directions). The pasta will finish cooking in the ragu. With a ladle or a measuring cup, scoop out about 1 cup pasta cooking water and then drain the pasta well.

Add the pasta to the ragu, along with the lemon juice, butter, and Parmigiano, and fold everything together. Taste and adjust with more salt, lemon, black pepper, or cheese, and adjust the texture to make it creamy by adding a splash or two of the reserved pasta water. Serve right away.

Cauliflower Steak with Provolone and Pickled Peppers

This is a novel, and flavor-packed, way to use cauliflower. It's also a great dinner party dish because it can be prepared ahead: Cook the cauliflower "steaks," pat on the topping, arrange them on a baking sheet, and refrigerate until just few minutes before serving. Then slide them into the oven, keeping in mind that the final cooking will take a little longer if they are cold.

» Serves 2 to 4 . . . or maybe 6, depending on the shape of your cauliflower and whether you serve a whole steak or a half per person

1 large head cauliflower (1½ to 1¾ pounds)

Extra-virgin olive oil

Kosher salt and freshly ground black pepper

1½ cups dried breadcrumbs (page 30)

1 cup grated (on large holes of a grater) aged provolone (3 ounces), plus ¼ cup finely grated aged provolone for dusting

½ cup chopped pickled sweet hot peppers (Mama Lil's is a great brand)

⅓ cup chopped mixed pitted olives

¼ cup capers

¾ cup lightly packed roughly chopped flat-leaf parsley

1 teaspoon finely grated lemon zest

Heat the oven to 450°F.

Trim the bottom of the cauliflower so that it sits steadily on the cutting board. Trim off about ½ inch from two opposite sides (to flatten them), then cut the cauliflower into 3 or 4 thick slabs—the number will be determined by the shape of your cauliflower. Brush both sides of each slab with olive oil and season generously with salt and black pepper. Chop and crumble the trimmings and set aside.

Figure out whether you need one or two baking sheets to fit the cauliflower steaks without crowding them, then heat the sheets in the oven for 10 minutes (this preheating will make the underside of the slabs nicely golden brown). Carefully lay the slabs on the sheet(s) and return to the oven quickly. Roast the cauliflower until it's tender all the way through, but not falling apart, 18 to 20 minutes.

While the cauliflower is roasting, make the topping by mixing together the breadcrumbs, large-grated provolone, pickled peppers, olives, capers, parsley, lemon zest, and crumbled cauliflower trimmings. Moisten with a small glug of olive oil, just to help the filling hold together. Taste and season generously with salt and black pepper until it's so delicious, you want to eat it all.

Take out the baking sheet(s) again and distribute the topping among all the slabs. Press and pat to make a thick layer. Return the cauliflower to the oven and roast until the topping is lightly browned and starting to crisp, and the cheese is starting to melt, 10 to 15 minutes.

With as wide a spatula as you have, transfer the slabs (they're delicate) to plates and top with a dusting of the finely grated provolone.

Baked Cauliflower with Salt Cod, Currants, and Pine Nuts

Salt cod is one of my favorite go-to ingredients, but it requires planning. At least a day ahead of cooking, it has to be soaked and rinsed several times, but after that it is quite easy to work with. The currants add a note of bittersweet to the dish that is a welcome contrast to the overall richness. This is perfect served with a simple leaf salad or bitter greens.

» Serves 4

1 pound salt cod fillet (start soaking this at least 1 day ahead)

1 cup heavy cream or crème fraîche

½ cup milk or water

3 garlic cloves, smashed and peeled

1 small bunch scallions, trimmed (including ½ inch off the green tops), cut into 1-inch lengths

1 bay leaf

1 small head cauliflower (about ¾ pound), cut into florets

¼ cup dried currants, soaked in water for 30 minutes and drained

¼ cup pine nuts, lightly toasted (see page 31)

¼ cup lightly packed flat-leaf parsley leaves

1 teaspoon finely grated lemon zest

Freshly ground black pepper

¼ teaspoon dried chile flakes or Aleppo pepper

½ cup dried breadcrumbs (page 30)

A day before you make this dish, desalt the cod: Rinse the salt cod with cool water, then put it in a large bowl or a big saucepan. Fill with more cool water and soak for 1 or 2 hours. Drain the water, refill with fresh water, and soak again. You'll want to drain and refill 5 or 6 times total. The fish should soak for a good 12 hours and up to 24 hours before it's ready to cook.

Once the cod is desalted, put it in a heavy-bottomed medium saucepan with the cream, milk, garlic, scallions, and bay leaf. Bring to a simmer and very gently simmer until the salt cod is tender and you can flake it apart with a fork, about 15 minutes. During this simmering time, the cream will reduce and thicken and the garlic and scallions will get soft.

Heat the oven to 425°F.

Scoop the cod out of the cream and crumble-flake it into a large bowl. Add the cauliflower, currants, pine nuts, parsley, and lemon zest to the bowl. Season with many twists of black pepper. Toss gently so all the ingredients are combined.

If the cream mixture still looks very liquidy, simmer for another few minutes until it is nice and thick. With a fork or wooden spoon, mash the garlic and scallion pieces into the cream. The garlic should crush into a puree and the scallions will just sort of smash. Pour this cream over all the ingredients and fold gently to combine. Taste and adjust your seasonings; you probably won't need salt because the cream will be salty.

Pile everything into a 3-quart baking or gratin dish (be sure to scrape all the cream from the bowl). Top the casserole with the breadcrumbs and bake until the cream is lightly browned and bubbling around the edges, about 20 minutes.

Let the dish cool for about 10 minutes, then sprinkle with the chile flakes just before serving.

Fried Cauliflower with Spicy Fish-Sauce Sauce

This recipe is the result of an experiment I did one day when I was working at a restaurant in New York City. I was cooking Brussels sprouts and trying to figure out what method to use to get them super crispy. I had sprouts going simultaneously in a sauté pan, the oven, the steamer, and I threw one into the deep fryer. I sort of forgot about that one, yanking it out only after it was almost burnt. And of course it was the winner—crisp, almost charred, and exceedingly sweet. Now I use the same method for many vegetables, cauliflower being ideal. You can serve it simply tossed with lemon, salt, and dried chile flakes; with a lime and freshly coarsely chopped garlic and parsley; or with a sauce or dip, as I do here.

» Serves 4

2 garlic cloves, minced

Extra-virgin olive oil

1 medium cauliflower cut into chubby florets

Vegetable oil, for deep-frying

½ cup finely chopped flat-leaf parsley

Spicy Fish-Sauce Sauce (page 43)

Put the garlic in a bowl large enough to hold all the cauliflower and add enough olive oil to cover.

Pour at least 3 inches of oil into a medium saucepan with tall sides (so that the oil can't bubble over when you add the cauliflower). Slowly bring the oil up to 365°F on a thermometer. Arrange a double layer of paper towels on a tray and set near the stove.

Carefully immerse a few of the cauliflower florets into the oil and fry until they are *really* dark brown, about 5 minutes. Remove with a slotted spoon and drain on the paper towels. Repeat to fry all the cauliflower, taking care not to add too many florets at once, which would lower the oil temperature and make the cauliflower greasy.

Toss the fried florets in the bowl with the chopped garlic and its oil, the parsley, and a big old glug of the fish-sauce sauce. You want enough to coat the florets and leave more for sopping up. You can also serve the cauliflower undressed, with the spicy fish-sauce sauce in a ramekin for dipping.

At the market Look for Romanesco, cauliflower's sexy cousin, especially at farmers' markets. Related to both cauliflower and broccoli, it has a flavor similar to cauliflower, is quite delicate, and is a shocking lime green. The most amazing thing about Romanesco is its fractal shape. Its endlessly repeating conical forms make it look like a rocket ship from a fever dream.

Cucumbers

A bite of cucumber brings you a refreshing juiciness and satisfying crunch that could almost be called thirst-quenching. The flavor, on the other hand, might kindly be called "subtle." Barely sweet with melon-y overtones, cucumbers benefit from supporting flavors in a dish.

Different on the outside, same on the inside. We're used to seeing green, slightly nubby cukes in the market, along with the "fancy" ones called English cucumbers, which almost always come imprisoned in a plastic sleeve. The main difference is the seeds, which are fewer and smaller in the English variety. But step away from the supermarket and into a farmers' market—or your garden—and you'll see a wide range of much prettier and more succulent cucumbers. Their shapes will range from round to submarine to slightly curved trumpets, in shades from ivory through lemon yellow, bronze, and green, striped, mottled, or uniform.

The flavors of all these are similar. However, pickling cucumbers (aka Kirby) are distinctly different. While you can pickle any cuke, Kirbys are cultivated to be drier and firmer than a salad-style cuke.

Chill. Cucumbers like the cold, so store them in the refrigerator, loosely wrapped in a plastic bag so that they get a bit of air—they will get slimy if they're tightly sealed.

Keep some peel, lose the seeds. Some cucumbers are waxed to keep them from drying out; I'll always peel a waxy cuke. Otherwise, my preference is to leave the skins on, unless they feel too nubby. Sometimes I'll peel them in alternating stripes, which leaves some color but removes much of the chewiness. Then I halve them lengthwise and scrape out the seeds using the tip of a spoon. Some people do this with a melon baller.

Add salt to tighten. A cucumber's juiciness also means that it can exude a lot of water into your dish, diluting flavors and making things soggy. So I always salt cucumbers before I use them to draw out some water while seasoning the flesh, making it tastier and firmer—it's like a gentle pickling.

Slice the cucumber according to the directions in the recipe and pile the slices into a bowl. Sprinkle generously with salt and arrange in a colander. Let sit for at least 1 hour (and up to 24). You'll see beads of moisture forming on the slices after a while. When the time is up, tumble the cuke slices onto paper towels and blot to remove the water and excess salt. Now you're ready to continue with your dish.

Versatile players. Cucumbers are so neutral that they fit in nicely anywhere you're looking for crispness and moisture, such as salads of almost any kind. I love cucumbers with dairy, such as yogurt, and I always use plenty of intensely flavored accents—dried fruit, hot chiles, fragrant herbs—to balance out their mildness. I mostly use cucumbers raw and chilled, but a lightly sautéed cucumber dressed with one of the flavored butters in this book (pages 33 to 37) makes a really delicious side dish to grilled meat, chicken, or fish.

Cucumbers, Celery, Apricots, and Pistachios

This dish hits every flavor note—sweet, sour, salty, bitter . . . and it's all kinds of crunchy. The more herbs you pack in there, the better. Mint, parsley, basil, and celery are just the beginning—you can add sorrel, every kind of basil you can find, chives, even some cooked grains or couscous. Serve this with grilled lamb, friends, the great outdoors, and cold pink wine.

» Serves 4

1½ pounds cucumbers (a mix of varieties if possible)

Kosher salt and freshly ground black pepper

4 medium celery stalks (leaves reserved)

½ cup dried apricots, quartered

1 garlic clove, smashed and peeled

¼ cup red wine vinegar

½ cup pistachios, lightly toasted (see page 31) and chopped

½ cup lightly packed mint leaves

½ cup lightly packed flat-leaf parsley leaves

½ cup lightly packed basil leaves

½ cup lightly packed celery leaves (if you have them)

¼ teaspoon dried chile flakes

Extra-virgin olive oil

Peel the cucumbers if their skins are tough or waxed. Trim the ends of the cucumbers, halve lengthwise, and scoop out the seeds. Cut the halves crosswise on an angle into very thin slices. Put the cucumbers in a colander and toss them with 1½ teaspoons salt. Set aside for at least 20 minutes to extract their water and give them a "quick-pickled" flavor.

Meanwhile, cut the celery crosswise on an angle into very thin slices and soak in ice water for 10 minutes. Drain, pat dry, and pile into a serving bowl.

Put the apricots, garlic, and vinegar in a small bowl. Let the apricots plump for 10 minutes.

Pat the cucumbers dry and add to the celery, along with the pistachios, mint, parsley, basil, and celery leaves (if using). Remove the garlic from the apricots and discard it. Add the apricots and vinegar to the bowl, along with the chile flakes and ¼ cup olive oil. Season with black pepper, but don't add more salt yet because the cucumbers will have absorbed a bit. Toss, taste, and adjust the flavors with more salt, vinegar, chile flakes, or black pepper until it's bright and zingy. Finish with another drizzle of olive oil. Serve right away.

Cucumbers, Yogurt, Rose, Walnuts, and Herbs

Be very careful with the amount of rose water you use—too much and the dish becomes overly floral. You can find rose water at well-stocked grocery stores and also at Middle Eastern stores. The salad is so beautiful, whether you build it on a big platter and serve it with a bunch of other dishes, or you plate it individually. If you can't find roses, use any edible flower (unsprayed, of course).

» Serves 4

1 pound cucumbers (as many varieties as you can find), unpeeled unless waxed

Kosher salt and freshly cracked black pepper

½ teaspoon rose water

¼ cup white wine vinegar

½ cup plain whole-milk or low-fat yogurt (not Greek)

1 bunch scallions, trimmed (including ½ inch off the green tops), thinly sliced on a sharp angle, soaked in ice water for 20 minutes, and drained well (see page 53)

¼ cup walnuts, lightly toasted (see page 31) and roughly chopped

1 small handful mint leaves

1 tiny handful pristine rose petals (from unsprayed roses)

Trim the ends of the cucumbers, halve lengthwise, and scoop out the seeds. Slice the cucumbers into shapes that echo their natural shape. Toss the cucumbers with 1 teaspoon salt and put in a colander so the salt can draw out excess moisture. Let them sit for 30 minutes. Blot the cucumbers on paper towels to remove the moisture and excess salt and transfer to a large bowl.

Mix the rose water and vinegar together, add to the cucumbers, and toss. Add the yogurt and toss again. Add the scallions, walnuts, mint, and rose petals. Season lightly with salt and lots of cracked pepper and toss again. Taste and adjust with more vinegar, salt, or pepper. Serve soon.

Lemon Cucumbers with Onion, Papalo, and Lots of Herbs

I don't run into new ingredients all that often, but when I do, it's like finding a favorite new rock band. Papalo is sometimes referred to as summer cilantro, because the plant can take the heat, unlike cilantro, which bolts (goes to seed) by the time true summer heat arrives. When you find papalo at your market—and you will more and more—this is the first salad you should make. You don't have to use lemon cucumber, but this is the perfect recipe to showcase its exceptional crunch. And if you can't find papalo, the salad is still delicious with all types of herbs. But take my word: Buy some papalo seeds and grow your own. You will be happy.

» Serves 4

1 pound lemon cucumbers or other cucumber varieties (preferably a mix of colors and shapes)

1 medium red onion

Kosher salt and freshly cracked black pepper

3 tablespoons white wine vinegar

¼ cup plain whole-milk yogurt (not Greek)

1 small handful papalo leaves or other fresh herbs

1 small handful basil leaves

1 small bunch chives, cut into 3-inch lengths

1 small cluster dill sprigs

Extra-virgin olive oil

Peel the cucumbers if their skins are tough or waxed. Trim the stem end of the cucumbers, halve them lengthwise, and scoop out the seeds. Set the flat side of a half cucumber on a cutting board and cut into ⅛-inch-thick slices. Put the cucumber slices in a large colander.

Cut off the ends of the onion, halve it lengthwise, and cut into thin half-moon slices as well. Add to the colander.

Salt the vegetables generously (about 2 teaspoons), tossing to distribute the salt. Let everything sit for about 40 minutes. This will soften the aggressive flavor of the onion and draw out excess moisture from the cucumber and cure it slightly.

Lift the cucumbers and onion out of the colander and pile onto a couple of paper towels. Blot to remove the excess moisture and salt, then pile into a large bowl.

Add the vinegar and toss well. Add the yogurt and toss again. Add the papalo (if using), basil, chives, and dill and toss again. Season with cracked pepper. Taste and add more salt, vinegar, or pepper to make the flavor pop. Finish with a nice shot of olive oil and toss again.

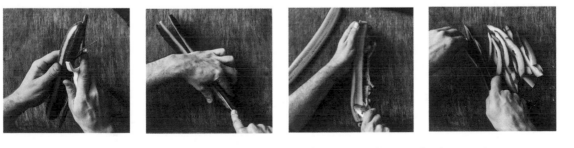

Peeling a cucumber in alternating strips offers some color but reduces any toughness. Halve the cucumber, scoop out the seeds, and slice at a sharp angle to create long crescents.

Cucumbers, Scallions, Mint, and Dried Chiles

This is my absolute go-to cucumber dish—you can throw it together in no time and the combination of cool cukes, hot chiles, and fragrant mint is definitely the whole being greater than the sum of its parts. Key here, however, is the vinegar, which is the slightly sweet, beautifully balanced late-harvest Sauvignon Blanc vinegar made by Albert Katz. (See more about KATZ vinegars on page 18.)

» Serves 4

1 pound cucumbers (preferably a mix of colors and shapes)

Kosher salt and freshly ground black pepper

1 bunch scallions, trimmed (including ½ inch off the green tops), sliced on a sharp angle, soaked in ice water for 20 minutes, and drained well (see page 53)

¼ red onion, very thinly sliced

1 small handful mint leaves (a mix of varieties is great!)

½ teaspoon dried chile flakes

3 tablespoons slightly sweet white wine vinegar, such as KATZ Sauvignon Blanc Vinegar

Extra-virgin olive oil

Coarse finishing salt, such as Maldon or Jacobsen (optional)

Peel the cucumbers if their skins are tough or waxed (for a typical green slicing cuke, peel the skin in alternating stripes). Trim the ends of the cucumbers, halve lengthwise, and scoop out the seeds. Slice the cucumbers into a variety of shapes: moons, angled slices, batons, small chunks. Toss the cucumbers with 1 teaspoon salt and put in a colander so the salt can draw out excess moisture. Let them sit for 30 minutes. Blot the cucumbers on paper towels to remove the moisture and excess salt. Pile them into a large bowl.

Salting cucumbers ahead of use reduces sogginess by pulling out moisture and gives them a tighter, "pickled" texture.

Add the scallions, onion, mint, chile flakes, vinegar, and a few generous twists of black pepper. Hold off on the salt for now. Toss to blend the ingredients. Taste and adjust with more chile flakes, black pepper, vinegar, and salt if needed. When the flavor of the salad is exciting and balanced, add ¼ cup olive oil and toss. Taste and add more oil if needed to balance the flavors. You want plenty of "dressing" pooling in the bottom of the bowl; the cucumbers will continue to drink that up, plus you want the juices to run into the other elements on your plate, such as grilled pork. Serve with a sprinkle of finishing salt, if you like, for some crunch.

String Beans

Kid-friendly, happily shaped, and with a flavor that pretty much defines "green," string beans—also known as snap beans—are amenable and versatile.

But not all are green. Most string beans are the color of grass, but it's not hard to find pale yellow wax beans and now some purple varieties (which will break your heart, by the way, because the purple fades to green once cooked). Other than color, the main difference among string beans is the shape, which ranges from thin, feminine haricots verts through the longer, sturdier Blue Lake variety to the flattened and slightly paler Romano bean, which is meaty and delicious but must be cooked a long time or else it's tough.

The "string" is a thing of the past. Prepping modern beans is easy, a simple snap rather than a snap and pull, which is what old-timey cooks did to remove the very fibrous string that ran down one side of the bean. You'll find a few varieties that still need their strings zipped off, but for most beans, all you do is bend the little stem end to snap it off.

Good from raw to cooked. When I get my hands on early-season, tender, young beans, I'll serve them raw, or just barely steamed—think of the phrase "crisp-tender." I find the grassy green notes dominate at this stage and I'll avoid masking that with competing ingredients. As the bean matures, the sweet earthy notes come forward, especially when I cook them until fully tender . . . even slightly burnt in some cases. More mature beans become really sweet and tender when roasted at high heat or grilled; and braising or stewing is ideal for very mature beans or Romano varieties.

String Beans, Pickled Beans, Tomatoes, Cucumbers, and Olives on Tonnato

This salad evolved from the classic *salade niçoise*: The potatoes and eggs are gone, but the fresh vegetables are still there, and the tuna is transformed from chunks to a creamy tonnato dip. I throw in arugula to have some greens, and top it all with crunchy torn croutons—the result is a main-dish salad that captures the vibrancy of the season. To serve this for guests, prepare all the elements ahead and assemble them at the last minute.

» Serves 4

1 medium cucumber

Kosher salt and freshly ground black pepper

½ pound string beans, trimmed

½ pound cherry tomatoes (a mix of colors if possible), halved

½ medium red onion, thinly sliced

½ cup pitted mixed olives (a mix of colors if possible)

2 tablespoons red wine vinegar

¼ teaspoon dried chile flakes

Extra-virgin olive oil

Tonnato (page 45)

8 ounces pickled string beans (page 59); choose a color that contrasts with the other beans

1 big handful arugula

1 small handful basil leaves

2 cups torn croutons (page 29; optional)

Peel the cucumber if its skin is tough or waxed. Trim the ends of the cucumber, halve lengthwise, scoop out the seeds, and cut crosswise into ¼-inch-thick slices. Toss the cucumber with 1 teaspoon salt and put in a colander so the salt can draw out excess moisture. Let it sit for 15 to 20 minutes. Blot the cucumber on paper towels to remove the moisture and excess salt. Pile into a medium bowl.

Meanwhile, bring a small amount of water to a boil in a skillet, add 1 teaspoon salt and the fresh beans, cover, and steam until the beans are tender but not soft, 5 to 6 minutes. Drain and cool the beans.

Add the tomatoes, onion, and olives to the cucumber. Add the vinegar and chile flakes and season well with salt and black pepper and toss. Taste and adjust with more of the seasonings. Finish by tossing with ¼ cup olive oil.

Spread the tonnato in a thick layer over a serving platter. Pile the steamed beans and the pickled beans on top, and tumble the tomato-cucumber salad on top of the beans. Drop the arugula and basil over the surface and top with the croutons (if using). Give the whole platter a nice drizzle of olive oil to finish and serve right away.

Roasted String Beans and Scallions with Pine Nut Vinaigrette

Roasting amps up beans' natural sweetness, and gives them a leathery yet tender texture. The scallions also get roasted because they're a partner vegetable in the dish, not simply an accent aromatic. The pine nut vinaigrette will last a week or more in the fridge.

» *Serves 4*

1½ pounds string beans (mix colors if you can!), trimmed

3 bunches scallions, trimmed (including ½ inch off the green tops), cut into lengths to match the beans

Extra-virgin olive oil

Kosher salt and freshly ground black pepper

1 tablespoon red wine vinegar

⅓ cup Pine Nut Vinaigrette (page 39)

Juice of ½ lemon

¼ teaspoon dried chile flakes

1 small handful mint leaves

1 small handful basil leaves

¼ cup pine nuts, lightly toasted (see page 31)

Heat the oven to 425°F.

Toss the beans and scallions with a healthy glug of olive oil, ½ teaspoon salt, and many twists of black pepper. Spread onto two baking sheets in a single layer, so the ingredients aren't too crowded. Roast until nicely softened and browned—even charred—in places, 20 to 30 minutes. (Rotate the pans during cooking if you need to so everything cooks evenly.)

Pile the beans and scallions into a large bowl and sprinkle with the vinegar. Toss to mix and let rest for about 10 minutes to cool slightly.

Whisk together the pine nut vinaigrette, lemon juice, and chile flakes in a small bowl. Pour over the beans and scallions and toss to coat evenly. Taste the beans and dress with more lemon juice, salt, black pepper, or chile flakes to make the dressing zingy. Add the mint, basil, and pine nuts and toss gently again.

Green Bean, Tuna, and Mushroom "Casserole"

One of my favorite things from my Midwestern upbringing is the green bean and mushroom casserole at Thanksgiving—probably the same one that was on your holiday table, thanks to the canned-mushroom-soup marketing campaign. This is my grown-up version of that casserole, which has all the comfort appeal of the childhood dish, but way better flavor and nutritional value. Make it with a one-to-one ratio of mushrooms to green beans, and have some fun with the beans, if you like—you can grill them, slice them thin and use raw, use pickled green beans, or use a mix of all of the above.

» Serves 4

Kosher salt and freshly ground black pepper

Extra-virgin olive oil

2 garlic cloves, smashed and peeled

1 pound wild mushrooms, wiped off and cut into bite-size pieces (about 6 cups)

One 5-ounce can oil-packed tuna, drained

1 pound green beans, trimmed

1 cup heavy cream

1 teaspoon finely grated lemon zest

1 tablespoon fresh lemon juice

⅓ cup dried breadcrumbs (page 30)

Bring a large pot of water to a boil and add salt until it tastes like the sea.

Meanwhile, add ¼ cup olive oil to a skillet that's large enough to hold all the mushrooms and beans and still have some room to stir the ingredients. Add the garlic and cook slowly over medium heat to toast the garlic so it's very soft, fragrant, and nicely golden brown—but not burnt—about 5 minutes. Scoop out the garlic and set it aside so it doesn't burn.

Increase the heat to medium-high and add the mushrooms. Season generously with pepper and salt and sauté, tossing frequently, until the mushrooms are nicely browned around the edges, 5 to 7 minutes. Add the tuna and toss to incorporate. Keep this warm until the green beans are ready.

Add the beans to the boiling water and boil until they are just a bit beyond crisp-tender, 4 to 7 minutes. Drain them thoroughly in a colander and then add them to the mushrooms and tuna.

Add the cream, toss all the ingredients to coat, and simmer until the cream has reduced to a nice cloaking consistency and all the flavors are nicely blended, 6 to 9 minutes.

Add the lemon zest and lemon juice and toss. Taste and adjust with more salt, pepper, or lemon juice. When the flavors are delicious, pile into a serving bowl and top with the breadcrumbs.

Grilled Wax and Green Beans with Tomatoes, Basil, and Spicy Fish-Sauce Sauce

Don't oil the beans before you grill them—this is one of my core cooking principles: Oiling vegetables before grilling gives them a burned chemical flavor, whereas dry vegetables will caramelize slowly all by themselves, giving you what you want—a sugary, grilled char flavor. Grilling a mix of colors is pretty, but you can make the dish with just one type of bean.

» Serves 4

1 bunch basil (try a mix of opal, lemon, lime, and bush basil)

½ bunch mint

½ pound yellow wax beans, trimmed

½ pound green beans, trimmed

1 bunch scallions, trimmed (including ½ inch off the green tops)

⅓ cup Spicy Fish-Sauce Sauce (page 43)

Kosher salt and freshly ground black pepper

Extra-virgin olive oil

1 pint cherry tomatoes (mixed colors), halved

½ cup hazelnuts, lightly toasted (see page 31) and roughly chopped

Heat a grill to medium-high.

While the grill is heating, pick the herbs and leave the leaves whole. If any of the herbs don't look pristine, discard them; these herbs are like leaves in a salad.

Once the grill is hot, grill the beans and the scallions directly on the grill grates, unoiled. (Um, make sure you place them perpendicular to the grates.) Grill until the beans and scallions are deeply charred and caramelized and quite tender. (You can also cook the beans in a hot cast-iron skillet in batches until evenly charred, slightly wilted, and tender.)

Take the vegetables off the grill, cut the scallions into shorter lengths, and toss the vegetables in a bowl with the spicy fish-sauce sauce. Taste and season with salt and pepper.

Drizzle on a glug of olive oil, fold in the tomatoes and herbs, and toss. Taste and adjust the seasoning again, adding more spicy fish-sauce sauce if needed to make the salad zingy. Top the beans with the chopped toasted hazelnuts. Serve on the warm side of room temperature.

Summer Squash

Here we go, into the land of fairy tale–size vines that take over the garden, and squashes that seem to multiply by magic. I'm always happy to accept surplus squash . . . as long as they're tiny. Summer squash has to be harvested young if you have any hope of enjoying it.

Big is bad. Squash generally has a mild (er, bland) flavor, with a pleasing not-quite-firm texture; but both of those attributes fade as squash matures. As seeds develop, squash becomes more bitter, watery, and fibrous—a lot of mushy unpleasantness if you wait too long to harvest.

Have fun with forms and colors. Most common is green zucchini, which has a bright golden counterpart. Smallish round varieties, such as Eight Ball and Ronde de Nice, are showing up at markets now. These are terrific halved, flesh scooped out a bit, and then stuffed and baked. Pattypan squash should get points just for its name and flying-saucer shape, but it's also quite delicious stuffed or grilled. Then there are the crooknecks, whose necks are the best part because they are dense, buttery, and seedless. The bulbous ends are sometimes a bit seedy. Whichever variety you choose, give it a squeeze and a bend . . . you want very firm squashes that aren't rubbery.

Be kind. They're sensitive. Squash keep for several days refrigerated in plastic bags, but their skins are tender, so take care not to bump or nick them. This tender skin means you don't need to peel them, and in fact it's best not to, because it holds the flesh together. There are a few heirloom varieties, however, that have nubbier skins, and in some cases are covered with tiny soft prickers. I just scrub those well, taking care not to abrade the skin.

Bland flavor needs intense heat. I like to use summer squashes raw when I get the truly young and fresh ones. These firm specimens are also perfect for pickling, very thinly sliced on a mandoline into flexible ribbons. When I cook squash, I always turn the heat up high—squash needs a hot, fast treatment, which will brown the outside and enhance the flavors while keeping the interior flesh from overcooking and becoming soggy. I'll usually salt squash in the same way that I do cucumbers (see page 195)—this draws out water and firms up the flesh. No need to peel before salting, and unless the seeds are well developed, don't scoop them out. For most of my squash recipes, you'll leave the halves intact, rather than slicing.

> **In the field** Both male and female squash plants produce flowers. But in your garden, you'll want to pick the males and leave the females to produce more squash. Male flowers stand up on tall stems (of course!), while the females stay closer to the plant.

Squash Ribbons with Tomatoes, Peanuts, Basil, Mint, and Spicy Fish-Sauce Sauce

Getting the squash ribbons really thin requires a mandoline slicer, but if you don't have one, do your best with a sharp knife to very thinly slice the zucchini. The flavors in this dish riff on those in the classic Thai green papaya salad—a deliciously vibrant collision of spicy, salty, tangy, herbal, and nutty. Once you have your spicy fish-sauce sauce made, the dish takes no time to assemble.

» *Serves 4*

4 firm medium zucchini or a mix of zucchini and yellow summer squash

Kosher salt

1 pint cherry tomatoes (a mix of colors is nice), halved

½ cup salted roasted peanuts, roughly chopped

1 bunch scallions, trimmed (including ½ inch off the green tops), sliced on a sharp angle, soaked in ice water for 20 minutes, and drained well (see page 53)

1 small handful basil leaves

1 small handful mint leaves

¼ cup Spicy Fish-Sauce Sauce (page 43)

Extra-virgin olive oil

Add the tomatoes, peanuts, scallions, basil, and mint. Pour in the spicy fish-sauce sauce and toss again. Taste and decide whether the salad needs more salt. Add ¼ cup olive oil and toss again. Do a final taste and toss, arrange on plates, and serve right away.

Using a mandoline, carefully slice the zucchini from the bottom to the top to create very thin ribbons of squash. (If you don't have a mandoline, just cut the zucchini into very thin crosswise slices, to create rounds.) Toss the squash with 1 teaspoon salt and put in a colander so the salt can draw out excess moisture. Let them sit for 30 minutes. Blot the squash on paper towels to remove the moisture and excess salt. Pile into a large bowl.

Grilled or Roasted Summer Squash with Caper-Raisin Vinaigrette

Recipe for a perfect midweek summer dinner: Prep the squash, sling some chicken thighs on the grill, and when the chicken is close to being done, add the squash halves. As the chicken rests a few minutes, toss the squash with the vinaigrette and the other ingredients. Bingo, you've got a meal that's both elemental and exciting, and took just about no time to prepare (you've got a batch of the caper-raisin vinaigrette in your fridge, right?).

» Serves 4

1½ pounds firm small summer squash (a mix of shapes and colors)

Kosher salt and freshly ground black pepper

1 pint cherry tomatoes, preferably Sun Golds

Extra-virgin olive oil

½ teaspoon dried chile flakes

2 tablespoons fresh lemon juice

¼ cup Caper-Raisin Vinaigrette (page 39)

¼ cup dried breadcrumbs (page 30)

Trim off the ends of the squash and halve lengthwise (with round or pattypans, cut through the "equator"). Salt the squash on their cut faces with 2 teaspoons salt and leave to drain for at least 1 hour or up to 24 hours (if for more than 2 hours, transfer to the refrigerator).

Blot the squash with paper towels to remove moisture and excess salt.

Heat a grill or the broiler to high.

Cook the squash—without oil—until both sides are lightly browned and the squash is just barely tender; you still want some resistance in the center.

Pile the squash into a bowl, tumble in the tomatoes, and drizzle with a glug of olive oil, the chile flakes, several twists of black pepper, and the lemon juice, and toss gently. Add the caper-raisin vinaigrette and toss again. Taste and adjust the flavors with more salt (though the squash is likely to be quite salty), chile flakes, black pepper, or lemon.

Arrange on a platter and shower with the breadcrumbs. Serve at room temperature.

Squash and "Tuna Melt" Casserole

Let's all just acknowledge that we love tuna melts, shall we? Here we capture the tuna-cheese flavor combo that is so good, and apply it to summer squash as a way to make a tuna melt more nutritious . . . and summer squash more flavorful!

» Serves 4

1½ pounds firm small summer squash (aim for different shapes and colors)

Kosher salt and freshly ground black pepper

Extra-virgin olive oil

4 bunches scallions, trimmed (including ½ inch off the green tops), thinly sliced

1 teaspoon fresh thyme leaves

¼ teaspoon dried chile flakes

Two 5-ounce cans oil-packed tuna

1½ cups shredded good-quality extra-sharp cheddar cheese

Trim off the ends of the squash and halve lengthwise (with round or pattypan squash, cut through the "equator"). Salt the squash on their cut faces with 2 teaspoons salt and leave to drain for at least 1 hour or up to 24 hours (if for more than 2 hours, transfer to the refrigerator).

Heat a big glug of olive oil in a skillet over medium heat. Add the scallions, thyme, chile flakes, ½ teaspoon salt, and several twists of black pepper. Cook until the scallions are soft and fragrant but not actually browned, 3 to 4 minutes. Take them off the heat, and when cool enough to taste, adjust the seasoning with more of any of the spices or the thyme.

Heat the oven to 450°F.

Spread the squash cut side down on a rimmed baking sheet (or two, if needed, to avoid crowding). Roast until slightly shrunken and browned on the cut sides, on the way to tender, but not at all mushy. Cooking time will depend on the size and shape of your squash, but for a typical slender 6-inch zucchini, this should take about 15 minutes. (Leave the oven on.)

Arrange the squash pieces in a baking dish that will fit them all snugly in one layer, this time cut side up. Distribute the scallions over the surfaces. Flake and crumble the tuna in an even layer over the scallions and then top evenly with the cheddar.

Return to the oven and bake until the cheese is nicely melted and beginning to bubble and brown, 10 to 15 minutes.

Let cool for about 5 minutes before serving.

Fried Stuffed Zucchini Flowers, Zucchini Jojos, and Zucchini Pickles

This recipe is a perfect triple threat: lightly battered and fried zucchini in three different forms, including long, fat wedges that we call Jojos in Oregon. Each is delicious on its own, if you're in the mood to be simple, but all three arrayed on a platter—crisp, golden, and showered with Parmigiano-Reggiano—make a stunning and delicious summer antipasto. The squash blossoms can be battered, fried, and served plain, or you can stuff them with a delicate ricotta filling, as I do here. The recipe for this dish looks long, but it's actually simple. The key is getting everything set up and in place before you start to fry.

» Serves 6

12 to 16 ribbons of zucchini pickle (page 59)

ZUCCHINI WEDGES

3 slender young zucchini or other summer squash, about 6 inches long, ends trimmed

Kosher salt

SQUASH BLOSSOMS

½ cup whole-milk ricotta cheese

2 tablespoons pine nuts, lightly toasted (see page 31) and roughly chopped

3 or 4 basil leaves, torn into pieces

6 to 8 medium mint leaves, torn into pieces

2 scallions, trimmed (including ½ inch off the green tops), finely chopped

1 tablespoon minced oil-packed sun-dried tomatoes

¼ teaspoon dried chile flakes

Kosher salt and freshly ground black pepper

6 squash blossoms

DEEP-FRYING AND BATTER

Vegetable oil, for deep-frying

½ cup cornstarch

½ cup all-purpose flour

¼ teaspoon dried chile flakes

Kosher salt and freshly ground black pepper

About 1 cup sparkling water

FOR SERVING

Kosher salt

1 small handful whole mint and basil leaves

Parmigiano-Reggiano cheese, for grating

6 lemon wedges

FOR THE ZUCCHINI WEDGES: Slice the zucchini lengthwise into quarters, like long Jojo-style fries. Arrange the quarters on a rack or platter and sprinkle the cut surfaces with 2 teaspoons salt. Let the slices sit for at least 1 hour and up to overnight (if for more than 2 hours, transfer to the refrigerator). Blot the zucchini with paper towels to remove moisture and excess salt.

FOR THE SQUASH BLOSSOMS: Stir together the ricotta, pine nuts, basil, mint, scallions, sun-dried tomatoes, and chile flakes. Taste and then season the filling generously with salt and pepper.

Gently pry open the petals of the squash blossoms and shake out any dirt or leaves. Pinch off the stamens (the brightly colored bits on the inside). If the flowers still have stems, leave them on.

Fill the flowers using your fingers and a small spoon (unless you want to get fancy and use a piping bag, which would make the job easy). Gently twist the tips of the petals together to seal the flowers.

FOR DEEP-FRYING: Arrange a double layer of paper towels on a tray or baking sheet and set it near your stove. Pour at least 3 inches of vegetable oil into a large pan (with tall enough sides to prevent the oil from bubbling over when you add the items). Slowly bring the oil up to 375°F on a thermometer. (Or fry a small piece of bread: When it takes 60 seconds to get nicely crisp and brown, but not burnt, your oil is just about right.)

As the oil is heating, make the batter: Whisk the cornstarch, flour, chile flakes, and salt and black pepper in a medium bowl so they're well blended. Whisk in the sparkling water a bit at a time until you have the consistency of thin pancake batter; you may not need all the water or you may need a touch more.

When the oil is ready, blot any remaining moisture from the salted zucchini wedges and all the moisture from the pickled zucchini ribbons and set them on plates.

Start with the zucchini wedges. Dip a wedge into the batter, let the excess drip off, and carefully immerse it in the hot oil. You can use tongs for this or, if you're handy with chopsticks, use wooden chopsticks. Fry until the coating is puffed and very light golden (these will not get deeply colored). Transfer to the paper towels to drain. Continue frying a few at a time; don't add too many wedges at once because that will cause the oil temperature to drop and the zucchini will get greasy.

Once all the zucchini wedges are fried, continue with the squash blossoms, and finally with the pickled zucchini. (If you're worried that the zucchini will get cold, you can hold things in a warm oven.) Turn off the heat under the oil.

Arrange the fried tasties on a serving platter, sprinkle with salt, mint and basil leaves, and finely grated Parmigiano, and serve with the lemon wedges.

Season Four

Late Summer

The days begin to grow shorter. The sunlight takes on a more golden glow as it streams from a lower angle, hinting that our warm days are numbered. The fields have had months of sunshine and warmth. Just about everything is going crazy. We still have the vegetables that joined the party early in the season, but now we get the quintessential hot-weather delights: corn, eggplant, tomatoes, peppers. Shell beans are in season now, too, and while not as succulent as these other late-summer entries, they are a treat to enjoy when fresh, and perfect for harvesting and storing for the fall and winter to come.

Throughout the year, my cooking is influenced not simply by the vegetables I have available but by the vibe of the season as well. At this point of the summer, the vibe is "party." The range of colors is full spectrum, and stone fruit, melons, and berries are on deck, too, great partners for the vibrant vegetables.

I know the nights will soon begin to cool, making me even more appreciative of the crazy good opportunities for deliciousness.

Recipes of Late Summer

Corn

I'm happy to see heirloom varieties of corn showing up at markets. That's something to celebrate, given that the vast majority of corn grown in this country is commodity corn grown for fuel or animal food.

Peek, don't pull. When choosing corn, don't do the pull-down-the-husk thing. That just exposes the kernels and causes them to dry out. Look for ears that are heavy for their size and whose husks feel moist and tight, not papery and loose. If the silks are still attached, they shouldn't be dried out or moldy (though if the corn was picked on a rainy day, the silks could be wet and yet the corn is perfect). If you must peek at the kernels, just pry open the top of the husk.

Caterpillars also like corn, so if you see one inside, don't freak out, just gently scooch it off the corn and into the compost.

A fleeting pleasure. The sugars and juice that make corn so amazing quickly convert to starch, especially if you refrigerate it. So try to buy corn the day you'll use it; farmers say not to pick the corn until the water is already boiling, but we can't all be that lucky.

Corn season is short because all the ears ripen and get harvested at about the same time. When it first shows up, I eat as much of it raw as I can, and when I do cook it, it barely sees any heat.

Off the cob. When eating corn on the cob, just peel off and tear away the husks and then get rid of the pesky silks. Grasp a section of silk at the tip and pull it away. Inevitably a few will remain, so live with them, or wipe them away with a damp paper towel.

To separate the kernels from the cob, lay the cob on a cutting board. With a sharp knife, slice the kernels off one side. Rotate the cob to that cut side and slice the kernels from the next side; continue until the cob is kernel-free. Slice deep enough to get most of the juicy kernel, but not so deep that you're including a lot of the tough mesh of the cob. Once all the kernels are off, scrape the cobs with the back side of the knife (the dull spine) to coax out the sweet milky juice.

Yank hard on two sides of the husk to pop out the ear. To remove kernels from the cob, just slice off one side, rotate the cob, and repeat until the cob is kernel-free.

Raw Corn with Walnuts, Mint, and Chiles

The classic grilled Mexican corn on the cob (*elote*)—served with chile powder, lime, mayo, and Cotija cheese—inspired this dish. You can eat this like a salad, served on a platter family-style, or you can serve it more like a relish.

» *Serves 4 as a first course*

2 ears sweet corn, husked, kernels sliced off into a bowl

⅓ cup roughly chopped lightly toasted walnuts (see page 31)

1 or 2 small fresh hot chiles, such as jalapeño, seeded, deribbed, and minced

4 scallions, trimmed (including ½ inch off the green tops), sliced on a sharp angle, soaked in ice water for 20 minutes, and drained well (see page 53)

Small handful mint leaves

½ lime

Kosher salt and freshly ground black pepper

Extra-virgin olive oil

¼ cup shredded Pecorino Romano cheese

Put the corn, walnuts, chiles, scallions, and mint in a bowl and toss to mix. Squeeze over the lime juice and season generously with salt and black pepper. Taste and adjust the seasoning so that the corn is lively with flavor. Add ¼ cup olive oil and toss. Taste and adjust with more oil, lime, salt, or black pepper.

Serve the corn salad in a bowl and top with the shredded pecorino.

MORE WAYS:

Dress up plain vegetables: Top roasted or grilled eggplant slices.

Garnish crostini: Spread garlic-rubbed grilled bread with Whipped Ricotta (page 37) and tumble corn on top.

Make a bright chunky salsa: Loosen with more lime juice and olive oil and use broken Whole-Grain Carta di Musica (page 46) as chips and dip.

Corn and Tomato Salad with Torn Croutons

This is a perfect hot-summer midweek meal, for which so little effort is required for such delicious reward. I love the crispness of the raw corn, but you can also make this dish by grilling whole ears of corn before cutting off the kernels.

» *Serves 4*

Kernels cut from 3 ears sweet corn, plus the milky pulp scraped from the cob (about 2 cups total)

1 pound tomatoes (all shapes and colors), cored and cut into wedges or chunks, or whatever looks pretty

3 to 4 scallions, trimmed (including ½ inch off the green tops), sliced on a sharp angle, soaked in ice water for 20 minutes, and drained well (see page 53)

¼ cup red wine vinegar

Kosher salt and freshly ground black pepper

2 cups torn croutons (page 29)

½ cup pistachios, toasted (see page 31) and roughly chopped

½ cup freshly grated Pecorino Romano cheese

1 handful basil leaves

1 handful mint leaves

Extra-virgin olive oil

Put the corn, tomatoes, and scallions in a large bowl. Add the vinegar and toss gently to mix. Season generously with salt and pepper and toss. Taste and adjust the seasoning so the salad is nicely bright.

Add the croutons, pistachios, pecorino, basil, and mint and toss again. Taste and adjust the salt and pepper. Moisten with ⅓ cup olive oil and toss again. Taste and adjust. Serve lightly chilled or at a little cooler than room temperature.

Sautéed Corn Four Ways

These four sautéed corn dishes are templates—delicious as written, but also meant to inspire you to create your own combinations. The idea is to simply eat corn every day when it's in season. The key to cooking corn is to cook it fast, over high heat. It's better to barely cook it, leaving it on the raw side so it stays sweet and crunchy, than to cook it too long and have it become tough and starchy.

» Serves 4

BASIC WITH SCALLIONS

1 tablespoon unsalted butter

4 ears sweet corn, kernels cut off (about 2½ cups)

1 bunch scallions, trimmed (including ½ inch off the green tops), thinly sliced on an angle

Kosher salt and freshly ground black pepper

Melt the butter in a large skillet over medium-high heat. Once the butter has melted and the foaming subsides, add the corn and scallions and a big pinch of salt and some pepper and cook, tossing and shaking the corn.

After a minute or so, you'll probably see some sugary corn juices start to stick to the bottom of the pan. Scrape those up with a metal spatula or wooden spoon as you cook. They are really tasty and you want to incorporate them into the sauté. Cook the corn until it's heated through and slightly caramelized, 3 to 4 minutes. Serve right away.

CREAM AND MELTING CHEESE

¼ cup heavy cream or crème fraîche

¼ cup freshly grated cheese, such as Fontina, cheddar, Parmigiano-Reggiano, Monterey Jack, or Gouda

Follow the basic recipe, but omit the scallions. Pour in the cream and let it boil about 30 seconds, then add the cheese and cook, stirring until the corn is cloaked in a lovely creamy sauce. Taste and adjust the salt and pepper. Serve right away.

PANCETTA, BLACK PEPPER, ARUGULA, AND HOT SAUCE

2 ounces pancetta, cut into small dice or lardons and fried until lightly browned and slightly crisp

1 handful arugula, washed and dried

A few dashes hot sauce, such as Sriracha

Follow the basic recipe, but omit the scallions. Toss in the pancetta and season the corn with a healthy dose of pepper. Add the arugula and a few shakes of hot sauce, and toss quickly just to incorporate the greens and begin to wilt them, but not actually cook them. Taste and adjust the salt, pepper, and hot sauce. Serve right away.

FRESH CHILES, RADISHES, AND PINE NUTS

1 large or a few small fresh green chiles, seeded, deribbed, and sliced into rings

4 or 5 radishes, trimmed, scrubbed, and cut into small chunks or wedges

¼ cup pine nuts, lightly toasted (see page 31)

1 large lime wedge

Follow the basic recipe, but omit the scallions. Add the chiles to the corn and cook, stirring and scraping, until the chiles lose a bit of their crunch and get fragrant, about a minute. Add the radishes and pine nuts, toss to mix, and squeeze the lime wedge over everything. Taste and adjust the salt and pepper. Serve right away.

Grilled Corn with Alla Diavola Butter and Pecorino

Not quite a recipe, this dish is a reminder that when you have a fridge stocked with good condiments, such as my alla diavola butter, great meals are minutes away. You can use any of the compound butters in the book (pages 33 to 37), and it's fun to set out several butters and let your friends choose their own.

» Serves as many people as you have ears of corn

Sweet corn, husked

Alla Diavola Butter (page 33)

Freshly grated Pecorino Romano cheese

Heat a grill to medium-high.

Arrange the corn—unoiled—on the grill and cook for only a couple of minutes, turning so that all sides get exposed to the heat. You just want to warm the exterior and maybe give it a kiss of smoke and flame, but you want the interior of the kernels to stay juicy and almost raw.

Arrange the corn on a platter and slather with the butter, turning the ears so they get entirely coated. Shower with grated pecorino and eat right away.

In the kitchen When grilling corn, you've got choices. You can remove all the husks and silks and grill "naked," or you can pull back the husks but leave them attached, and remove the silks. Or for less-charred results, pull back the husks, remove the silks, and then pull the husks back into position—the corn will steam rather than grill, but it will still pick up some smoky flavor.

Corn, Tomatoes, and Clams on Grilled Bread, Knife-and-Fork–Style

People always want bread to dip into their clam broth, so why not put the clams right on the bread from the get-go? And you don't need to use a knife and fork; hands are perfectly fine. I was just being polite.

» Serves 4

Extra-virgin olive oil

3 garlic cloves, smashed and peeled

1 tablespoon Tomato Conserva (page 272) or tomato paste

1 bunch scallions, trimmed (including ½ inch off the green tops), sliced on a sharp angle

8 ounces cherry tomatoes (a mix of colors and varieties), halved if large

½ teaspoon dried chile flakes

2 tablespoons unsalted butter

Kosher salt and freshly ground black pepper

1 pound small clams, such as Manila, rinsed

½ cup dry, unoaked white wine

½ cup lightly packed flat-leaf parsley leaves

2 large ears sweet corn, husked, kernels sliced off into a bowl (about 1⅓ cups kernels)

Juice of ½ lemon

Four ½-inch-thick slices country bread, grilled, rubbed with garlic, and kept warm

Heat a large skillet over medium heat. Add a couple of tablespoons of olive oil and the garlic and cook slowly to toast the garlic so it's very soft, fragrant, and nicely golden brown—but not burnt—about 5 minutes.

Add the tomato conserva and cook for another 30 seconds or so, stirring and scraping so the tomato doesn't burn but does get a bit darker. Add the scallions and cook, stirring, until they start to get fragrant and soft, another minute or so.

Add the tomatoes, chile flakes, and butter, and season generously with salt and black pepper. Cook, stirring the tomatoes occasionally, until they start to burst and render their juices, another 3 to 4 minutes.

Add the clams and wine, cover the pan, and cook until the clams all open; this could take as little as 2 minutes or up to 6 minutes, depending on the size and type of clams. When the clams are open (toss out any that refuse to open even after another couple of minutes cooking), add the parsley, corn, and lemon juice. Taste and adjust the sauce with more salt, black pepper, chile flakes, or lemon juice.

Arrange the grilled bread on plates or in shallow bowls and spoon the corn and clams over the top, dividing the juices evenly, too. Finish with a generous drizzle of olive oil, and serve with a knife and fork, and a bowl for empty shells.

Corn Fritters with Pickled Chiles

Think hush puppies and you'll get the idea. When you're frying the fritters, be sure not to add too many at once to the oil or it will lower the temperature and make the fritters soggy. Fry them in batches and let them sit in a low oven on a baking sheet lined with paper towels until all are cooked.

» *Makes about 24 fritters*

1 teaspoon fast-acting yeast

1 cup all-purpose flour

1 cup fine cornmeal

Kosher salt and freshly ground black pepper

½ cup plain whole-milk or low-fat yogurt (not Greek)

½ cup water

2 ears sweet corn

⅔ cup finely chopped pickled chiles, store-bought or homemade (page 59)

3 scallions, trimmed (including ½ inch off the green tops), sliced on a sharp angle

½ cup freshly grated Parmigiano-Reggiano cheese

Vegetable oil, for deep-frying

Compound butters (pages 33 to 37; optional), for serving

Whisk together the yeast, flour, cornmeal, 1½ teaspoons salt, and many twists of black pepper in a large bowl. Whisk in the yogurt and water to make a mostly smooth batter (a few lumps are okay; add more water if the dry ingredients aren't fully moistened).

Cover the bowl and keep in a warm place for at least 1 hour and up to overnight (if for more than 2 hours, put it in the refrigerator, and then let it warm at room temperature for about 30 minutes before you continue).

When the batter is bubbling and puffed up a bit, husk the corn, slice off the corn kernels, and add them to the batter. Then, with the back of a table knife, scrape the milky juice from the cobs into the batter too. Gently fold in the chiles, scallions, and Parmigiano.

Arrange a double layer of paper towels on a tray. Pour at least 2 inches of oil into a large pan (with tall sides, so that the oil can't bubble over when you add the batter). Slowly bring the oil up to 375°F on a thermometer. (Or fry a small piece of bread: When it takes 60 seconds to get nicely crisp and brown, but not burnt, your oil is just about right.)

Using two tablespoons, scoop up some batter and carefully lower it into the oil. Continue until you have added enough fritters to fill the pan but not crowd it. Cook the fritters, turning with your spoon in order for all sides to get nicely browned. When puffy and a rich brown, scoop them out with a slotted spoon and drain on the paper towels. Season lightly with salt.

Serve the fritters warm (not piping hot), with one or more of the compound butters, if desired.

Eggplant

Eggplant may be the trickiest vegetable to cook, and therefore it can inspire some ambivalence. But when handled correctly, it is sublime.

Younger specimens have fewer seeds. Choose eggplant whose flesh will be dense, creamy, and as seedless as possible. That means young, firm, heavy-for-their-size eggplants. The more time on the vine, the pithier the flesh and the more bitter the flavor. Another contributor to eggplant unpleasantness is time spent in cold storage. Eggplant doesn't like the cold, and if stored poorly by the distributor or grocer, the bitter compounds can be nasty. One more reason to shop at a farmers' market or grow your own.

I prefer the slender Asian varieties, which I like for their relative lack of seeds but also because one Asian eggplant split lengthwise makes a perfect portion and looks great on the plate. The larger globe eggplants can be delicious, too, but will be seedier.

Salt and cook well to improve texture. Eggplant is like a damp sponge. Deal with the "damp" aspect by salting the cut surfaces of eggplant an hour or two ahead to draw out bitter liquid. The "sponge" part means that eggplant will absorb other flavors in your dish, making it a good team player, but it can absorb too much oil during cooking. To avoid this, be sure your oil is hot enough when you add the eggplant.

Eggplant is one of the few vegetables that I won't tell you to eat raw; when cooked, you never want it crisp-tender. Only when it is fully tender will you achieve the creaminess that is eggplant's hallmark.

Peel. Most eggplant skin is tender enough to eat, so whether you peel is up to you. I'll sometimes peel the eggplant in stripes, leaving a bit of skin to provide structure.

Carta di Musica with Roasted Eggplant Spread, Herbs, and Ricotta Salad

I serve this dish as an appetizer or as part of a trio of antipasti. A good-quality feta would be a nice swap out for the ricotta salata, and a few small edible flowers would make the dish look stunning on a cocktail spread.

» Serves 4

1 bunch scallions, trimmed (including ½ inch off the green tops), sliced on a sharp angle, soaked in ice water for 20 minutes, and drained well (see page 53)

1 big handful mixed fresh herbs (mint leaves, flat-leaf parsley leaves, basil leaves)

1 tablespoon fresh lemon juice

Kosher salt and freshly ground black pepper

Extra-virgin olive oil

Roasted Eggplant Spread (recipe follows)

4 Whole-Grain Carta di Musica (page 46) or other large, very thin cracker breads

½ cup crumbled ricotta salata

Put the scallions and herbs in a bowl, toss with the lemon juice, and season with salt and pepper. Taste and adjust with more of any of the ingredients until the salad is bright and zingy. Drizzle on a couple of tablespoons of olive oil and toss again.

Spread a thick layer of the eggplant onto the cracker breads. Top with the salad and sprinkle the ricotta salata over the top. Finish with another generous drizzle of olive oil and serve.

Roasted Eggplant Spread

Use this delicious spread as a crostini topping, a dip, or a sandwich spread. Here I roast the eggplant in a hot oven, but you can also grill-roast it over charcoal, which will give it a smoky flavor, much like a Middle Eastern baba ghanoush. Either way, be sure you cook it fully—if the eggplant is at all undercooked, the spread won't be creamy and the flavor will be a bit too "green."

» Makes about 1½ cups

1 pound globe eggplant

2 teaspoons fish sauce or Italian colatura

1 teaspoon red wine vinegar

¼ teaspoon dried chile flakes

Extra-virgin olive oil

½ lemon (optional)

Heat the oven to 450°F.

Prick the eggplant a couple of times so it doesn't burst during roasting. Set it on a baking sheet and roast until totally tender and starting to collapse, 30 minutes to 1 hour depending on size. Let the eggplant cool on the pan until you can handle it, then split it open.

Scrape the flesh into a food processor (compost the skin). Pulse a couple of times to make a rough puree. Add the fish sauce, vinegar, chile flakes, and ¼ cup olive oil. Pulse until is smooth.

Taste (watch out for the processor blade!) and adjust with more fish sauce, chile flakes, and olive oil until the spread is rich and creamy. Serve with a squeeze of lemon if you like.

Grilled Eggplant with Tomatoes, Torn Croutons, and Lots of Herbs

Eggplant is amazing on the grill, but sometimes the exterior can char before the inside is fully cooked and creamy-tender. Let the eggplant sit in a warm place for a few minutes after you've pulled it from the grill. This allows the interior to steam a bit more—carryover cooking—guaranteeing the lush texture you're looking for.

» Serves 4

1½ pounds eggplants (aim for a nice variety of small Asian types)

Extra-virgin olive oil

¼ cup red wine vinegar

Kosher salt and freshly ground black pepper

1 pound tomatoes (go for variety here, too, in colors and sizes), cored and cut into chunks if large

1 bunch scallions, trimmed (including ½ inch off the green tops), sliced on a sharp angle, soaked in ice water for 20 minutes, and drained well (see page 53)

1 cup torn croutons (page 29)

A couple handfuls mixed herb leaves: basils (lemon, opal, Genovese, etc.), mints, flat-leaf parsley, minutina, chives (cut into 2-inch lengths), cilantro, and, if it's still around, papalo

Trim the ends off the eggplants, halve them lengthwise, and sprinkle with a generous dose of salt. Set them on a rack or in a big colander and leave for at least 1 hour and up to 12 hours (if longer than 2 hours, put them in the fridge).

Heat a grill to medium-high.

Blot the moisture and excess salt from the surface of the eggplants. Grill the eggplants—unoiled—until they are lightly charred on the outside and tender on the inside, about 10 minutes total, though this will depend on the variety of eggplant. (Alternatively, to roast them: Heat the oven to 450°F, and heat a baking sheet for 15 minutes to get it ripping hot. Toss the eggplants in a couple of tablespoons of extra-virgin olive oil and place them cut side down on the hot—be careful!—pan, and blast it back in the oven. Roast until both sides are nicely browned and the eggplants are tender, about 18 minutes.)

When the eggplants are cooked, pile them into a large bowl. Add the vinegar, ½ teaspoon salt, and lots of twists of pepper and toss to distribute all the seasonings. Add the tomatoes, scallions, croutons, and herb leaves and toss gently. Add ½ cup olive oil and toss. Taste and adjust the seasoning. Let the dish sit for a few minutes so the tomato juices soak into the croutons and serve at room temperature.

At the market Keep an eye out for the numerous varieties of Asian eggplants, many of which are about the size of small tomatoes or skinny cucumbers, with skins ranging from purple to green, striped, red, orange, and white. While the skin color will fade with cooking, using a variety of shapes makes a dish attractive.

Rigatoni and Eggplant alla Norma

The traditional Sicilian dish pasta alla Norma was named after a tragic character in an opera, but I like to think of Norma as an Italian grandmother who loves being in the kitchen. She's the type of cook who can turn simple ingredients into something marvelous, like this quick dish.

» Serves 2

1 medium globe eggplant (about ¾ pound), cut into ½-inch-thick rounds, each cut across into ½-inch-wide strips

Kosher salt and freshly ground black pepper

Extra-virgin olive oil

2 garlic cloves, smashed and peeled

½ pound Italian sausage (mild or hot), bulk or with casings removed

1 pint cherry tomatoes, halved if large

1 tablespoon fresh oregano leaves, or 1 teaspoon dried

½ teaspoon dried chile flakes

8 ounces rigatoni

½ cup finely grated Pecorino Romano cheese

½ cup crumbled ricotta salata cheese

Put the eggplant strips in a colander and sprinkle with 1 teaspoon salt. Leave for at least 1 hour and up to 2 hours to draw out the excess moisture. When it's time to cook them, blot off the moisture and excess salt from the surface with a paper towel and give them a gentle squeeze to really wring out the water.

Heat a glug of olive oil in a large skillet over medium heat. Add the garlic. Cook slowly to toast the garlic so it's very soft, fragrant, and nicely golden brown—but not burnt—about 5 minutes.

Shape the sausage into 3 patties. Add the sausage to the pan and cook, flipping a few times, until gently browned on the outside and almost cooked on the inside, about 5 minutes total. Break up the sausage into bite-size chunks. Scoop the sausage out of the pan and set aside.

If the pan looks slightly dry, add another couple of tablespoons of olive oil, bring the heat up to medium-high, and add the eggplant in a single layer (cook it in batches if necessary). Cook the eggplant, turning the strips as they become browned on each side, until they're fairly tender and nicely colored all over, 6 to 8 minutes.

Add the tomatoes, oregano, and chile flakes and season with salt and a generous dose of black pepper. Cook, stirring and scraping the bottom of the pan, until the tomatoes break down a bit and the whole mess gets nicely juicy and saucy, another 6 to 8 minutes. Return the sausage to the pan.

Meanwhile, bring a large pot of water to a boil and add salt until it tastes like the sea. Add the rigatoni and cook until al dente (1 minute shy of the time listed on the package). With a ladle or a measuring cup, scoop out about ½ cup of the pasta cooking water.

Drain the pasta and add it to the pan with the eggplant. Stir and cook for another minute or two so the pasta absorbs the flavors. Add the pecorino and toss. Taste and adjust with more salt, black pepper, or chile flakes, along with a few spoonfuls of the pasta water if needed to make the sauce cling to the pasta.

Pile into bowls, top with the ricotta salata, and finish with a drizzle of olive oil.

Braised Eggplant and Lamb with Yogurt and Spiced Green Sauce

I use lamb shoulder in this dish because the flavor is rich and the cut contains a lot of connective tissue, which melts into a fork-tender texture. Sometimes lamb shoulder is hard to find in one piece, but you can use shoulder chops and just cut the meat into chunks, provided the chops aren't too thin. While the dish is cooking, make a batch of fresh flatbreads; you can serve the stew folded up in the bread—like the best gyro you've ever had. Or serve it with a big bowl of couscous and a tomato salad, perfect for a late-summer meal.

» Serves 4 to 6

Extra-virgin olive oil

2½ pounds lamb shoulder, cut into 1½-inch chunks

Kosher salt and freshly ground black pepper

3 garlic cloves, smashed and peeled

1 medium onion (about 8 ounces), finely chopped

1 tablespoon ground cumin

½ teaspoon ground allspice

½ teaspoon ground cinnamon

½ teaspoon ground coriander

¾ teaspoon dried chile flakes

1 bay leaf

2 pounds firm eggplant, preferably a slender variety with few seeds, peeled and cut into 1-inch chunks

4 cups Israeli couscous, or 4 Slightly Tangy Flatbreads (page 48), for serving

1 cup plain whole-milk or low-fat yogurt (not Greek)

¾ cup Spiced Green Sauce (page 44)

Heat a glug of olive oil in a large skillet or Dutch oven (the pan needs to be large enough to eventually hold all the ingredients) over medium-high heat. Pat the lamb chunks dry with a paper towel and then add half of them to the pan. (It's best to do this in batches because often lamb exudes a lot of water, which would take too long to evaporate if you had the full quantity in the pan at once.) Season generously with salt and black pepper and sauté the lamb until it's nicely browned on all sides, 5 to 7 minutes. Scoop the lamb out of the pan and set aside and repeat with the rest.

Reduce the heat to low and add a bit more oil. Add the garlic and cook gently for 2 to 3 minutes to soften and very lightly toast the garlic. Add the onion, season lightly with salt, and cook over medium-low heat, stirring and scraping the pan, until the onion is fragrant and soft and lightly golden, but not browned, 4 to 5 minutes.

Add the cumin, allspice, cinnamon, coriander, chile flakes, and bay leaf. Cook, stirring and scraping the pan so the spices get distributed and lightly toasted but don't burn, about 1 minute.

Return all the lamb chunks and any accumulated juices to the pan and add just enough water to barely cover the lamb but not to drown it (about 1½ cups). Bring to a simmer, adjust the heat to a low simmer, cover, and cook until the lamb is approaching tenderness, yet still resists a bit when you poke it with a knife. Depending on your lamb, this could take 45 minutes or as long as 2 hours, so start testing early.

Add the eggplant to the lamb and fold to distribute. If the stew looks dry, add another ¼ cup water. Cover again and simmer everything until the lamb and eggplant are fully tender, 20 to 30 minutes, depending on the eggplant.

Take a taste of the lamb and the eggplant, along with some of the braising liquid, and adjust with more salt, black pepper, or chile flakes if you like. If it's very liquidy or not concentrated enough in flavor, you can scoop out the lamb and eggplant and simmer the braising liquid for a few more minutes to reduce and concentrate it.

Serve the stew on couscous or on a piece of flatbread. Top with a generous spoonful of the yogurt and top that with the spiced green sauce.

Preserved Eggplant

Not your typical pickle, preserved eggplant is tangy but also lush from being preserved in olive oil as well as vinegar. Once you taste it, you'll find so many uses for this versatile condiment. Make sure you keep this refrigerated.

» Makes about 1 quart

1 pound firm eggplant, preferably Asian, peeled

Kosher salt and freshly ground black pepper

½ cup red wine vinegar

6 garlic cloves, smashed and peeled

3 sprigs rosemary

Extra-virgin olive oil

You'll need a couple of widemouthed pint-size canning jars and lids. Wash thoroughly and then sterilize in boiling water.

Whether you peel the eggplant is up to you and the tenderness of the slices. You can peel in stripes if you like. If your eggplant is slender, cut it into long halves or quarters. If your eggplant is round, cut it into thick coins or chunks. The shape is not critical.

Toss the eggplant with 2 teaspoons salt and tumble into a colander. Let sit for at least 2 hours and up to 8 if possible (if more than 2 hours, put it in the refrigerator) to pull out excess water.

Blot the eggplant pieces with paper towels to remove the surface moisture and excess salt. Put the eggplant back in the colander and press to squeeze out as much moisture as possible. Lay a double layer of plastic wrap over the eggplant and arrange some heavy cans or jars on top to apply more weight and press more water from the eggplant. Press for a couple of hours.

Blot the eggplant dry and put it in a bowl. Add the vinegar and toss to distribute. Pile the eggplant into the canning jars, layering in the garlic and tucking the rosemary sprigs upright into the jars.

Cover the eggplant with olive oil, tapping the jars to be sure the oil finds its way into the crevices. Seal the jars and keep in the refrigerator for up to 1 month. Let the preserves rest for at least 1 week before you serve them.

MORE WAYS:

Roll up savory meatballs: Finely chop the eggplant and fold into a meatball mixture of ground lamb, pine nuts, raisins, breadcrumbs, and crumbled feta.

Pair with grilled meats: Slice or dice the eggplant, fold it into the Classic Salsa Verde or the pickle version (page 44), and spoon over slices of grilled flank steak, lamb chops, or grilled chicken thighs.

Make a simple but spectacular pasta: Chop the eggplant and toss with cooked pasta, fresh oregano, chile flakes, ricotta salata, and loads of extra-virgin olive oil.

Sweet Peppers and Chiles

With a range of hues like a box of crayons, sweet peppers are one of the most vivid vegetables in the garden. Midnight black, chocolate brown, yellow, orange, and lipstick red, their colors are part of their appeal. And so is their flesh—crunchy when raw, and silky when roasted, peppers and chiles are just plain succulent.

Explore the sweet and the heat. Have some fun and sample whatever peppers look good. I find the biggest differences among sweet peppers are in the thickness and juiciness of the flesh rather than the flavors. Your basic bell pepper is predictably good, with a nice large cavity that's perfect for stuffing. When it comes to sweet pepper varieties, however, I stay away from green. They are immature and haven't developed enough sugars to balance out the harsher flavor compounds. I love green chiles but not green bell peppers.

Be ready to take a chance. When you get into hot chile territory, flavor and heat levels vary unpredictably. The variety will dictate the heat level to a degree, but once the plant is in the soil, it's the boss, with most of the chiles moderately spicy, but with a few incendiary rogues. Growing conditions affect heat level, too, with hotter and drier weather generally meaning hotter chiles.

My favorite sweet pepper varieties include Lipstick and pimiento, which are thick-walled and meaty, and the scrawnier but ultrasweet Jimmy Nardello. On the chile side, a good Anaheim offers chile flavor without much heat, and poblanos are gorgeous, glossy, and British racing green, with a heat level that can range—unpredictably—from mild to searing. Their large cavity also makes them good stuffers.

Sweet peppers and chiles last several days in the fridge; and once you roast and peel them, they can last another 4 to 5 days covered in a bit of olive oil and kept cold.

Roast and peel. Sweet peppers and chiles are at their best when roasted and peeled. At West Coast and New Mexican farmers' markets in the fall, you'll see vendors roasting the chiles in big gas-fired rotating drums, which is so cool to see and smell, but at home, the broiler or an outdoor grill is your best bet: Heat the broiler or grill. Arrange peppers on a baking sheet and broil, turning occasionally, until the skins are blackened all over, 10 to 12 minutes. If using a grill, position the peppers on the grates directly over the flame. Transfer to a large bowl, cover with a kitchen towel, and let them sit about 15 minutes to steam and cool. This will allow the flesh to fully soften and the skins to be peeled off easily.

Once the peppers are cool, gently pull on the stem to release the core and most of the seeds and discard. Work in or over a bowl so that you capture all the sweet-smoky juices from the pepper. Peel or rub off the charred skin; it's okay if a bit of skin still clings. Now open up the flesh and scrape out any remaining seeds. To tame the heat of a hot chile, slice out the ribs as well, which is where much of the heat resides.

Roasted Pepper Panzanella

A perfect lunch to eat outside in August, this bread salad will be at its peak of flavor and texture when the bread has had time to drink up some of the pepper juices, oil, and vinegar, but not so much time that the bread is totally mushy. To bring it on a picnic or to a potluck, pack up the torn croutons and mozzarella separately and toss them in at the end. Not eating meat? Leave out the salami.

» Serves 4

4 large red or orange bell peppers or other sweet, thick-fleshed peppers, such as pimiento (about 2 pounds)

½ small red onion, thinly sliced

2 garlic cloves, finely chopped

2 tablespoons red wine vinegar

¼ teaspoon dried chile flakes

Kosher salt and freshly ground black pepper

1 tablespoon oregano

1 tablespoon savory (or more oregano)

¼ cup lightly packed mint leaves

Extra-virgin olive oil

2 ounces thinly sliced spicy salami (such as soppressata), roughly chopped

2 recipes torn croutons (page 29)

4 ounces fresh mozzarella, preferably buffalo, torn into pieces

Heat the broiler.

Arrange the whole peppers on a baking sheet and broil them, turning occasionally, until the skins are blackened in spots and blistered all over, 10 to 12 minutes. (If you have another method for doing this, such as charring the peppers on the grill, feel free to use it.) Transfer the peppers to a large bowl, cover with a kitchen towel, and let them sit for about 15 minutes to steam. This will allow the flesh to fully soften and the skins to be peeled off easily.

Reduce the oven temperature to 400°F.

When the peppers are cool enough to handle, peel and seed them and then cut them into 1-inch-wide strips. Toss the peppers in a large bowl with the onion, garlic, vinegar, chile flakes, 1 teaspoon salt, several twists of black pepper, the oregano, the savory, and half the mint. Add ¼ cup olive oil, toss again, and set aside.

Add the salami and croutons to the large bowl and toss to mix. Let the salad rest for at least 15 minutes and up to 30; you want the juices from the peppers to soak into the bread. Arrange the salad on a platter and distribute the mozzarella on top. Shower with the remaining mint. Serve at room temperature or slightly chilled.

In the field That red chile isn't a separate variety; it's simply the green chile's older sister. All fresh chiles, sweet or hot, start out green. As they mature, they develop their final color, usually red, but you'll find yellow, orange, purple, and even chocolate brown cultivars. Don't get too excited, though—as you cook the purple or brown ones, the color fades to greenish.

Peperonata

Peperonata is a staple in my home pantry and it should be one in yours, too. If only we had had this to slather on all of the grilled sausages during my Wisconsin childhood. In my version, I add a variety of cherry tomatoes near the end of the cooking process. The late addition brightens everything up and adds a nice texture. Plus, they look beautiful.

This recipe makes a big batch because you can serve peperonata on everything. In its simplest form, pile it on some grilled bread and go to town.

» *Makes about 8 cups*

4 pounds peppers, mostly sweet but a few hot are nice, too (use a mix of colors and varieties, if possible)

Extra-virgin olive oil

5 garlic cloves, smashed and peeled

3 bunches scallions, trimmed (including ½ inch off the green tops), cut into 1-inch lengths

½ teaspoon dried chile flakes

Kosher salt and freshly ground black pepper

2 pounds tomatoes (about half regular tomatoes, cut into chunks, and half cherry tomatoes)

1 tablespoon sherry, balsamic, or red wine vinegar

6 big sprigs fresh thyme or oregano, or a mix

Core and seed all the peppers. Cut them into slices, some thick and some thin, for the best texture. Set aside.

Heat ½ cup olive oil in a large pot such as a Dutch oven over medium heat. Add the garlic and cook slowly to toast so it's very soft, fragrant, and nicely golden brown—but not burnt—about 5 minutes.

Dump in all the peppers, half the scallions, and the chile flakes and season generously with salt and black pepper. Cook over medium-high heat, stirring frequently, until the peppers start to relax a bit, about 5 minutes. Add half the tomatoes (use the cut-up larger tomatoes here).

Cook and stir until the peppers and tomatoes get very soft, about 30 minutes. The tomato pulp should become a nicely thick sauce, and you should see the juices start to stick to the bottom and sides of the pan. Be sure to frequently scrape this up and down so that nothing burns and these delicious reduced juices get incorporated into the mix.

After about 30 minutes, add the cherry tomatoes, the rest of the scallions, the vinegar, and the thyme. Keep cooking until these tomatoes burst and their juices thicken also, and the whole mess is thick and savory.

Taste and adjust the salt, black pepper, vinegar, and chile flakes. And of course, add a bit more olive oil. Serve warm or at room temperature.

MORE WAYS:

Dress up breakfast: Spoon over a simple cheese omelet.

Create an instant comfort food: Top a bowl of creamy polenta.

Add a savory topping: Serve with slices of braised pot roast.

Transform simple seafood: Spoon over a fillet of cod or halibut and bake.

Red Pepper, Potato, and Prosciutto Frittata Topped with Ricotta

At its heart, this is a Denver omelet in frittata form . . . but I daresay a lot better. Loaded with sweet roasted peppers, potatoes, and fluffy ricotta, the frittata is slightly fragile because of all the moist ingredients, so I never do the classic flip when getting it out of the pan. Instead, I just loosen it from the pan and slide it onto a plate. I love this served with a simple spicy green salad.

» Serves 3 or 4

½ pound potatoes, peeled if the skins are mature

Kosher salt and freshly ground black pepper

2 tablespoons unsalted butter

2 red bell peppers or other large sweet peppers, seeded and cut into julienne strips

1 bunch scallions, trimmed (including ½ inch off the green tops), sliced on a sharp angle

4 ounces prosciutto, cut into thin strips

6 eggs

½ cup finely grated Parmigiano-Reggiano cheese

Extra-virgin olive oil

½ cup whole-milk ricotta cheese, seasoned lightly with salt and pepper and stirred so it's creamy

Put the potatoes in a large pan of water and add salt until it tastes like the sea. Bring to a boil and cook until they are tender but not mushy, 15 to 20 minutes, depending on their size. Drain.

When cool enough to handle, cut into small chunks.

Heat the oven to 400°F.

Heat the butter in a 10-inch skillet (nonstick if you have one, with an ovenproof handle) over medium-high heat. Add the bell peppers, scallions, and prosciutto, season lightly with salt and black pepper, and cook until fragrant and the bell peppers are softening but not browning, 5 to 7 minutes. Add the potatoes.

Crack the eggs into a large bowl, add 1 teaspoon salt, many twists of black pepper, and the Parmigiano. Whisk until the eggs are nicely blended. Pour the eggs over the ingredients in the skillet, scraping everything out of the bowl with a rubber spatula.

Reduce the heat to medium and let the eggs sit peacefully for about 2 minutes. Then carefully slip the spatula around the edges of the eggs, releasing them from the pan, allowing more liquid egg to flow underneath. Let that new layer of egg set up a bit and then repeat the process. You are building layers of cooked egg, which will help the frittata have a lighter texture than if you simply let the whole thing set as one.

After most of the liquid egg has cooked, but the top is still runny, dollop the ricotta over the top

For a neat julienne, cut away the top and bottom of the pepper. Slice open, cut out the seedy core, and lay flat. Cut away interior ribs, then cut into strips.

of the frittata in 8 blobs, evenly spaced so each slice will get some ricotta. Transfer the pan to the oven and finish cooking the frittata all the way through, about 5 minutes or so. It should puff a bit and the top will get lightly browned.

Let the frittata sit in the pan for a couple of minutes, then run the spatula or a small knife around the edge of the frittata and as far under the center as you can go. Slide the frittata onto a cutting board or cooling rack. If a bit sticks to the pan and rips, don't worry, just piece it back together.

Serve the frittata on the warm side of room temperature, cut into wedges. It's delicious the next day, too.

Cheese-Stuffed and Pan-Fried Sweet Peppers

A bit like a Mexican chile relleno, this dish takes advantage of the natural container that a pepper provides, once you've cored and seeded it. I like this combination of cheeses—feta for tang, Fontina for melting, ricotta for sweet dairy flavor—but you can play with whatever you have on hand.

» Serves 2 as a main dish, 4 as a first course

½ cup crumbled feta cheese

1 cup whole-milk ricotta cheese

½ cup grated Fontina cheese

2 tablespoons chopped flat-leaf parsley

2 scallions, trimmed (including ½ inch off the green tops), thinly sliced

Kosher salt and freshly ground black pepper

4 large bell peppers or 8 smaller chiles, such as poblano or Anaheim, roasted, peeled, and seeded (page 243), but don't slit the sides—keep the "container" shape of the pepper intact

Flour, for dredging

1 egg, beaten well

Extra-virgin olive oil

Pickle Salsa Verde (page 44; optional)

Mix together the feta, ricotta, and Fontina cheeses in a small bowl. Add the parsley and scallions and season generously with salt and black pepper. Taste and adjust the seasoning.

Carefully fill each bell or chile pepper with the cheese mixture, pinching the tops to seal in the cheese as well as you can. Put the flour on a plate and the beaten egg in another plate or shallow bowl. Lay out a double layer of paper towels on a tray or plate to drain the finished peppers.

Heat ½ inch of olive oil in a large skillet over medium-high heat. As the oil is heating, you can prep the peppers: Dredge a pepper through the flour to coat it lightly and evenly, then dip into the egg. Let the excess egg drip off and carefully lay the pepper into the hot oil in the pan. Be careful; the oil may pop.

Fry until the pepper is nicely browned on one side, 2 to 3 minutes, then carefully flip and fry the other side. Repeat with the remaining peppers, but don't add too many at once, as that will lower the oil temperature and make the peppers greasy.

Transfer the peppers to the paper towels to drain and serve warm on their own or with the salsa verde.

Sweet and Hot Peppers, 'Nduja, and Melted Cheese

'Nduja is an spreadable fresh sausage from Calabria, with a spicy bite and the tang of a good salami. If you can't find it, you could substitute a small dice of Spanish chorizo or soppressata. The dish is best eaten right out of the oven, so have some cold white wine or good beer and crusty bread at the ready.

Serves 4

Extra-virgin olive oil

3 or 4 garlic cloves, smashed and peeled

1 bunch scallions, trimmed (including ½ inch off the green tops), cut into 3-inch slices

1 to 3 jalapeños (depending on how hot you want the dip), seeded, deribbed, and thinly sliced

¼ pound 'nduja

1 large sweet red pepper, roasted (see page 243), seeded, peeled, and cut into thin strips

A few sprigs thyme

¼ pound Fontina cheese, grated on the coarse holes of a box grater

½ pound Taleggio cheese, cut into chunks

Toasted country bread, Whole-Grain Carta di Musica (page 46), or vegetables, for serving

Heat a large skillet over medium heat. Add a couple of tablespoons olive oil and the garlic and cook slowly to toast the garlic so it's very soft, fragrant, and nicely golden brown—but not burnt—about 5 minutes.

Add the scallions and jalapeños and cook until they are soft, fragrant, and lightly browned, another 5 minutes (if the garlic threatens to burn, scoop it out and then return it to the pan when the other ingredients are ready). Smash the garlic as you're cooking so it breaks up into little bits.

Heat the oven to 450°F.

Spread the 'nduja in an even layer on the bottom of a small casserole dish, something that holds about 4 cups, or among 4 individual baking dishes. Layer on the roasted red pepper and the cooked scallions, garlic, and jalapeños. Sprinkle the thyme all over and then mix the two cheeses together and pile them in. Drizzle with a healthy shot of olive oil and bake until bubbling and melty, about 10 minutes.

Serve hot with toasted bread or carta di musica or as a dip with raw vegetables.

Shell Beans

Fresh shell beans were a revelation to me many years ago when I first realized that those hard, dry things in plastic bags actually start out as fresh, moist beans. Shell beans are grown primarily to be processed for long storage, but there's a short window when you can eat them fresh. Immediately after a summer in the sun, shell beans are plump with just enough starch to make them creamy.

Get 'em while you can. Shell beans are still a specialty, to be found only at a few stalls of your farmers' market, though I'm starting to see some varieties even in grocery stores in late summer. I love any variety, but borlottis are favorites of mine because my cooking is strongly Italian inflected. Also called cranberry beans, they are meaty and sweet, creamy but with enough integrity to hold their shape. Cannellini, purgatorio, and other white beans are also incredible, and lately I've had fun experimenting with fresh chickpeas.

Buy as many as you can, and shell them within a day or two so they don't get moldy inside. Shell beans freeze well, so pack up the overflow in a freezer bag and stash it for fall or winter.

The recipes in this section will also be delicious made with dried beans, so don't let unavailability of the fresh version stand in your way.

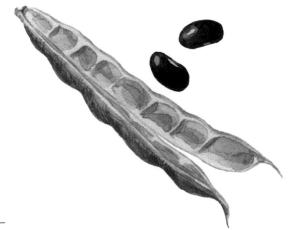

In the kitchen Salt isn't the culprit that prevents dried beans from cooking properly—acid is. Salt your cooking water generously, so the beans get seasoned all the way to the interior, and don't add tomatoes, wine, or other acidic ingredients to a bean dish until the beans have reached tenderness.

Perfect Shell Beans

The exact quantities and times will vary depending on what type of bean you're using and whether it's fresh or dried, and even within those categories, each batch of beans will have its own personality and behavior.

But that doesn't matter! This method will guide you to perfectly cooked beans no matter what, as long as you pay attention. The key is to obsessively watch them as they cook over low heat. You need to cook the beans right until the point that they are almost done, allowing carryover cooking to bring them to the exact doneness as they cool. This way of cooking also helps the beans retain their shape, especially if you're reheating or using them in another dish. There is really nothing better than a perfectly cooked bowl of beans with good extra-virgin olive oil.

» Makes 5 cups cooked beans and liquor (the flavorful cooking liquid)

4 cups fresh shell beans (from 3 pounds beans in the pod), or 2 cups dried beans	**1 bay leaf**
	1 garlic clove, smashed and peeled
1 big sprig rosemary	**Kosher salt**
1 small whole dried red chile	**8 to 10 cups water**
	Extra-virgin olive oil

If you're using dried beans, put them in a bowl or pot and add cool water to cover by a couple of inches. Soak them overnight on the counter. Drain and rinse; you should have about 4 cups now. Continue with the recipe.

Put the beans, rosemary, chile, bay leaf, garlic, and 1½ teaspoons salt in a large pot. It needs to be big enough for the beans to expand, so

make sure there's plenty of room. Add water to cover the beans by 1 inch—about 8 cups for fresh beans, 10 cups for dried.

Bring everything just barely to a boil over high heat, then immediately reduce the heat and adjust so that the beans are simmering merrily, but not actually boiling hard at all. Cook uncovered until the beans are about halfway soft. You can tell by biting into a few   they will be soft enough for you to easily bite them with no crunch, but they'll still be quite dry and crumbly inside. This could take as little as 30 minutes for fresh or 1 hour for dried, so taste early and often!

At this point, add another heaping teaspoon of salt and a glug of olive oil. Keep cooking at a gentle simmer and check frequently—the closer you get to doneness, the more frequently you should check. You want to stop cooking the beans when they are very creamy and tender all the way through but not yet mushy or broken up (though a few will split).

When you are just about at that perfect point, move the pot off the heat and let the beans cool in their liquid. They'll finish softening the last few degrees as they cool. (If you worry that you've gone a bit too far and the beans risk getting mushy, as soon as you take them from the heat, transfer them from the pot to a bowl set

into some ice water and stir gently to cool things down quickly.)

Once the beans are starting to cool, taste and add more salt if needed, and add another nice glug of olive oil. Once cool, you're in business. Be sure to keep the bean cooking liquid, because you'll use it in several of the recipes here.

MORE WAYS:

Bake a quick cassoulet: Pile some beans into a baking dish, slice some good garlic sausage and nestle it into the beans, cover the top with breadcrumbs, drizzle with olive oil, and bake until bubbling.

Puree to make a dip: Scoop out some beans and liquid and puree in a food processor. Add roasted garlic, a touch of spice such as cumin or smoked paprika, and olive oil of course. Serve slightly warm with hunks of bread or vegetables for dipping.

Make a hearty soup: Brown some diced bacon or pancetta in a soup pot. Add a few diced tomatoes (canned are fine) and cook a few minutes to concentrate. Add several ladlefuls of beans and liquid, some chicken or vegetable broth to thin, and a big sprig of thyme. Simmer until nicely married and flavorful. Puree half and leave the rest chunky.

Beans on Toast

When you have great beans and the beans are cooked right, this is a perfect dish. My great beans are Ayers Creek Farm borlotti beans, grown by Anthony and Carol Boutard from Gaston, Oregon. Every year Anthony and Carol grow more and more and we buy them all. So source some good beans in your area, eat as many as you can while they're still fresh, and then freeze the rest.

» Serves 4

2 garlic cloves

Extra-virgin olive oil

1 tablespoon very roughly chopped fresh rosemary leaves

Dried chile flakes

Kosher salt and freshly ground black pepper

3 cups Perfect Shell Beans (page 254), with some bean cooking liquid or water

4 thick slices country bread

Slice one of the garlic cloves as thinly as you can. Cut the other garlic clove in half and set aside.

Pour ¼ cup olive oil into a small saucepan. Add the sliced garlic, rosemary, a pinch of chile flakes, and a pinch of salt. Warm gently over low heat until nicely fragrant (whatever you do, don't overheat to the point where the garlic browns). Set aside for about 15 minutes for the flavors to infuse the oil.

Put 2 cups of the beans into a food processor and puree them. Once they're relatively smooth, drizzle in a splash of the bean cooking liquid and another ¼ cup olive oil. Check the consistency and add more liquid or oil to make a smooth, thick, but spreadable puree—stiff enough to hold the marks of your spoon, but not thick like refried beans. Taste and adjust with salt, black pepper, or chile flakes.

Toast, broil, or grill the bread so it's lightly browned but still chewy inside. Rub the slices with the cut side of a garlic half.

Spread the puree thickly all over each piece of toast, like you're frosting a cupcake. Put the toasts on plates and then spoon over the remaining whole beans and drizzle with the infused oil and some of the bits in it. Serve right away.

Beans and Pasta

Beans and pasta—or *pasta e fagiole* in Italian—is a Roman classic. What may sound like an unlikely combination at first—two starches in one bowl—leads to a rich, creamy, and well-balanced dish with the addition of tomato. I love to make this with fresh shell beans in late summer, because in my part of the country, the nights are already cooling. If you can't find fresh beans, any small, dried white bean will work just as well throughout the year.

» *Serves 2 or 3*

Kosher salt

4 ounces pasta (huge rigatoni is great here, as are small shapes such as ditalini)

Extra-virgin olive oil

3 garlic cloves, smashed and peeled

2 tablespoons Tomato Conserva (page 272) or tomato paste

2 teaspoons chopped fresh rosemary

¼ teaspoon dried chile flakes

½ cup canned crushed tomatoes

2 cups Perfect Shell Beans (page 254), plus about ½ cup bean liquid or pasta cooking water

½ cup freshly grated Parmigiano-Reggiano cheese or a mix of Parmigiano-Reggiano and Pecorino Romano

Bring a large pot of water to a boil and add salt until it tastes like the sea. Add the pasta and cook according to the package directions, but stop just shy of al dente (the pasta will cook a bit longer once added to the beans). Right before you drain, scoop out about a cup of the pasta water and set it aside.

Heat a glug of olive oil in a large pot over medium-low heat. Add the garlic and cook slowly to toast the garlic so it's very soft, fragrant, and nicely golden brown—but not burnt—about 5 minutes. You want it cooked enough so that it will easily smash and blend with the other ingredients.

Add the tomato paste, rosemary, and chile flakes and stir and spread it around as you cook it. You want the paste to lightly caramelize and take on deeper flavors and start smelling slightly toasty, which should take 5 to 8 minutes. Use a heatproof silicone spatula to scrape up anything that sticks to the bottom of the pan.

Add half the crushed tomatoes and cook down in the same manner until it is concentrated, too, another 3 to 4 minutes. Everything should be dark red and nicely oily now.

Add the cooked beans and about ½ cup of the bean liquid or pasta water. Simmer, stirring, until the liquid is reduced and concentrated to a creamy, cloaking texture, 4 to 5 minutes.

Add the drained pasta and the last bit of crushed tomatoes and fold everything together. Let everything simmer together for a minute or two. The dish should be moist but not at all soupy. If it feels too dry, add a few spoonfuls of the pasta water. Taste and add more salt or chile flakes (if you used pasta water instead of bean cooking liquid, you'll probably need to add more seasoning). Finish with a healthy drizzle of olive oil and the grated cheese.

Risotto with Shell Beans, Sausage, and Bitter Greens

Not a traditional risotto, this dish is more of a creamy beans and rice. It's an adaptation of a Marcella Hazan recipe, my twist being the addition of tons of spicy greens.

» Serves 4 to 6

1 small head radicchio (about 8 ounces), cored, leaves torn into pieces

1 cup Perfect Shell Beans (page 254) plus 5 cups cooking liquid (or if you didn't make beans from scratch, low-sodium chicken broth, homemade meat broth, or water)

Extra-virgin olive oil

½ small onion, finely chopped

Kosher salt and freshly ground black pepper

½ pound fresh garlicky sausage, such as mild Italian sausage, casings removed, meat pulled into small pieces

1½ cups Arborio or carnaroli rice

2 large handfuls arugula

¼ cup lightly packed roughly chopped flat-leaf parsley

½ cup freshly grated Parmigiano-Reggiano cheese

½ cup freshly grated Pecorino Romano cheese

Put the radicchio in a bowl of ice water and let it soak at least 30 minutes; this will take away some of the bitterness.

Put the bean liquid or broth in a saucepan and bring to just below a simmer.

Heat a glug of olive oil in a very large skillet or a Dutch oven (the pan needs to be big enough to hold all the ingredients and allow you to stir easily) over medium-high heat. Add the onion and a pinch of salt and cook, stirring a lot, until the onion is fragrant and translucent, but not browned at all, about 2 minutes. Add the sausage and cook until the sausage has lost its pinkness, another 3 to 4 minutes. While you're doing this, try to break up the sausage even more so you don't have any large clumps.

Reduce the heat to medium-low and add half the cooked beans and about ¼ cup of the bean liquid and smash the beans into a paste, stirring to incorporate the liquid to make everything creamy. The goal is to have the ingredients cloaked in nice creamy bean puree.

Add the rice and stir to distribute, then add the rest of the beans and stir again. Add a ladleful (about 1 cup) of bean liquid and stir. Adjust the heat so that the liquid is definitely bubbling but is not boiling like crazy—if it's too hot, the liquid will evaporate too quickly and the rice won't get tender. Cook, stirring occasionally (contrary to the myth, risotto doesn't need that much stirring!), until the liquid has reduced a lot and you can see the bottom of the pan as you stir.

Add another ladleful and repeat the process. Keep adding, stirring, and cooking down until the rice is no longer chalky in the center when you bite it (but not more tender than that or the final dish will be a bit mushy), 20 to 25 minutes, depending on your rice. If you run out of bean liquid, don't worry, just add some warm water.

When the rice is done, check the amount of liquid: The risotto will stiffen up a bit when you add the cheese and also during the time between the pan and the table, so keep it fairly loose now. Do this by stirring in more bean liquid or water, up to ½ cup or so. Taste and adjust the seasoning with salt and pepper.

Once the risotto is at the right consistency, drop the radicchio, arugula, and parsley into the pan and fold in so that the heat starts to wilt the greens. Fold in half the cheeses, adjust the seasoning and liquid again, and serve immediately. Pass the rest of the cheese at the table.

Crunchy Mixed-Bean Salad with Celery and Tarragon

The traditional three-bean salad, but with crunch and complexity. If you're lucky enough to find more than one variety of shell bean, use a mix. The different sizes, shapes, and colors add to the pleasure.

» Serves 4

Kosher salt and freshly ground black pepper

½ pound wax beans, green beans, or a mix, trimmed

2 cups Perfect Shell Beans (page 254), preferably a mix of types, drained and rinsed

4 to 6 medium inner celery stalks with leaves attached

1 bunch flat-leaf parsley, thick stems trimmed off and reserved, leaves left whole

½ cup lightly packed tarragon leaves

Extra-virgin olive oil

½ bunch scallions, trimmed (including ½ inch off the green tops), thinly sliced, soaked in ice water for 20 minutes, and drained well (see page 53)

½ cup roughly chopped pepperoncini, plus a splash of the pickling liquid

1 lemon

2 tablespoons capers, rinsed, drained, and roughly chopped

Kosher salt and freshly ground black pepper

4 Soft-Cooked Eggs (page 52)

Bring a medium pot of water to a boil and add salt until it tastes like the sea. Add the wax beans and boil for just about 1 minute (longer if the beans are mature); you want the beans to be crisp-tender. Drain and immediately run under cold water to stop the cooking. Pat dry.

Pile the wax beans into a large bowl. Add the shell beans.

Roughly chop the leaves on the celery stalks, then cut the stalks crosswise at a sharp angle into ¼-inch pieces and add all to the bowl of beans.

Measure out half the parsley stems (compost the others or save for another use), trim off the dried ends of the stems, and very finely slice them crosswise, as you would chives. Add the parsley stems, leaves, and the tarragon to the bowl, along with the scallions and pepperoncini, plus a splash of the pickling liquid. Gently mix all the ingredients. Grate the lemon zest into the bowl, add the capers, season generously with black pepper, add about ½ cup olive oil, and toss again. Tear the eggs into pieces and distribute over the bowl.

When you're ready to serve, give the salad a final spritz of lemon juice.

Tomatoes

The comparison between in-season, local vegetables and industrially grown ones is never as stark as with a tomato. Only the former is capable of moving your soul.

Take your pick. Fortunately, many growers are bringing all shapes, sizes, and colors to market. Cherry tomatoes, technically called "small-fruited tomatoes," are bright and high in acid, though some yellow varieties can be bland. The genius of the bunch is the Sun Gold, which is tangerine-orange and super sweet, with fruity overtones that are a bit like a tangerine's. Good eaten as a snack or flash-sautéed to make a quick sauce, Sun Golds will never let you down. I love many other varieties of tomatoes—Brandywine, Black Krim, and Old German are favorites.

An unripe tomato has a lot to offer, too. While I'm waiting for things to rosy up (and as the season wanes), I'll use green tomatoes to bring juicy crunch and bright acid to a dish.

Do taste tomatoes before you buy. Easy to do with cherry tomatoes, not so easy with a big beefsteak type, but if you're planning to buy a large quantity, such as for Tomato Conserva (page 272), buy a sample and taste it. Nothing is worse than realizing that your preserving project isn't going to be as good as you thought. Even local/seasonal isn't perfect every time.

Storing and prepping. There's still some debate as to whether tomatoes and refrigeration are compatible. Some food scientists maintain that a flavor compound degrades in the cold, dulling the wonderful complexity of the tomato. Others say nonsense, but it's agreed that if your tomato isn't fully ripe but you wish it were, you should not refrigerate it. Keep those tomatoes on the counter, under a light cloth, if you're worried about summer insects. You should try to consume your tomatoes within a day or two anyway, so you needn't worry about spoilage.

Other than coring, I don't do much in the way of prep for tomatoes. Some cooks like to peel and seed them, but I like texture, I like rusticity, so why waste time taking away a natural part of the tomato?

Tomato-Rubbed Grilled Bread Topped with Tomato Salad

The Spaniards have a snack called *pan con tomate*, which is simply grilled bread rubbed with olive oil, garlic, and ripe tomato. That's my starting point here, but I'm doubling down on the tomatoes and topping the whole thing with a tumble of juicy cherry tomato salad.

» *Serves 4 as a first course*

1 pint cherry tomatoes (a mix of colors if possible), halved or quartered if large

1 tablespoon red wine vinegar

Kosher salt and freshly ground black pepper

4 thick slices country bread

2 garlic cloves, halved

Extra-virgin olive oil

1 large tomato, halved

Whipped Ricotta (page 37)

Put the cherry tomatoes in a bowl and season with the vinegar and generous amounts of salt and pepper. Toss to mix and let sit.

Grill the bread on both sides in the broiler, toaster, or on a grill. Rub both sides of each slice of bread with the cut garlic cloves and then brush the bread with a bit of olive oil.

Take a tomato half and rub it over one side of a piece of bread. You want the tomato to be abraded by the grilled bread, so that the juices soak into the bread and bits of tomato flesh form a light coating on the bread. Ideally, you'll have used up both tomato halves on the 4 pieces of bread.

Spread the whipped ricotta over the tomatoed sides, arrange on plates, and then tumble the cherry tomatoes with their juices over the breads. Finish with a healthy drizzle of olive oil.

Farro with Tomatoes, Raw Corn, Mint, Basil, and Scallions

I keep cooked farro in my refrigerator all summer long so I can use it as a foundation for quick meals. This recipe can be your blueprint and then you can improvise with other vegetables, fruits, leaves, nuts, and whatever other yummy things you have a hankering for. It's important to include tomatoes, however, because they provide a lot of moisture and brightness, and they are so nutritious.

» *Serves 4*

3 cups cooked and cooled farro (page 50)

2 cups torn croutons (page 29)

1 bunch scallions, trimmed (including ½ inch off the green tops), sliced on a sharp angle, soaked in ice water for 20 minutes, and drained well (see page 53)

1 pint cherry tomatoes, halved

4 ears sweet corn, husked

1 handful fresh mint leaves

1 handful fresh basil leaves

¼ cup red wine vinegar

1 teaspoon dried chile flakes

Kosher salt and freshly ground black pepper

Extra-virgin olive oil

Put the farro in a big bowl. Add the croutons, scallions, and tomatoes. Using a paring knife, cut the corn kernels off the cobs into the bowl. Once the kernels are removed, scrape the cobs with the back of the knife blade so that you also capture all the milky pulp.

Add the mint and basil and toss everything together. Add the vinegar, chile flakes, 1 teaspoon salt, and a lot of twists of black pepper and toss again. Taste and adjust any of the seasonings to get the flavors nice and vibrant.

Finish with ⅓ cup olive oil and toss. Taste and adjust again. Serve lightly chilled or a little cooler than room temperature.

Tomato, Melon, and Hot Chile Salad with Burrata

When you join tomatoes, melons, and hot pickled peppers, the sweet, tart, and spicy juices mingle into a delicious complexity. The salad is beautiful, too, especially when you use a mix of tomato and melon colors—an ideal party dish. Make the salad with burrata or mozzarella—buffalo if you can find it—or without cheese at all. If you do use burrata, it's best to toss this with your hands so you can get the creamy burrata to coat the tomatoes and melon.

» Serves 4

1½ pounds tomatoes (a mix of larger tomatoes, cut into wedges, and cherry tomatoes, halved)

1½ pounds melon, seeded, rind cut away, and cut into crescents or half-crescents

Kosher salt and freshly ground black pepper

¼ cup chopped hot pickled peppers, such as oil-packed Calabrian peppers, or something milder such as pepperoncini

¼ cup white wine vinegar or red wine vinegar

1 small handful basil leaves

Extra-virgin olive oil

2 balls burrata or very fresh mozzarella

Put the tomatoes and melon into a large bowl, season generously with salt and black pepper, and toss gently. Add the hot pickled peppers and vinegar and toss again. Taste and adjust the salt, black pepper, pickled peppers, and vinegar to make a wonderful sweet-tart-hot balance.

Add the basil and ¼ cup olive oil and toss again. Right before serving, pull apart the burrata and distribute it over the salad, and toss gently with your clean hands. It will get nicely runny and messy as people serve themselves.

Israeli-Spiced Tomatoes, Yogurt Sauce, and Chickpeas

When people come to my house for a meal, I lay out big platters of these spiced tomatoes, chickpeas, and yogurt sauce, and then grill the flatbreads to order. If you can't find sumac, squeeze a few drops of lemon onto the tomatoes.

» Serves 6

1 teaspoon ground sumac

½ teaspoon ground coriander

½ teaspoon ground cumin

½ teaspoon dried chile flakes

Kosher salt and freshly ground black pepper

1 or 2 garlic cloves, minced

6 small or 3 big tomatoes, cored and cut into ¼-inch-thick slices

¾ cup plain whole-milk or low-fat yogurt (not Greek)

1 small cucumber, peeled, seeded (if necessary), and chopped

2 cups lightly packed mixed basil, mint, and flat-leaf parsley leaves, half roughly chopped and half torn or left whole

Hot sauce, such as Sriracha

1 cup cooked chickpeas (canned is fine)

½ small red onion, thinly sliced

2 tablespoons red wine vinegar

Extra-virgin olive oil

Slightly Tangy Flatbreads (page 48), preferably freshly cooked and still warm

Mix the sumac, coriander, cumin, chile flakes, 1 teaspoon salt, and the garlic in a little bowl. Lay out the tomatoes on a baking sheet and sprinkle the spices all over them. Let them sit for up to 1 hour while you fix the rest of the dish.

Stir together the yogurt, cucumber, and mixed fresh herbs. Season generously with salt, black pepper, and a few dashes of hot sauce. Let the sauce sit for at least 15 minutes and up to 1 hour, if you can, then taste and adjust the seasoning so the sauce is nicely savory.

Toss the chickpeas, onion, vinegar, and parsley leaves. Season with salt and black pepper, taste, and adjust the seasoning. Add a glug of olive oil and toss again.

Arrange a layer of the marinated tomatoes on a platter, and pour any accumulated juices over the tomatoes. Drizzle or dollop the yogurt sauce onto the tomatoes and tumble the chickpea salad on top. Serve with freshly grilled flatbreads.

At the market You can find sumac in Middle Eastern shops and, with increasing frequency, at well-stocked grocery stores. This ground dried berry from a wild bush looks a bit like coarse chile powder, but it's tart rather than hot.

Spaghetti with Small Tomatoes, Garlic, Basil, and Chiles

This is inspired by the classic *pasta al pomodoro*, and it could not be simpler nor more perfect for all the varieties of small-fruited tomatoes (the real name for cherry tomatoes) in the summer. You can make this sauce in the time it takes the pasta to boil. With my method, you get both the cooked tomato flavor and the brightness of a warm, raw tomato, which creates a vibrancy that a long-cooked sauce will not have.

» Serves 2

Kosher salt and freshly ground black pepper

Extra-virgin olive oil

1 or 2 garlic cloves, smashed and peeled

3 cups cherry tomatoes (aim for a mix, but definitely include Sun Golds if you can)

½ teaspoon dried chile flakes

1 big handful basil leaves

8 ounces spaghetti or linguine

1 tablespoon unsalted butter

Dried breadcrumbs (page 30; optional)

Parmigiano-Reggiano, for serving (optional)

Bring a large pot of water to a boil and add salt until it tastes like the sea.

Heat a large skillet over medium heat. Add a couple of tablespoons of olive oil, add the garlic, and cook slowly to toast so it's very soft, fragrant, and nicely golden brown—but not burnt—about 5 minutes. (You want a nice toasted piece of garlic that you smash into the sauce in a minute.)

Add a little more than half of the tomatoes to the pan (about 1½ cups). They will sizzle and spatter because of the moisture meeting the oil, so have a lid handy to cover the pan if things get too lively. Cook until the tomatoes burst and break open. (If some are stubborn and aren't bursting, poke them to move things along.) This will take 5 to 8 minutes.

Take the pan off the heat and gently smash the tomatoes with the back of a spoon. Add the chile flakes and season generously with salt and black pepper. Return to the heat, add half the basil, reduce the heat, and cook down to thicken the sauce a bit more, another 5 minutes.

Meanwhile, add the pasta to the boiling water and cook until 1 to 2 minutes shy of al dente according to the package directions. With a ladle or a measuring cup, scoop out about a cup of the pasta water and set it aside. Drain the noodles well.

Increase the heat under the sauce to medium-high, add the pasta, and toss it in the pan along with a good splash of the pasta water. Add the rest of the tomatoes and cook the sauce, stirring everything around so the pasta drinks up the sauce and finishes cooking and the newly added tomatoes get warm.

Once the noodles are properly cooked, add the remaining basil, a healthy drizzle of olive oil, and the butter. Take the pan off the heat and toss, toss, toss. Taste and adjust your seasoning. Serve as is, or with a handful of breadcrumbs and a shower of grated Parmigiano.

Tomato Soup with Arugula, Torn Croutons, and Pecorino

Play with other herbs, such as some rosemary instead of the thyme, as well as adding fresh basil, mint, or parsley. Parmigiano can take the place of the pecorino, or skip the cheese altogether to keep this vegan. You can serve this soup cold or warm, and it freezes well, so make a triple batch and freeze some to have a taste of summer when the snow falls again.

» *Serves 4 as a cup, 2 as a bowl*

Extra-virgin olive oil

1 medium onion, thinly sliced

2 garlic cloves, smashed and peeled

1 teaspoon thyme leaves

Kosher salt and freshly ground black pepper

2½ pounds red tomatoes, cored and cut into wedges

A few shakes of hot sauce, such as Sriracha

2 handfuls arugula, large stems trimmed off

1 cup torn croutons (page 29)

Pecorino Romano cheese, for grating

Heat a glug of olive oil in a large skillet over medium heat. Add the onion, garlic, and thyme. Season lightly with salt and cook until soft and fragrant, about 5 minutes (you are not looking for color; this is called "sweating").

Add the tomatoes, increase the heat a bit, cover the pan, and cook for about 5 minutes to get the tomato juices flowing.

Pour the whole mixture—or in batches—into a blender or food processor and process to make a smooth puree. Blend in the hot sauce. Taste and adjust the seasoning with more salt and pepper.

To serve, pour some soup into a deep bowl, toss in a handful of arugula and some torn croutons. Grate some pecorino over the top and finish with a couple of twists of pepper and a nice drizzle of olive oil.

MORE WAYS:

Make a quick cioppino: Add 2 cups of mixed seafood—such as peeled and deveined shrimp, scallops, chunks of halibut, or cooked crabmeat—to the hot soup and simmer just until cooked. Omit the arugula and pecorino, and finish with lemon.

Build a heartier soup: Fold in cooked white beans, sliced cooked sausage, and a handful of torn basil leaves.

Add complexity: Include a roasted red pepper with the tomatoes and add a tablespoon of smoked paprika when you add the thyme.

Grilled Green Tomatoes with Avocado, Feta, and Watermelon

Make this dish at the end of the summer, when you or your neighbors have a lot of green tomatoes around and the melons are still sweet. I love to throw purslane into salads whenever I find it at the market or in my garden. If you can't find purslane (though it's probably growing in your yard, really), make this salad anyway.

» Serves 4

4 medium green tomatoes, cored and halved through the equator

1 bunch scallions, trimmed (including ½ inch off the green tops), sliced on a sharp angle

Kosher salt and freshly ground black pepper

½ teaspoon dried chile flakes

4 tablespoons balsamic vinegar

1 firm-ripe avocado, halved and pitted

Two 1-inch-thick slices watermelon (or if your watermelon has a small diameter, use 3 or 4 slices), flesh cut into 1-inch cubes (about 2 cups)

1 small handful basil leaves (use a variety, if you can)

1 small handful mint leaves

1 small handful purslane sprigs (tough ends and stems snapped or cut off; optional)

Extra-virgin olive oil

1 cup diced feta cheese

Heat a cast-iron skillet (or a grill) until it's very hot. Place the tomatoes cut side down in the skillet (you might have to do this in batches) and sear them until they are slightly softened and the surface is nicely charred, about 5 minutes. Let them cool slightly.

Add the scallions to the pan (or grill) and do the same with them, cooking until softened and charred around the edges, 5 to 7 minutes, turning once or twice.

Cut the tomatoes into chunks, cut the scallions in half, and pile them both into a large bowl. Season with salt, black pepper, the chile flakes, and 2 tablespoons of the vinegar and toss gently.

Using a spoon, scoop out curls of the avocado and drop them into the bowl. Add the watermelon chunks, basil, mint, and purslane and toss again gently. Season with the remaining 2 tablespoons vinegar, salt, pepper, and ¼ cup olive oil. Taste and adjust with more salt, black pepper, chile flakes, or vinegar. Finish by sprinkling the feta chunks over the top and drizzling on another shot of olive oil.

In the field Purslane is a weed that grows in abundance this time of year, though you may never have noticed it before. It's also a superfood, extremely high in vitamin E, beta-carotene, vitamin C, minerals, and loads of omega-3 fatty acids.

Tomato Conserva

Who knew that tomato paste could be exciting? That's essentially what *conserva* is, but because you're making it with fresh tomatoes at their peak, good olive oil, and care and attention, the result is like no canned tomato paste you've ever had. Deep and sweet with just a hint of caramelized sugars, a big batch of conserva is an excellent preserve to make when you're feeling crafty.

» Makes about 2 cups

About 8 pounds tomatoes

Extra-virgin olive oil

Core the tomatoes and roughly chop them. Pile into a large pot, preferably one with a wide surface, which will speed up cooking. Add ¼ cup olive oil and bring to a boil over high heat.

Reduce the heat to medium or whatever temperature keeps the tomatoes simmering (you need to be careful not to scorch the tomatoes on the bottom) and cook until you've got the consistency of tomato sauce, 30 to 50 minutes. Work the tomatoes through a food mill to remove the skins and seeds. If you don't have a food mill, you can do this by pressing the tomatoes through a fine-mesh sieve or very fine colander, but a food mill makes the job much easier.

Heat the oven to 300°F. Oil a rimmed baking sheet (a 13 x 18-inch half-sheet pan or two smaller pans), a couple of 9 x 13-inch baking dishes, or a large Dutch oven.

Add the conserva and bake until the consistency goes from liquidy to a thick puree, about 3 hours. You'll need to tend to the conserva several times during cooking because the tomato close to the edges will brown more quickly. Use a heatproof silicone spatula to move the tomato from the edges of the pans into the center (and vice versa) to promote even cooking and create deep flavors.

Reduce the heat to 200°F and bake slowly for as long as you can, even overnight. You won't need to give the conserva as much attention at this point, but you should check it now and then anyway. The finished conserva should be very thick, like tomato paste, and deeply tomatoey.

You can freeze in small freezer bags, or put into jars and refrigerate, or even can in a pressure-canner (follow the instructions in a good canning manual).

Season Five

Fall

Bittersweet. That's fall in a nutshell. Leaves are dropping, along with the temperatures, and the lush plants bursting with life such a short time ago look all used up.

Yet after summer's frenetic growth, I can't help but welcome fall's slower pace. I'm ready to be indoors, spending a little longer by the warm stove, braising the fall crop of artichokes, roasting the last of the chiles, and sautéing a fresh haul of mushrooms, newly emerged after a rain. Vegetables that love the cold—like Brussels sprouts and braising greens—are coming into their prime, sweetened by the cold nights and occasional fall frosts that encourage sugar development. Roots are sweeter now as well. I do still serve some fall vegetables raw, especially those first Brussels sprouts and kale leaves. But I'm more likely now than in early months to turn up the stove and transform the vegetables with heat.

Recipes of Fall

Beets (Late Season)

By fall, beets have been in the ground for a few months, growing large and luscious. While small spring beets are great for tossing into dishes whole or halved, the big bruisers are perfect for chunking up and roasting. A roasted beet salad using deep magenta Bull's Blood beets mixed with golden beets is a glorious thing.

It's all about the root. What I don't see as much of in fall, however, are beet greens. They're generally a bit tired and beaten up by this time, and may not make it to the market, so I focus on roots-only dishes this time of year. To balance out their earthy sweetness, I like to pair fall beets with sharp accent flavors like citrus, hot chiles, and horseradish—a fellow underground denizen.

Weather watch. Be cautious about late-season beets if your region has been really hot in the preceding summer months—the beets can be a touch woody or fibrous, though still sweet.

Ready and waiting. Like all root vegetables, beets are good keepers—under the right conditions. Don't have a root cellar? Your fridge is fine, but beets need some humidity to keep from getting squishy, so just wrap them lightly in plastic and tuck them in the crisper drawer.

Roasted Beet, Citrus, and Olive Salad with Horseradish

Italians like to make a simple citrus salad with red onion and olives, and that's the root of the idea here. The color of the beets bleeds into the citrus segments and looks so pretty. The horseradish functions as a catalyst, bringing all the flavors together in a surprisingly delicious way.

» Serves 4

1½ pounds beets (a mix of colors if possible)

Kosher salt

1 navel orange or 2 smaller tangerines, satsumas, or other sweet citrus

1 lime

2 tablespoons red wine vinegar

¼ teaspoon dried chile flakes

⅓ cup roughly chopped pitted black and green olives

1 cup lightly packed flat-leaf parsley leaves

¼ small red onion, thinly sliced

Extra-virgin olive oil

A couple of inches fresh horseradish root

Heat the oven to 375°F.

Trim the top and bottom of the beets and rinse the beets to remove any mud or grit. Cut any large beets so that they are all about the same size.

Put the beets in a baking dish that's large enough to accommodate all of them in a single layer. Season with some salt and pour ¼ cup water into the dish. Cover tightly with foil and steam-roast until the beets are fully tender when pierced with a knife. Depending on the size and density of the beets, this could take between 30 minutes and 1 hour.

When the beets are cool enough to handle, slide off the skins with your fingers or peel them off with a paring knife. Cut the beets into whatever jolly shape you like—wedges, chunks, rounds—and pile them into a large bowl. Keep them warm.

Segment the orange (see page 344), reserving the juice. Using the same method, peel the lime, but don't segment it. Once you've cut away the peel and pith, slice the lime crosswise into thin rounds.

Whisk together the reserved orange juice, vinegar, ½ teaspoon salt, and chile flakes. Pour over the warm beets and toss. Let them sit and absorb the dressing for a few minutes, then toss again. Add the olives, parsley, onion, orange segments (and any accumulated juices), and lime slices and toss. Drizzle in a healthy glug of olive oil and toss again. Do a final taste.

If you have time, chill the salad for about 1 hour (or as long as overnight) before serving. Taste the dressing and adjust the vinegar, salt, and chile flakes until the flavor is quite zesty.

To serve, grate a fine layer of horseradish onto each serving plate. Pile a portion of beet salad on top, and then finish with another nice showering of finely grated horseradish.

Roasted and Smashed Beets with Spiced Green Sauce

A warm beet is a wonderful thing, which is one reason I love this dish. The other reason is the smashing. The texture produced allows the addictive herb-laden sauce to integrate right into the beet flesh. If you don't have early-season beets, older storage beets are fine, too, but peel them before roasting.

» Serves 4

8 small to medium beets (about 1½ pounds)	**Kosher salt and freshly ground black pepper**
Extra-virgin olive oil	**Spiced Green Sauce (page 44)**

Heat the oven to 375°F.

Trim and scrub the beets (or peel them if the skins are tough). If necessary, cut large ones in half or quarters to make them all about the same size. Toss them in a bowl with a small glug of olive oil, and season generously with salt and pepper.

Arrange the beets in a baking dish or a cast-iron skillet, cover the pan with foil, and roast until the beets are almost fully tender, 35 to 55 minutes, depending on the size and freshness of the beets.

Take off the foil and keep roasting until the beets are completely tender and have taken on a nice roasty texture, another 10 to 12 minutes.

When the beets are cooked and completely tender, smash them by pressing firmly but gently on each one with the bottom of a juice glass, measuring cup, or other flat object. You want to crush the beets to the point where they are still holding a roughly spherical shape but the tops are cracked and craggy, so that the sauce will penetrate in a most delicious way.

Arrange the beets on a serving platter—or serve right from the skillet if that looks good—and spoon the spiced green sauce over the tops. Serve warm or at room temperature.

Roasted Beets and Carrots with Couscous, Sunflower Seeds, Citrus, and Feta

Roasted roots love to play together, and especially beets and carrots, which are the sweetest. A tangy dressing and briny cheese bring delicious tension to the dish.

» Serves 4 to 6

1 pound beets (a mix of colors if possible)

Extra-virgin olive oil

Kosher salt and freshly ground black pepper

½ pound carrots (a mix of colors if possible), cut into thick coins

⅓ pound onions, shallots, or a mix, cut into chunks

½ cup **Citrus Vinaigrette** (page 39), plus more if needed

1 cup Israeli couscous

1 garlic clove, smashed and peeled

1 large sprig thyme

½ teaspoon dried chile flakes

½ cup salted roasted sunflower seeds

1 cup lightly packed cilantro leaves

½ cup crumbled feta cheese

Heat the oven to 450°F.

Trim the top and bottom of the beets, peel them, and cut into bite-size chunks. Toss with a small glug of olive oil, season lightly with salt and black pepper, and spread on a rimmed baking sheet. Roast for 10 minutes. Toss the carrots and onions with a glug of olive oil and season with salt and black pepper. Spread everything on a rimmed baking sheet and add to the oven. Roast all the vegetables until tender and lightly browned, 12 to 15 minutes more. Pile the roasted vegetables into a bowl and toss with ½ cup citrus vinaigrette.

Bring a medium saucepan of water to a boil and add salt until it tastes like the sea. Add the couscous, garlic, thyme, and chile flakes. Cook according to the package directions. Drain and remove the thyme sprig and garlic clove. Let cool.

Add the couscous, sunflower seeds, and cilantro to the vegetables and gently toss everything together. Taste and season with more vinaigrette, salt, black pepper, and chile flakes until the salad is nicely balanced and zingy. Crumble the feta over the top and serve slightly warm or at room temperature.

Brussels Sprouts

At long last, most people have discovered that when you cook them right (i.e., don't boil them into oblivion), Brussels sprouts are nuggets of sweet, nutty flavor.

Tiny cabbages. Much of a sprout's sweetness comes from riding in and out of warm—but not hot—days and cool nights. Frost makes them super sweet, but too much heat makes them bitter. Sprouts are essentially tiny cabbages, so choose those that look like a good cabbage should—tightly closed and firm. The size itself doesn't really affect the flavor.

Trimming. If you bought sprouts still on the stalk—which is a remarkable sight—cut them away with a sharp knife. When you buy them already liberated, the cut end is usually dried out, so trim that off. Peel off any outer leaves that are bug bitten, yellow, or otherwise the worse for wear. For roasting, cut in half. For braising, halve them, put them cut side down, and cut through the core into ¼-inch-wide slices. For salads, use the same process but slice them as thinly as you can.

Go hot or go raw. Like other brassicas, sprouts take well to high-heat methods like roasting or sautéing, which caramelize their sugars and make them irresistible. But when I want to eat them raw—and yes, there are still plenty of green things to eat raw even in fall—I slice the sprouts very fine into a slaw or salad. It's time-consuming, but worth it.

Raw Brussels Sprouts with Lemon, Anchovy, Walnuts, and Pecorino

I love this salad—it's like a very citrusy version of a Caesar salad, but of course with incredibly nutritious Brussels sprouts. The early-season sprouts, which are compact with tender outer leaves, shaved thin, are perfect for eating raw. Do take your time slicing them—either with a mandoline or a sharp knife—to get them absolutely as thin as possible.

» Serves 2

½ pound Brussels sprouts, trimmed

4 or 5 anchovy fillets

1 garlic clove, smashed and peeled

Extra-virgin olive oil

¾ cup hazelnuts or walnut halves and pieces, lightly toasted (see page 31)

½ lemon

Kosher salt and freshly ground black pepper

2 tablespoons dried breadcrumbs (page 30)

Pecorino Romano cheese, for grating

If you have a mandoline, now's the time to use it to get very thinly sliced Brussels sprouts. But if you're using a knife, here's how you'll do it: Trim off the stem ends of the Brussels sprouts if they look dry. Cut each one in half lengthwise through the core, and then put a half, cut side down, on a cutting board. Using a nice sharp knife, slice as thin as you can from the core to the top. Repeat with the rest. This step will take

you some time, but it's worth the effort, because the salad is best when the sprouts are almost "shaved." Don't worry about getting the slices a consistent thickness—just go for thin! Pile the shaved sprouts into a large bowl.

Chop the anchovies very fine and smear them into a paste. Chop the garlic as fine as you can, and drizzle with just a bit of olive oil to keep the garlic from oxidizing. Chop or smash the nuts so that some pieces are small and some are coarser.

Squeeze the lemon half onto the sprouts and toss to distribute. Add the anchovy and garlic (including the oil that was drizzled on the garlic) and toss well to fully distribute—the best way to do this is to massage everything with your hands. Season lightly with salt and generously with pepper. This salad likes a lot of pepper, but you may not need quite as much salt because the anchovies and cheese are both salty.

Pour in a healthy glug of olive oil and toss again. Taste and adjust the seasoning with more salt, pepper, or lemon juice. Add the nuts and breadcrumbs and toss again. Arrange on plates or a platter. Grate lots of pecorino over the top and serve.

The fluffy texture of shaved Brussels sprouts is worth the work.

Brussels Sprouts with Pickled Carrots, Walnuts, Cilantro, and Citrus Vinaigrette

Serve this dish warm or at room temperature, but not cold. If you make it ahead, pull it out of the fridge 20 minutes before you serve it. Make it a full meal by folding in some toasted cooked farro (page 50). The citrus vinaigrette will easily keep for 2 weeks in the fridge.

» *Serves 2 to 3*

Extra-virgin olive oil

1 garlic clove, smashed and peeled

¾ pound Brussels sprouts, trimmed and halved lengthwise

Kosher salt and freshly cracked black pepper

About ⅓ cup roughly chopped or slivered pickled carrots, store-bought or homemade (page 58)

½ cup walnuts, hazelnuts, or pecans lightly toasted (see page 31) and smashed or roughly chopped

1 bunch scallions, trimmed (including ½ inch off the green tops), thinly sliced

¼ cup Citrus Vinaigrette (page 39)

½ cup lightly packed roughly chopped cilantro leaves

½ cup lightly packed roughly chopped flat-leaf parsley leaves

Heat a large skillet over medium heat. Add ¼ cup olive oil and the garlic and cook to toast the garlic so it's very soft, fragrant, and nicely golden brown—but not burnt—about 5 minutes. Scoop out the garlic and set it aside (to prevent it from burning while you're cooking the sprouts).

Increase the heat a bit and add the Brussels sprouts, cut side down. Season well with salt and pepper and cook gently until the sprouts are tender all the way through, but not mushy, 8 to 10 minutes. Reduce the heat midway if the sprouts are getting too brown. Return the garlic to the pan, crushing it to break it up and disperse among the sprouts.

When the sprouts are cooked, pull the pan from the heat and add the pickled carrots, half the nuts, and all the scallions and toss thoroughly to mix and warm the new ingredients slightly.

Spoon the vinaigrette over the sprouts and toss again. Add half each the cilantro and parsley and toss again. Taste and adjust with more salt, pepper, or vinaigrette so the salad is very vibrant.

Right before serving, add a little more vinaigrette if you like, along with the rest of the nuts, cilantro, and parsley. Serve slightly warm or at room temperature.

At the market At farmers' markets, you'll often see Brussels sprouts still attached to their stalk. It's dramatic looking (and I've even seen a stalk roasted and served whole), but they're not any better on the stalk, and now you're stuck composting a cumbersome bit of brassica.

Gratin of Brussels Sprouts, Gruyère, and Prosciutto

This dish takes its cue from the classic Brussels sprouts-and-bacon combo, and it is addictive. You'll probably find yourself eating leftovers, cold, standing up in the kitchen . . . quite happy and not willing to share.

» Serves 4

1½ pounds Brussels sprouts, trimmed and halved lengthwise

1 medium onion (6 to 8 ounces), cut into small chunks

Extra-virgin olive oil

Kosher salt and freshly ground black pepper

2 ounces prosciutto, chopped

1 cup heavy cream or crème fraîche

¼ pound Gruyère cheese, grated

¼ cup dried breadcrumbs (page 30; optional)

Heat the oven to 400°F.

Put the Brussels sprouts and onion chunks into a large bowl, drizzle in a glug of olive oil, season with ½ teaspoon salt and many twists of pepper, and toss to distribute the oil.

Spread over a rimmed baking sheet and roast until the sprouts are mostly tender but still have a bit of resistance when you poke them with a knife, 15 to 20 minutes. (Leave the oven on.)

Transfer the vegetables to a gratin or baking dish that's large enough to hold the sprouts in mostly a single layer. Sprinkle the prosciutto around the vegetables, pour the cream over everything, and top with the Gruyère.

Bake until the cheese and cream are bubbling, 15 to 20 minutes. Top with the breadcrumbs (if using). Let cool for about 5 minutes. Serve hot.

Roasted Brussels Sprouts with Pancetta Vinaigrette

Wednesday night and you're not sure what's for dinner? This is. Roast up a bunch of sprouts, season with this meaty dressing—or any other vinaigrette or even simple oil and vinegar—and you have a substantial side dish without much work. Serve over a mound of wild rice, or next to some pork tenderloin medallions.

» Serves 4

1½ pounds Brussels sprouts, trimmed, and cut through the core into quarters

Extra-virgin olive oil

1½ teaspoons chopped thyme

Kosher salt and freshly ground black pepper

½ cup Pancetta Vinaigrette (page 39)

Heat the oven to 425°F.

Toss the sprouts with a healthy glug of olive oil and the thyme in a medium bowl. Season generously with salt and pepper. Spread out the sprouts evenly on two rimmed baking sheets. Roast until the sprouts are tender but not mushy, 20 to 22 minutes, stirring the sprouts once or twice during roasting. Note that any loose leaves will get browned and even slightly charred—delicious!

Slide the sprouts into a medium bowl, add the vinaigrette, and toss to coat. Taste and adjust any seasoning with more salt or pepper.

Carrots
(Late Season)

As with other root vegetables that we meet early in the spring (see young carrots starting on page 136) and then again in the fall, carrots are bigger, firmer, denser, and occasionally woodier by the time autumn rolls around. But they're very, very sweet, with less of the piney-lemony flavor of young spring specimens.

Forget the tops and the skins. What a late-season carrot does not have are greens. Carrot tops are only good, in my opinion, early in the season when they are still quite delicate and very moist and fresh. And their skins are tougher, too, so in most cases, I peel fall carrots.

Mature yes, old no. You'll still find a colorful array of carrots later in the season, though orange predominates. Whatever the color, be sure it's bright, not faded. The carrots should be firm, not flabby, with no splits or cracks. Fall carrots are mature, but you don't want them to be old.

Fall carrots are also large carrots. These big boys are good for grating, cutting into chunks, pureeing, and definitely roasting. While a young spring carrot is about tender, bright sweetness, a carrot that has seen some serious time underground—especially some cold nights—is about deep, mellow sweetness. It's a very rooty character.

Farro and Roasted Carrot Salad with Apricots, Pistachios, and Whipped Ricotta

The combination of the nutty farro, carrots, apricots, and ricotta makes this dish savory-sweet— almost carrot cakey. You can swap out the apricots for dates, dried cherries, or a combination of both. Take your time to toast the farro until it's deeply flavored.

» *Serves 4*

½ pound carrots, trimmed, peeled, and cut into small chunks

Extra-virgin olive oil

¼ teaspoon dried chile flakes

Kosher salt and freshly ground black pepper

2 cups cooked farro (page 50)

4 ounces dried apricots (preferably Turkish), roughly chopped

3 tablespoons white wine vinegar

½ cup lightly packed flat-leaf parsley leaves

½ large red onion, thinly sliced

½ cup pistachios, lightly toasted (page 31)

Whipped Ricotta (page 37)

½ cup crumbled ricotta salata or feta cheese

Heat the oven to 375°F.

Toss the carrots with a small glug of olive oil, the chile flakes, 1 teaspoon salt, and a few twists of black pepper. Spread out evenly on a baking sheet and roast until tender and lightly browned, about 15 minutes. Let cool slightly.

Pile the roasted carrots, farro, and apricots into a bowl. Season with the vinegar and toss. Taste and add more salt or chile flakes. Add the parsley, onion, and pistachios and toss. Taste again and adjust with more salt, chile flakes, or vinegar. Finish by tossing with ¼ cup olive oil.

Spread the whipped ricotta onto 4 plates or a platter in a nice schmear. Distribute the salad on top of the whipped ricotta, dress with the crumbled ricotta salata, finish with another tiny thread of olive oil, and serve.

Grated Carrot Salad with Grilled Scallions, Walnuts, and Burrata

Fall carrots are dense and sweet, thanks to the cool nights, and mature carrots' large size makes them easy to grate. Don't be put off by the anchovy in this dish—it works so well with the grilled scallion and the burrata. In fact, this could be the dish that helps you understand why people love anchovies so much.

» Serves 4

2 bunches scallions (about 16), trimmed (including ½ inch off the green tops)

¾ pound carrots (a mix of colors will be lovely), trimmed and peeled

1 cup walnuts, lightly toasted (see page 31) and chopped so that some are quite fine and some are still chunky

2 anchovy fillets, finely chopped

½ cup lightly packed very roughly chopped flat-leaf parsley

¼ cup fresh lemon juice

½ teaspoon dried chile flakes

Kosher salt and freshly ground black pepper

Extra-virgin olive oil

1 ball burrata or very fresh mozzarella

Heat a cast-iron or other heavy skillet over medium-high heat (or heat a grill). Cut the scallions into lengths that will fit into the skillet, or leave whole if you're grilling them. Char or grill the scallions—dry, no oil—turning them frequently, until they are blackened on the outer layer and very soft and collapsed and juicy inside, 8 to 10 minutes. Chop the scallions into ½-inch pieces and set aside.

As the scallions are cooking, prep the carrots by grating them on the large holes of a box grater or shredding them using a mandoline or other appliance. You can also cut them into julienne by hand, but the finer, the better, because the seasonings will penetrate more deeply into carrots cut to a finer gauge.

Put the carrots in a bowl and add the scallions, walnuts, anchovies, parsley, lemon juice, chile flakes, ½ teaspoon salt, and about 20 twists of black pepper. Toss well and let the salad sit for a few minutes so the seasonings can marry and the salt can draw out a bit of the carrot juices.

Toss again, taste, and dial in the flavors so they are really lively by adding more of any of them. Pour in ¼ cup olive oil and toss. Taste again, then distribute on your plates or a platter.

Pull the burrata or mozzarella into shreds or little blobs and distribute it over the salad. Drizzle on a bit more oil to finish and serve.

Burnt Carrots with Honey, Black Pepper, Butter, and Almonds

Roasting carrots concentrates their already sweet flavor, and roasting them so dark that they burn a bit adds a bitter edge that is fantastic, especially when balanced by the butter and honey. You can add fresh herbs, if you like. A little fresh thyme or winter savory would be an excellent partner.

» Serves 4

1½ pounds carrots, trimmed and peeled, but left whole

Extra-virgin olive oil

2 tablespoons white wine vinegar

Kosher salt and freshly ground black pepper

2 tablespoons unsalted butter, cut into small pieces

2 tablespoons honey

½ cup almonds, toasted (see page 31) and chopped

Heat the oven to 475°F.

Spread the carrots on a rimmed baking sheet, drizzle on a tablespoon or so of oil, and roll the carrots to coat them. Roast until they are very dark brown, even a bit burnt on the edges, but not fully tender, 10 to 12 minutes. (Leave the oven on but reduce the temperature to 300°F.)

When the carrots are cool enough to handle, cut them on a sharp angle into ½-inch-thick slices and transfer to a large bowl. Add the vinegar, season with salt and lots of pepper, and toss to coat. Let the carrots sit for 5 minutes to absorb the vinegar.

Spread them out on the baking sheet again, distribute the butter bits on top, and drizzle the honey over all. Roast until they are fully tender and the butter and honey are making a lovely mess, 5 to 7 minutes. Scrape everything into a serving bowl, taste, and adjust with more vinegar, salt, or pepper. Top with the almonds. Serve warm.

Carrot Pie in a Pecan Crust

I eat a lot of carrots—by themselves, pickled, in salads, grilled, in cake—and so why not in a pie? The pie has a soft, delicate texture reminiscent of a pumpkin pie (though the slices won't hold their shape as well as pumpkin pie), but it's distinctly carrot and deliberately not too sweet. The pecan crust adds a touch of richness.

» *Make one 9-inch pie (serves 6 to 8)*

2 pounds carrots (about 6 large), trimmed, peeled, and cut into 1-inch chunks

Kosher salt

½ cup sugar

1½ cups heavy cream or crème fraîche

2 tablespoons unsalted butter

2 eggs

1 egg yolk

Pecan Dough (page 49)

Put the carrots in a large saucepan, cover with water, add 2 teaspoons salt, and bring to boil. Adjust the heat to a gentle boil and cook until the carrots are thoroughly tender, 20 to 35 minutes, depending on the age and shape of your carrots. Drain well and transfer to a blender.

Put the sugar and ¼ cup water into the saucepan, stir to moisten the sugar, and cook over medium-high heat, without stirring but with a few swirls of the pan, until the sugar syrup has turned a dark amber and smells very caramel-y, 5 to 6 minutes. Be careful because this caramel is very hot.

Carefully add ¼ cup cream—things may get quite spattery—and whisk until the caramel is smooth. Add the butter and a pinch more salt. Pour the caramel sauce into the blender with the carrots. Add the remaining 1¼ cups cream, the whole eggs (which you've cracked one at a time into a separate bowl, just in case any shell gets in them), and egg yolk. Blend on high until the filling is really smooth. Set aside until your pie shell is ready.

Lightly flour the work surface and roll out the pecan dough to a 14-inch round. Roll it gently around your rolling pin, move it over a 9-inch pie plate, and gently unroll it into position, allowing it to drape into the corners without stretching. Tuck the excess pastry under itself to make a neat thicker edge. Using two fingers of one hand and one finger of the other hand, work your way around the edge to flute it. Chill the pie shell for 30 minutes in the freezer or 1 hour in the refrigerator.

Heat the oven to 400°F. Line the pie shell with foil or parchment paper and fill with dried rice or beans. If you're using foil, fold it toward the center so it doesn't get stuck in the pastry. Bake until the edges are puffed and very light brown, about 10 minutes. Reduce the oven temperature to 325°F. Carefully remove the foil and weights and bake for another 20 minutes to dry out the center of the crust. Make sure the crust edges aren't getting too brown. If so, reduce the oven temperature to 300°F.

Pour the filling into the partially baked crust and bake at 325°F until the filling is just set. It will still be very soft, but the top will have puffed a bit and when you shake the pie, you won't see actual rolling liquid in the center, just a bit of a jiggle. This should take about 1 hour.

Let the pie cool completely before cutting. It is very good for breakfast.

In the field Eliot Coleman of Four Season Farm calls his late-season carrots "candy carrots" because the frost has made them so sweet.

Swiss Chard

If you don't like beets, you may not like Swiss chard. The two vegetables are in the same family and in fact a bunch of beet greens can pass for Swiss chard in a pinch. Their common trait is a mineral earthiness—as in they taste a bit like dirt—which you either love or hate.

Sturdier than spinach. That earthiness in chard is balanced by a green flavor, with just a hint of bitterness from oxalic acid, a substance also contained in spinach. Given a choice between chard and spinach, I always go for chard because it maintains the textural integrity of the leaves even after long cooking. Spinach, on the other hand, can be wimpy and almost slimy . . . hence no spinach in this book!

Cook the ribs. The central rib on a chard leaf is thick and fibrous, so cut it away from the leaf to cook separately. Lay the leaf flat and slice along either side of the rib. Use the leaves whole, as is, or stack them, roll them into a loose cylinder, and slice across into ribbons, thick or thin as you like. Slice the ribs crosswise, lengthwise in strips, or on an angle and sauté them first, so they'll have a chance to soften and integrate into the dish by the time the leaves are ready.

Rainbow Chard with Garlic and Jalapeños

When I was at Four Season Farm, I thought it would be a good idea to grow a lot of chiles. Well, Maine has cold nights, and Mainers don't seem to like chiles much anyway, so in fact it was a bad idea, but as a result, the farm staff got to eat plenty of chiles in our staff meals. This was a favorite. Be generous with the garlic, vinegar, and extra-virgin olive oil.

» Serves 4

1 bunch Swiss chard (rainbow chard, sold as Bright Lights, is beautiful in this dish), dried ends trimmed

Extra-virgin olive oil

3 garlic cloves— 2 smashed and peeled, 1 halved

1 or 2 medium jalapeños, seeded, deribbed, and cut crosswise into thin slices

Kosher salt and freshly ground black pepper

4 teaspoons red wine vinegar

4 thick slices country bread

If the chard stems are very slim and tender, you can just sauté them along with the leaves. If they are thicker, prep them this way: Fold the leaves in half lengthwise and slice along the edge of the center rib and stem to cut away the stems. Cut the stems across into thin slices, or if very slender, split lengthwise into strips. Rinse the stems well in a colander and pat dry. Stack a few leaves, roll them into a loose cylinder, and cut or tear them into wide ribbons. Repeat with all the leaves. Rinse the leaves well in a colander and shake dry.

Heat ¼ cup olive oil in a large skillet or Dutch oven over medium heat. Add the smashed garlic and cook slowly to toast the garlic so it's soft, fragrant, and nicely golden brown—but not burnt—about 5 minutes. Add the jalapeño slices

and cook another minute or so until slightly softened. Then add the chard stems, season with salt and black pepper, and sauté until they lose about 75 percent of their crunch, 4 to 5 minutes.

Add the chard leaves; if they won't all fit into the pan, just add a few handfuls and toss them with tongs until they're wilted, and then add the rest. Add a splash of water and cover the pan. Cook over medium heat until the chard is tender, 8 to 10 minutes. If there is a lot of liquid in the pan at this point, increase the heat and boil most of it off. Add the vinegar, season with salt and black pepper, and toss well. Taste—the chard should have an appealing sweet-and-sour flavor.

Remove from the heat, pour in a healthy glug of olive oil, and let the chard rest so all the flavors and textures meld nicely. This is best served 1 to 2 hours later. It's also fine to make a day ahead; just be sure to bring it to room temperature.

Toast or grill the bread slices, then rub the surface with the halved garlic. Put the toast on plates or a board and arrange the greens and their juices on top. Finish with a ribbon of olive oil and serve.

Spaghetti with Swiss Chard, Pine Nuts, Raisins, and Chiles

All these ingredients come together to create a simple, sweet, salty, spicy, earthy pasta that is dead simple to make. Leftovers make a great frittata: Warm them in an ovenproof skillet, add some cheese, pour in beaten eggs, and bake. The bits of pasta that stick out will get crunchy in the oven.

» Serves 3 to 4

½ cup raisins

Red wine vinegar

Kosher salt and freshly ground black pepper

8 ounces spaghetti, tagliatelle, or angel hair

Extra-virgin olive oil

2 garlic cloves, thinly sliced

½ cup pine nuts

½ teaspoon dried chile flakes

1 bunch Swiss chard, dried ends trimmed, stems thinly sliced, leaves torn into strips

3 tablespoons unsalted butter

Parmigiano-Reggiano cheese, for grating

Combine the raisins, a splash of vinegar, and warm water just to cover in a bowl and plump for 20 minutes. Drain.

Bring a large pot of water to a boil and add salt until it tastes like the sea. Add the spaghetti and cook according to the package directions. Start tasting a minute or so ahead of time so you don't overcook it. With a ladle or a measuring cup, scoop out about ½ cup of the cooking water, and drain the pasta well.

Meanwhile, pour a healthy glug of olive oil into a large skillet over medium-low heat. Add the garlic and pine nuts and let them toast very slowly until lightly browned, about 5 minutes. Add the chile flakes and cook for another 10 seconds so they can bloom, then add the drained raisins.

Increase the heat to medium, add the chard stems, season with a bit of salt and black pepper, and cook slowly until the stems are slightly tender, 3 to 4 minutes. Add the torn chard leaves and a splash of water (use the pasta water, if the timing works), cover the pan, and cook until the leaves are wilted, 2 to 3 minutes.

Add the drained pasta and the butter to the chard and toss well. Taste and adjust the seasoning with more salt, black pepper, or chile flakes. Grate a bit of Parmigiano over everything, drizzle with more olive oil, and pile into bowls. Serve with more grated cheese.

Swiss Chard, Leek, Herb, and Ricotta Crostata

Leafy greens are meant for pies and tarts, like this chard crostata—an open-faced, freeform tart that doesn't require a tart pan. Here I pair wilted chard with sweet leeks and lots of fresh herbs. It's at once fresh tasting and comforting, perfect with a glass of cider.

» Serves 4 to 6

1 bunch Swiss chard, dried ends trimmed

Extra-virgin olive oil

3 garlic cloves, smashed and peeled

2 leeks, trimmed, halved lengthwise, cleaned well, and cut crosswise into ¼-inch-thick half-moons

½ teaspoon dried chile flakes

Kosher salt and freshly ground black pepper

1 cup whole-milk ricotta cheese

1 cup freshly grated Parmigiano-Reggiano cheese

1 cup lightly packed fresh herbs: a mix of dill, cilantro, mint, and parsley

2 teaspoons lightly packed grated lemon zest

2 eggs

1 recipe Walnut Dough (substitute walnuts for pecans in Pecan Dough, page 49)

If the chard stems are very slim and tender, you can just sauté them along with the leaves. If they are thicker, prep them this way: Fold the leaves in half lengthwise and slice along the edge of the center rib and stem to cut away the stems. Cut the stems crosswise into thin slices. Rinse the stems well in a colander and pat dry. Stack a few leaves, roll them into a loose cylinder, and cut or tear them into wide ribbons. Repeat with all the leaves. Rinse the leaves well in a colander and shake dry.

Heat ¼ cup olive oil in a large skillet or Dutch oven over medium heat. Add the garlic and cook slowly to toast the garlic so it's soft, fragrant, and nicely golden brown—but not burnt—about 5 minutes. Add the chard stems, leeks, and chile flakes, and season with salt and black pepper. Sauté until the leeks are soft and fragrant and the chard stems are soft, 8 to 10 minutes.

Add the chard leaves; if they won't all fit in the pan, just add a few handfuls and toss them with tongs until they're wilted, and then add the rest. Add a splash of water and cover the pan. Cook over medium heat until the leaves are tender, 8 to 10 minutes. If there is a lot of liquid in the pan at this point, uncover the pan, raise the heat, and boil most of it off.

Transfer the vegetables to a bowl or platter to cool. Meanwhile, put the ricotta, Parmigiano, herbs, lemon zest, and eggs in a bowl and stir to blend well.

Add the cooled chard and fold together. Taste and adjust the seasoning with more salt, black pepper, or chile flakes.

Line a large baking sheet with parchment paper or a silicone baking mat. Lightly dust the work surface and roll out the dough to a rough 15-inch round. Roll the dough gently around your rolling pin, move it over the baking sheet, and gently unroll it into position, allowing it to drape over the sides of the sheet.

Pile the ricotta-chard filling into the middle of the dough and gently spread it in an even layer to within about 3 inches of the edge. You should have a round of filling that's about 9 inches in diameter.

Gently fold the border of dough up and over the filling, pleating loosely as you work your way around the crostata. Don't aim for perfection.

Bake the crostata until the dough is nicely browned, on the underside as well as the edges, 25 to 30 minutes. Reduce the heat to 325°F and bake until the crust is cooked all the way through, another 15 to 20 minutes.

Carefully slide the parchment onto a rack and let the crostata cool for at least 15 minutes before cutting. You can serve it slightly warm or at room temperature.

Collards

Mention "collards" and everyone thinks of a big pot of greens, simmered all day long with a meaty ham bone. They're a Southern staple. Soul food. Something we eat alongside a big plate of barbecue. That's all true, but it's also just the beginning.

Collards are like kale. You know that kale salad you love, or those kale chips you can't get enough of, or that braised kale gratin that had you licking your fork clean? You can totally swap out the kale for collard greens. They're similar in flavor and texture, both providing a sturdy backdrop for a wide range of assertive ingredients. They don't have to be simmered all day, although they'll stand up to it just fine if you do, and become exquisitely tender in the process. But really, just remove the ribs (see page 308) and slice the leaves into shreds for salads, or toss into pasta or soups. Blanch them whole and use them like wraps, and of course you can braise them into silky submission.

Color is key. Size doesn't matter when it comes to leafy greens (unless you're talking immature baby leaves or microgreens). A medium collard leaf will have the same flavor as a big one. What you want to look for are perky leaves with a deep green color. Any evidence of yellowing, wilting, or slimy edges means they're past their prime. Wrapped in plastic in the fridge, they'll keep for several days.

Shaved Collard Greens with Cashews and Pickled Peppers

Collards are a member of the brassica family, closely related to kale. So if we can make a raw kale salad, why not a raw collards salad? The cashews and cashew butter are unexpected with collards, but after one bite you'll see that they make perfect sense.

» *Serves 4*

6 ounces mushrooms (creminis are fine, or use wild mushrooms if you have them)

Kosher salt and freshly cracked black pepper

¾ pound collard greens

6 ounces red or green cabbage (about ¼ small head)

6 tablespoons cashew butter

2 tablespoons white wine vinegar

2 tablespoons pickle liquid (from the pepperoncini jar)

Extra-virgin olive oil

⅓ cup seeded and chopped pepperoncini or other pickled peppers

¼ cup roughly chopped toasted cashews (see page 31)

Heat the oven to 400°F.

Spread the mushrooms on a baking sheet and roast them—with no oil—until they have lost much of their moisture and are slightly dry around the edges. The timing could range from 15 to 30 minutes, depending on the type and moisture content of the mushrooms. Toss them with some salt after they're roasted and set aside to cool.

Meanwhile, cut out the thick rib from each collard leaf and compost or discard it. Stack a few leaves on top of one another and roll them into a tight cylinder. With a sharp knife (all your knives are sharp, aren't they?), slice across the roll to cut the collards into very thin strips, pretty much as thin as you can get. (This technique is called chiffonade.) Put the collards in a bowl.

Cut out the core from the cabbage and slice in the same way as the collards. Add to the bowl.

In a small bowl, whisk together the cashew butter, vinegar, and liquid from the pickled peppers. When the ingredients are blended, whisk in 2 tablespoons olive oil and season generously with salt and black pepper. Taste and tinker with the balance until the sauce is irresistible.

Add the mushrooms and pickled peppers to the greens, pour on the dressing, and toss until it's completely integrated. Because the dressing is thick, you'll need to toss a lot; using tongs makes this easier. Taste and adjust with more vinegar, pickle juice, salt, or black pepper. Top with the chopped cashews and serve.

Collards with Freekeh, Hazelnuts, and Grapes

In this salad, the freekeh itself provides plenty of chewiness, so I add cooked collards rather than raw. The grapes add juiciness, but also the flavor of fall. If you can't find hazelnuts, use roasted almonds or lightly toasted walnuts.

» *Serves 4*

1 cup freekeh

4 garlic cloves, smashed and peeled

Red wine vinegar

1 bunch collards, ribs cut out, leaves sliced into 2-inch-wide ribbons

2 cups red seedless grapes, halved

½ cup hazelnuts, lightly toasted (see page 31) and roughly chopped

1 bunch scallions, trimmed (including ½ inch off the green tops), sliced on a sharp angle, soaked in ice water for 20 minutes, and drained well (see page 53)

Extra-virgin olive oil

Kosher salt and freshly ground black pepper

Dried chile flakes

Cook the freekeh (see page 50) and when you drain it, drain the water into a large saucepan in which you'll cook the collards. Spread out the freekeh to cool, as per the recipe.

Put the cooking liquid pan back on the stove and add the garlic, a splash of vinegar, and the sliced collards. Adjust the heat to a lively simmer, cover, and cook until the collards are tender but still retain some tooth to them, 12 to 20 minutes depending on their maturity. Drain the collards and let them cool.

Combine the collards and freekeh in a large bowl. Add the grapes, hazelnuts, and scallions and toss. Add ¼ cup vinegar, season well with salt, black pepper, and ¼ teaspoon chile flakes, and toss again. Taste and adjust the seasoning. Finish with ¼ cup olive oil or more if needed. This salad tastes best after the flavors have had at least 15 minutes to mingle.

Stewed Collards with Beans and a Parmigiano Rind

The classic Southern dish has you stew the collards with a ham hock or some other pork product. In my version, I keep the greens vegetarian, but I don't give up one bit of the savory umami flavor of meat—a Parmigiano rind does the trick. Not to mention that you now have something to do with all those bits of leftover cheese!

» Serves 6

Basic Recipe for Perfect Shell Beans (page 254)

3 garlic cloves, smashed and peeled

1 sweet onion, such as Walla Walla or Vidalia, sliced

1 rind from a wedge of Parmigiano-Reggiano

1 big sprig rosemary

1 small whole dried chile, such as chile de árbol

1 bunch collards, ribs cut out, leaves cut into wide ribbons

Grilled bread, for serving (optional)

Extra-virgin olive oil

Follow the recipe for the perfect shell beans, but once the beans are about half-cooked, add the garlic, onion, cheese rind, rosemary, chile, and collards. It may take a few minutes for the collards to wilt enough to actually submerge them in the bean liquid, but add a bit of water if you need to.

Simmer until the beans are fully tender as well as the collards. The cheese will just soften and contribute its flavor to the dish.

When the beans are fully cooked, take the pot from the heat and let everything rest for at least 30 minutes. Remove the rosemary sprig and whole chile. You can reheat a bit before serving, if you like, but the flavors and textures will be best if the dish is warm, not hot.

Serve in a bowl on its own or ladled over a piece of grilled bread. Finish with a nice drizzle of olive oil on top.

MORE WAYS:

Stew with Southern-inflected chicken and sausage: Brown some chicken pieces and some spicy sausage slices in a skillet and then nestle them into the beans and collards. Add a bit more water so the meats are barely covered. Be sure to cook long enough for the chicken to cook thoroughly. Season with some hot sauce.

Pair with polenta: Make a batch of polenta, seasoning it with Parmigiano and plenty of dried chile flakes so that it's warmly spicy. Top with the collards and beans and plenty of pot liquor.

Bake with a crunchy cornbread topping: Pour into a baking dish, crumble cornbread over the top, drizzle with olive oil or dot with butter (or both!), and bake in a hot oven until the topping is browned and crisp on the edges.

Kale

For a while there, all the food mags were saying the same thing: "Kale is having a moment." But that moment has lasted for several years now, and kale shows no sign of losing status. In fact, I think it's safe to say the leafy green is now firmly entrenched on American plates, both at home and in restaurants—and with good reason.

Kale can do anything. We typically think of kale as a braising green, because its leaves aren't as delicate as spinach or lettuce. But by now we all know that braising is just half the story. Almost everyone has encountered, and fallen in love with, some version of kale salad. When thinly sliced and dressed, the raw leaves become tender but still retain a satisfying chew and provide a bitter backdrop that can stand up heroically to bold flavors. I use kale from its earliest young leaves in spring to the more generous leaves of a mature plant, and I especially love the late-season last gasp of the plant—the bolted shoots and flowers called rabe.

Play with texture. There are three main types of kale, and they vary more in texture than flavor, though lacinato (also called Tuscan kale or cavolo nero) is the sweetest of the bunch. It also has the flattest leaves, making it the easiest to work with. Curly kale is really, really curly, with the most pronounced bitter flavor. Russian kale has magenta stems and lobed leaves, almost like an elongated oak leaf, and the mildest flavor of the bunch. Like other greens, avoid those that are wilted, yellowed, or slimy. They'll keep in a plastic bag in the fridge for several days.

Prep is simple. Slice or strip the leaves from the ribs and slice or chop the leaves depending on what you plan to do with them. The ribs are perfectly edible, but too woody to eat raw. They take longer to cook, so chop them up and get them going before you add the leaves, or simply toss them in olive oil and roast them into a crispy snack.

Slice kale very finely when serving raw—you want it toothy but not tough.

The Kale Salad That Started It All

This is the raw kale salad that changed my life. I was the chef de cuisine at Franny's in Brooklyn back in 2007. I was mad that I couldn't find good salad greens in the middle of winter, and I especially hated (still hate) the "mesclun mix" that lines the shelves of supermarkets—no flavor, no texture. I created this kale salad in rebellion against those miserable greens, having no idea it would take the world by storm. But once it got written up in the *New York Times*, the world seemed to have an unending hunger for kale salads!

» Serves 2 to 4

1 bunch lacinato kale (aka Tuscan kale or cavolo nero), thick ribs cut out

½ garlic clove, finely chopped

¼ cup finely grated Pecorino Romano cheese, plus more to finish

Extra-virgin olive oil

Juice of 1 lemon

⅛ teaspoon dried chile flakes

Kosher salt and freshly ground black pepper

¼ cup dried breadcrumbs (page 30)

Stack several kale leaves on top of one another and roll them up into a tight cylinder. With a sharp knife, slice crosswise into very thin, about ¹⁄₁₆ inch, ribbons (this is called a chiffonade). Put the kale in a salad spinner, rinse in cool water, and spin until completely dry. Pile the kale into a bowl.

Put the chopped garlic on a cutting board and mince it even more until you have a paste (you

can sort of smash and scrape the garlic with the side of the knife as well). Transfer the garlic to a small bowl, add ¼ cup pecorino, a healthy glug of olive oil, the lemon juice, chile flakes, ¼ teaspoon salt, and plenty of twists of black pepper, and whisk to combine.

Pour the dressing over the kale and toss well to thoroughly combine (you can use your clean hands for this, to be efficient). Taste and adjust with more lemon, salt, chile flakes, or black pepper. Let the salad sit for about 5 minutes so the kale softens slightly. Top with the

breadcrumbs, shower with more cheese, and drizzle with more oil.

In the kitchen A trick to ensure tender kale without long cooking: Freeze the kale raw (and trimmed) for a few hours; freezing will break down the fibers. Cook it straight from the freezer.

Wilted Kale, Alone or Pickled on Cheese Toast

I use this agrodolce method with many vegetables, especially leafy greens. I love the layers of flavor you can create and the delicious tension between the sweet and sour, the earthy green kale, and the creamy foil of the whipped cheese on the toast. And of course you bring all those flavors into balance with a proper glug of good extra-virgin olive oil.

» Serves 2

3 tablespoons white wine vinegar	Kosher salt and freshly ground black pepper
¼ cup golden raisins	¼ teaspoon dried chile flakes
Extra-virgin olive oil	2 slices bread, grilled
1 garlic clove, smashed and peeled	Whipped Ricotta (page 37) or fresh sheep or goat cheese
½ pound kale (preferably lacinato, aka Tuscan), thick ribs cut out, leaves torn into big pieces	¼ cup roughly chopped lightly toasted walnuts (see page 31)

Put the vinegar and raisins in a little bowl and let the raisins plump for 1 hour.

Heat ¼ cup olive oil in a large skillet or Dutch oven over medium heat. Add the garlic and cook slowly to toast the garlic so it's very soft, fragrant, and nicely golden brown—but not burnt—about 5 minutes.

Add the kale leaves to the pan; if they won't all fit at once, just add a few handfuls and toss them with tongs until they're wilted, and then add the rest. Season with salt and black pepper, add a splash of water, and cover the pan. Cook over medium heat until the kale is tender, 8 to 10 minutes. If there is a lot of liquid in the pan at this point, uncover the pan, increase the heat, and boil most of it off. Add the raisins and vinegar and chile flakes and toss well. Taste.

Remove from the heat, pour in a healthy glug of olive oil, and let the kale cool. This is best served 1 to 2 hours later. It's also fine to make a day ahead; just be sure to bring it to room temperature.

Spread the grilled bread with a thick layer of the whipped ricotta or fresh cheese. Top with a juicy mountain of kale and sprinkle the walnuts on top. Finish with a thread of olive oil.

In the field Plants that can withstand cold temperatures are also those with the deepest colors and most potent nutrients. I learned from greens expert Frank Morton (he was the first farmer to grow the now ubiquitous "mesclun mix") that leaves of cold-hardy plants contain dissolved solids, including colorful pigments, that act as antifreeze for the plants. So pick winter vegetables with rich color to get a big dose of healthy.

Kale Sauce with Any Noodle

This sauce can be made in the same time it takes to cook the pasta, so it's a perfect midweek dinner or nice weekend lunch. The color is just brilliant, and the flavor is so perfectly balanced. When transferring the kale to the blender, don't worry about the excess liquid—you may even find a need for another little spoonful of water to get everything moving.

» Serves 2 as a main dish, 4 as a first course

Kosher salt and freshly ground black pepper

2 garlic cloves, smashed and peeled

Extra-virgin olive oil

1 pound kale (any variety, though lacinato is wonderful), thick ribs cut out

½ pound rigatoni, pappardelle, or any noodle

¾ cup freshly grated Parmigiano-Reggiano cheese

Bring a large pot of water to a boil and add salt until it tastes like the sea.

While the water is coming to a boil, put the garlic and ¼ cup olive oil into a small heavy pot or skillet over medium heat and cook until the garlic begins to sizzle. Reduce the heat to low and gently cook until the garlic is light golden, soft, and fragrant, 5 to 7 minutes. Pour the oil and garlic into a bowl so it can cool quickly.

When the water is boiling, add the kale leaves and boil until they are tender but not mushy or overcooked, about 5 minutes. Pull them out with tongs or a slotted spoon and transfer them to a blender. It's fine if they are still wet.

Add the pasta to the still-boiling water and cook until al dente according to the package directions. With a ladle or a measuring cup, scoop out about a cup of the pasta water, then drain the noodles.

Process the kale in the blender with the oil and garlic, adding just a bit of the pasta water to help the process along and to make a nice thick puree. Season with salt and pepper.

Transfer the drained pasta back to the pot and pour in the kale puree. Add half the Parmigiano and toss well. Add a touch more pasta water and toss until the pasta noodles are well coated with a bright green, creamy-textured sauce. Serve right away with a big drizzle of olive oil and the rest of the cheese.

Colcannon with Watercress Butter

Colcannon is a traditional Irish dish mainly consisting of mashed potatoes with kale or cabbage and leeks. I finish mine with a big dollop of watercress butter for some pop. If you find kale still in the market in early spring, make this with Green Garlic Butter (page 34) instead.

» Serves 4

2 pounds Yukon Gold potatoes, peeled and cut into chunks

1 bunch lacinato kale (aka Tuscan kale or cavolo nero), leaves torn from the stems and then torn into 3-inch pieces

1 leek, trimmed, halved lengthwise, cleaned well, and cut crosswise into ¼-inch-thick half-moons

2 tablespoons unsalted butter

½ cup heavy cream or crème fraîche

Kosher salt and freshly ground black pepper

4 tablespoons Watercress Butter (page 36)

Put the potatoes in a large pot of water and add salt until it tastes like the sea. Bring to a boil and cook until they are tender but not mushy, about 15 minutes.

Add the kale and cook for another minute, then add the leeks and cook everything for another minute, or until all the vegetables are very tender. With a ladle or a measuring cup, scoop out about a cup of the cooking water and drain the vegetables.

Return the potatoes, kale, and leeks to the pot. Smash everything together and add the unsalted butter and cream. Season with salt and lots of pepper and taste. Place in a bowl piping hot and put the watercress butter right in the middle so it melts and people fight for it at the table.

In the field The phrase "gone to seed" generally implies something negative, but when the brassicas head that way, I'm positively psyched. Called rabe (or raab), you'll see them in your garden or at the farmers' market in spring, from overwintered brassicas like turnip, kale, cabbage, and mizuna. Brassicas will bolt in early fall, too, if you planted them in the spring. While these skinny shoots topped with tiny clusters of florets—and eventually blooming flowers—might look rangy, they are remarkable sweet and tender, with a snappable texture much like an asparagus spear. I eat them raw in salad or I give them a quick sauté. While the flavor of a rabe echoes the plant, any spiciness or bitterness is generally softer.

Kale and Mushroom Lasagna

Lighter and more delicate than a typical tomato-and-meat lasagna, this green lasagna is nonetheless bursting with flavor. You could use a mix of cooking greens instead of all kale; just be sure you wilt them until quite tender so the texture harmonizes with the other layers.

» *Serves 6*

6 tablespoons unsalted butter

¼ cup all-purpose flour

2 cups chicken or vegetable broth, homemade or low-sodium store-bought

1 cup whole or 2% milk

Kosher salt and freshly ground black pepper

¾ pound white or cremini mushrooms, wiped clean and finely chopped

1 pound kale, thick ribs cut out, leaves cut into very thin strips, rinsed, and shaken dry

Grated zest of 1 lemon

1 pound whole-milk ricotta cheese

One 9-ounce box no-boil lasagna noodles (you may have a few left over)

1½ cups freshly grated Parmigiano-Reggiano cheese

Melt 4 tablespoons of the butter in a medium saucepan over medium heat. Add the flour, stir to make a smooth paste, and cook for a minute or two so the raw flour flavor cooks out. Whisk in the broth and the milk. Bring the mixture (called a velouté) to a boil, whisking to eliminate lumps. Reduce the heat and simmer for 5 minutes to thicken slightly. Season lightly with salt and pepper (if you've used store-bought broth, remember that it can be salty).

Melt the remaining 2 tablespoons butter in a large skillet over medium-high heat. When the sizzling stops, add the mushrooms, season with salt and pepper, and cook, stirring and scraping the pan, until all the moisture from the mushrooms has been released and evaporated and they begin to brown and stick a bit to the pan, 10 to 12 minutes. Scrape into a bowl and let cool slightly.

Return the skillet to medium-high heat, add the kale, season lightly with salt, and cook, tossing frequently, until the kale is wilted and very tender, 12 to 15 minutes. You may need to add a few splashes of water along the way if the pan gets dry. Taste and adjust the seasoning with more salt and some pepper.

Stir the lemon zest into the ricotta in a bowl.

To assemble the lasagna, spread a bit less than half the velouté in an even layer on the bottom of a 9 x 13-inch baking dish. Arrange the lasagna noodles in an even layer, breaking the noodles to fit as needed. Spread the mushrooms evenly over the noodles and then top with the kale, distributing it evenly.

Arrange a second layer of noodles, then top with evenly spaced dollops of the ricotta. Gently spread the dollops to make an even layer without disturbing the noodles. Add one more layer of noodles, top with the remaining velouté, and sprinkle the Parmigiano over the top.

Bake until the cheese is golden brown and the juices are bubbling around the edges, 40 to 50 minutes. Let the lasagna cool for at least 20 minutes before cutting and serving.

In the kitchen The mushroom mixture used here is called a duxelles. It's a handy flavor bomb that you can add to omelets, pastas, stuffed chicken breasts, or anywhere that you'd like a hit of mellow umami.

Mushrooms

Meaty porcinis, delicate chanterelles, frilly hen-of-the-woods, sexy truffles. Wild mushrooms are a constant source of inspiration for me, and since you can't farm them into being, they always seem like a gift from the weather gods. You'll find wild mushrooms in the spring as well as fall, but I'm addressing them in the fall section of this book as I think their woodsy flavors work best in hearty, cool-weather dishes. That being said, reliable, versatile, cultivated mushrooms like creminis always have a place in my kitchen.

Plump, not wizened. Mushrooms contain a lot of water, so if they're looking at all wrinkly and dried out, you know they're over the hill. But you don't want them to be wet and slimy, either. Plump and fresh is what you're going for, with no bruises or browning, which is why I try to avoid wild mushrooms foraged during a rainy week: They're waterlogged. Store mushrooms in the fridge in a paper bag. Plastic bags encourage condensation, which leads to rot.

In the kitchen Mushrooms can be like little sponges, holding on to lots of water, which can make it tough to brown and crisp them. To remove some of that water, arrange your mushrooms on a tray lined with paper towels and leave them in the refrigerator, uncovered, overnight.

To wash or not to wash? Wild mushrooms grow in meadows or forests, and cultivated mushrooms grow in a sterile medium that's sort of like soil, so both types of mushroom will have a few things clinging to them. But rinsing isn't a good option. Mushrooms are like sponges and they'll soak up the water and become even more water-filled than they naturally are. So just take a damp cloth or paper towel and wipe off any obvious bits of nature and leave it at that. The only exception is the morel, which has a honeycombed cap that harbors lots of grit. With morels, you should rinse them and then carefully pat dry.

Most mushroom stems are perfectly wonderful to eat, so all you need to do is trim off the dried end. The one exception is the shiitake. Shiitake stems are very fibrous and not great to eat, though they are delicious in stock or as the base for Mushroom Butter (page 35).

When cooking those massive portobellos, it's sometimes a good idea to scrape away the black gills under the cap, as they add a lot of moisture.

Blast them with heat. No matter what you plan to use mushrooms in, they'll offer the most flavor if you cook the moisture out of them first. To do that, you need to cook them in a generous amount of fat over high heat in a single layer until browned on both sides. But don't crowd the pan or they'll just steam. It's the same technique you'd use when searing chunks of beef for a stew.

Double-Mushroom Toast with Bottarga

Bottarga is a salted and cured fish roe, usually mullet but sometimes tuna. Finely grated or sliced, use it as a salty, intensely umami-ish seasoning. Mushrooms are also high in natural glutamates—compounds that contribute to the delicious intensity of umami—creating a doubly savory, meaty umami dish. If you can't find bottarga, substitute grated Parmigiano-Reggiano.

» *Serves 4 as a first course*

Extra-virgin olive oil	2 tablespoons unsalted butter
3 garlic cloves—2 smashed and peeled, 1 halved	¼ cup chopped flat-leaf parsley
1 pound wild mushrooms, such as maitake, chanterelle, black trumpet (or a mix of creminis and wild), wiped clean and dry, cut into chunks if large	1 teaspoon finely grated lemon zest
	4 thick slices country bread
	Mushroom Butter (page 35; optional)
Kosher salt and freshly ground black pepper	Bottarga, for grating
	Lemon wedges

Heat a large skillet over medium heat, add a glug of olive oil and the smashed garlic, and cook slowly to toast the garlic so it's very soft, fragrant, and nicely golden brown—but not burnt—about 5 minutes. Add the mushrooms, increase the heat a bit, season with salt and pepper, and sauté the mushrooms until their juices have rendered out and then been reabsorbed, 5 to 8 minutes, depending on your mushrooms.

Now the mushrooms will be able to brown and crisp a bit, so cook until that happens, another 3 to 4 minutes. Remove from the heat, add the butter, parsley, and lemon zest, and shake the pan to incorporate. Taste and adjust the seasoning (keep in mind that the bottarga will be salty).

Grill or toast the bread, rub one surface of each piece with the halved garlic, then spread on a thin layer of mushroom butter (if using). Spoon the sautéed mushrooms on top and grate the bottarga generously over everything. Serve with a lemon wedge.

Roasted Mushrooms, Gremolata-Style

A light hand with the seasonings lets the forest-y mushroom flavor lead the way. I use this as a side dish or as a topping for grilled fish, braised meats, or meatballs. The basic roasted mushrooms without the gremolata seasoning are even more versatile.

» *Serves 4 as a small side dish*

1½ pounds mixed mushrooms (a combination of cremini and wild or wild-cultivated)

Extra-virgin olive oil

4 garlic cloves—
2 smashed and peeled,
2 chopped

Kosher salt and freshly ground black pepper

Grated zest and juice of ½ lemon

2 tablespoons dried breadcrumbs (page 30)

1 tablespoon capers, rinsed, drained, and chopped

2 tablespoons chopped flat-leaf parsley

Heat the oven to 400°F.

Brush or rinse off any bits of debris from the mushrooms and trim off any dried stems or spoiled bits. If using shiitakes, discard the stems. Cut or tear the mushrooms so they are all approximately the same size.

Pile the mushrooms into a bowl, then add a glug of olive oil and the smashed garlic. Season generously with salt and pepper and toss everything really well, massaging the oil and seasonings into the mushrooms.

Spread them in an even layer, no overlapping, on one or two baking sheets. Roast until they are browned and crisp around the edges; either flip them or otherwise scoot them around the baking sheets during roasting to promote even browning. Depending on the moisture content of your mushrooms, this should take between 10 and 25 minutes.

Toss the roasted mushrooms (and roasted garlic) with the chopped garlic, lemon zest and juice, breadcrumbs, capers, and parsley. Taste and adjust with more salt and pepper.

MORE WAYS:

Make an instant stroganoff: Sear a tender steak such as rib-eye or tenderloin. Thinly slice, return to the pan with the gremolata-style roasted mushrooms, add crème fraîche and a bit of broth, and simmer to marry the flavors. Serve over gloriously buttered egg noodles.

Fill an omelet: Pile the plain roasted mushrooms, dollops of goat cheese, and fresh dill and parsley into the center of an omelet before you fold it.

Toss with pasta: Cook pasta, scoop out some pasta water, and fold the cooked pasta together with plain roasted mushrooms, minced garlic, chopped parsley, a touch of butter, and lots of grated cheese. Use the pasta water to make everything creamy. Finish with lots of cracked black pepper.

In the kitchen Gremolata is the name for an Italian seasoning that includes grated citrus zest, chopped garlic, and fresh herbs, usually parsley. It's a good tool to have in your flavor toolbox.

A variety of mushrooms creates complexity of texture and flavor. Here we used cremini, porcini, hedgehogs, and oysters.

Mushrooms, Sausage, and Rigatoni

As a kid, I used to pick off the mushrooms from the mushroom and fennel-sausage pizza that would hit the family dinner table. So while I didn't eat the mushrooms back then, I was imprinted by the flavor combination. Get all your ingredients prepped before you start cooking this dish so that by the time the pasta is cooked, you are ready for action.

» Serves 2 or 3 as a main dish, 4 as a first course

Kosher salt and freshly ground black pepper

½ pound rigatoni

½ pound fresh garlic sausage, bulk or with casings removed

Extra-virgin olive oil

2 garlic cloves, smashed and peeled

1 pound wild mushrooms, such as maitake, chanterelle, black trumpet (or a mix of creminis and wild), wiped clean and dry, cut into chunks if large

1 tablespoon unsalted butter

¾ cup freshly grated Parmigiano-Reggiano cheese

½ cup freshly grated Pecorino Romano cheese

¼ cup dried breadcrumbs (page 30)

Bring a large pot of water to a boil and add salt until it tastes like the sea. Add the pasta and cook according to the package directions, but start tasting a minute or so ahead of time to be sure you don't overcook it. With a ladle or a measuring cup, scoop out about a cup of the pasta cooking water, then drain the pasta well.

A walk in the woods yields a basket of black trumpet mushrooms.

Meanwhile, shape the sausage into 3 patties and heat a large skillet or Dutch oven (it needs to be big enough to hold all the ingredients in the final phase) over medium heat. Add the sausage and cook, flipping occasionally, until browned on the surface and just cooked on the inside. Break into bite-size chunks with a spoon. Take care not to let the juices on the surface of the pan (called the "fond") get too dark. Scoop out the sausage and set it aside.

Pour the sausage grease out and set the pan over medium-low heat. Add ¼ cup olive oil and the smashed garlic and cook slowly to toast the garlic so it's very soft, fragrant, and nicely golden brown—but not burnt—about 5 minutes.

When the garlic is good, increase the heat to medium-high and drop in the mushrooms. Season generously with salt and pepper and sauté until the mushrooms are fragrant and getting browned around the edges, 6 to 12 minutes depending on the variety and size

and moisture content of the mushrooms. (Take care that you're not letting the garlic get too brown during this phase; if so, just pluck it out.)

Pull the pan from the heat and drop in the butter, along with a few spoonsful of the pasta cooking water. Shake the pan around a bit to incorporate it and begin making a creamy emulsion. Add the pasta and the sausage to the pan, toss again, add the cheeses and a bit more pasta water, and toss more, adding more pasta water if needed to keep everything lovely and creamy. Taste and add more salt or pepper if needed. Top with breadcrumbs and serve the pasta right away.

At the market Some "wild" mushrooms are now cultivated, but they still have deep woodsy flavors and interesting shapes and textures. Look for maitakes, shiitakes, and oyster mushrooms.

Sautéed Mushrooms and Mussels in Cream on Sliced Steak

My version of surf and turf. The mushrooms and mussels alone are delicious—double the recipe and skip the steak to make this pescatarian.

» Serves 4

1 pound rib-eye or New York strip steak, preferably grass-fed but as nicely marbled as you can get

Kosher salt and freshly ground black pepper

3 tablespoons unsalted butter

2 garlic cloves, roughly sliced

Extra-virgin olive oil

1 small handful mixed hearty herb sprigs, such as sage, thyme, rosemary, and savory

1 pound wild mushrooms, such as maitake, chanterelle, black trumpet (or a mix of creminis and wild), wiped clean and dry, cut into chunks if large

½ teaspoon dried chile flakes

1 pound mussels, rinsed well and debearded

¾ cup heavy cream

1 teaspoon fresh lemon juice

Generously season all sides of your steak with salt and black pepper. Do this as far ahead as you can, up to a day in advance, keeping the steak in the fridge.

Take the steak out of the refrigerator about 30 minutes before cooking. When you're ready to cook, blot the steak dry with paper towels.

Heat a heavy skillet over high heat until it's very hot. Add the steak—don't use any oil. Turn the heat down to medium-high or medium, so that the steak is browning nicely but not getting too crusty or dark. Cook until it's about half done, 3 to 4 minutes depending on the thickness and temperature of your steak.

Add the butter, garlic, and 1 tablespoon olive oil to the pan. Cook, basting the steak by spooning the hot butter and juices over the top. After another minute or so, flip the steak, add the herbs, and keep basting away, letting the herbs and butter get all flavorful together.

When the steak is medium-rare, 8 to 10 minutes total for a 1-inch-thick steak, transfer it to a cutting board and let it rest while you cook the mushrooms.

Take the herbs out of the pan (but keep the fat) and discard or compost them. Bring the heat back up to medium-high. Add the mushrooms and chile flakes and sauté until the mushrooms are slightly wilted and crispy, about 8 minutes, shaking the pan a bit.

Add the mussels (yes, in their shells). Cook, shaking and tossing the pan so the mushrooms don't burn and the mussels get even heat, until the mussels open, about 10 minutes, then pour in the cream. Fold the mussels and mushrooms together until they are nicely cloaked in cream. If there are mussels that just won't open, toss them out.

Add the lemon juice. Taste a mushroom and adjust the seasoning with more salt, black pepper, or chile flakes as needed.

Slice the steak, arrange it on a platter, and pour the mushrooms and mussels over the top. Serve right away, with a bowl for discarded mussel shells.

In the kitchen Mussels are easy to cook with because they don't need much prep. Just give them a rinse and then scrape or cut away the small tangle of fibers, called the beard, that attaches them to their home.

Crispy Mushrooms with Green Herb Mayonnaise

Frying a mushroom seals its woodsy flavor and fleshy texture inside a crisp shell—exactly the kind of contrast that keeps you coming back for more. I often eat these simply with lemon and grated cheese, but a bowl of potent herb mayonnaise elevates the experience.

» Serves 4 to 6 as an appetizer

Vegetable or olive oil, for deep-frying

½ cup cornstarch

½ cup all-purpose flour

1 cup sparkling water

¼ teaspoon dried chile flakes

Kosher salt and freshly ground black pepper

1 pound wild mushrooms, such as maitake, chanterelle, black trumpet (or a mix of creminis and wild), wiped clean and dry, cut into bite-size chunks

Parmigiano-Reggiano cheese, for grating

4 big lemon wedges

Green Herb Mayonnaise (page 42)

Arrange a double layer of paper towels on a tray or baking sheet and set it near your stove. Pour 2 inches of oil (vegetable oil or a mix of olive and vegetable) into a saucepan, making sure there are at least 3 inches of headroom (because the oil may bubble up a bit during cooking, and you don't want any spillovers—dangerous!). Slowly bring the oil up to 375°F on a thermometer. (Or fry a small piece of bread: When it takes 60 seconds to get nicely crisp and brown, but not burnt, your oil is just about right.)

As the oil is heating, whisk together the cornstarch and flour in a bowl. Whisk in enough sparkling water to make a thin batter. Season with the chile flakes and some salt and black pepper.

When the oil is ready, dip a mushroom into the batter, let the excess drip off, and carefully immerse it in the hot oil. Take care to not add too many at once because that will cause the oil temperature to drop and the mushrooms will get greasy. (To make things go faster, you can use a wire mesh spoon, called a spider, to add a bunch of the mushroom chunks to the batter, tapping to encourage the excess batter to drip off.) Fry until the coating is puffed and very light golden (these will not get deeply colored) and the mushrooms are cooked through (it's important to have your wild mushrooms thoroughly cooked). Transfer to the paper towels to drain and give a quick seasoning of salt and black pepper.

Once all the mushrooms are fried, take the oil off the heat and arrange the mushrooms on a serving plate. Shower with the Parmigiano, and serve right away with lemon wedges and a bowl of the green herb mayonnaise for dipping.

Season Six

Winter

Expectations are low for fresh produce in the dead of winter. Yet the range of what's available in the cold months is stunning: roots, potatoes, the whole crazy world of winter squash, and, of course, cabbage.

The winter flavor palette is subtle, however. Gone are the assertive green flavors of early-season vegetables. What winter brings is a lot of earthiness, mellowness, and, believe it or not, sweetness.

Many winter-hardy vegetables gain a boost of sweet once the weather dips below freezing. When a plant's starches turn to sugar during a frost, it's called cold-sweetening. For roots like beets, carrots, and parsnips, and brassicas like broccoli, cabbage, and Brussels sprouts, the sugar acts like antifreeze, protecting their cells from damaging ice crystals. For the rest of us, that first frost is a delicious call to the kitchen.

Recipes of Winter

Cabbage

Cabbage is often in the shadows of its sexier brassica-family kin, such as kale and Brussels sprouts, but cabbage has many talents, especially in winter months when the cold weather has enhanced its natural sugars.

East meets West. Cabbage can be divided into two main categories: European and Asian. European cabbages include green cabbage (also called white), red or purple cabbage, and savoy. The most common Asian varieties are napa and bok choy. The differences relate more to texture than flavor, though the Asian cabbages are less sweet.

Hefty and plentiful. A head of European cabbage should feel heavy and dense, and the outer leaves shouldn't be too torn or yellowed. Asian cabbages will be lighter and leafier. One head of cabbage yields a lot, so plan on having it around for a while. Fortunately, they are good keepers, loosely wrapped in a plastic bag in your fridge.

It can take a punch, and the heat. Whatever variety you choose, raw cabbage makes a crunchy and refreshing salad or slaw that can stand up to a big range of bold flavors—think chiles and limes, or fish sauce and sesame oil. It also cooks up juicy with a slight bite when steamed, and takes on a sweetness when grilled or pan-roasted until browned, or just simmered low and slow in soups or stews.

In the field As temperatures drop, many vegetables prepare to survive the freeze by converting their starches into sugars. More sugar lowers the freezing point and hence helps them survive. The consequence of their survival tactic is of course a boon for the cook. All root vegetables, fall artichokes, and many brassicas such as cabbages and leafy greens grow sweeter after a few rounds of winter frost.

Coring round cabbage. Ever accommodating, cabbage doesn't need much prep. For most preparations, start by quartering the cabbage through the base. Slice the triangle of core away from the leaves. Now you're ready to cut through the leaves to make slices from angel-hair fine to thick, depending on your recipe, or simply use the leaves whole. If some leaves have thick, hard ribs, simply shave them off with a paring knife.

Steamed Cabbage with Lemon, Butter, and Thyme

Cabbage has a wonderful character when you treat it simply, and of course the texture is fantastic—silky and crunchy at the same time—and this shallow-steaming method gets that texture just right. While I love the simplicity of this basic version, I also like to juice it up a bit with hot sauce, grated Parmigiano, and breadcrumbs.

» Serves 4

1 pound cabbage, savoy or green (but not red), quartered, cored, and cut into thick wedges

2 garlic cloves, smashed and peeled

Kosher salt and freshly ground black pepper

Juice of ½ lemon

2 to 3 tablespoons unsalted butter, at room temperature

½ teaspoon thyme leaves

Bring ½ inch of water to a boil in a large saucepan. Add the cabbage, garlic, and 1 teaspoon salt. Cover and steam-simmer rapidly. After about a minute, uncover, stir the cabbage around so it's getting evenly steamed (it's okay if some of the leaves fall off the wedges), add a touch more water if necessary, cover, and cook until the cabbage is mostly tender but still has some crunch, 4 to 6 minutes total depending on your cabbage.

Drain the cabbage well, give it a quick chop or two to make it easier to eat, and pile it into a bowl. Season with the lemon juice, butter, thyme, and several twists of pepper.

Roasted Cabbage with Walnuts, Parmigiano, and Saba

I like serving this with a big roast. The walnut garnish makes the dish interesting and special, but it's not overly rich. It's also easy to pull together: Once your roast is cooked, pull it out of the oven and let it rest, crank up the oven temp, and roast the cabbage. Both dishes will be ready to serve at the same time.

» *Serves 4 to 6*

1 head savoy cabbage, quartered and cored

4 tablespoons unsalted butter, at room temperature

Kosher salt and freshly ground black pepper

1 tablespoon saba or balsamic vinegar, plus more for drizzling

2 garlic cloves, minced

Extra-virgin olive oil

⅓ cup walnuts, lightly toasted (see page 31) and chopped

⅓ cup dried breadcrumbs (page 30)

½ cup freshly grated Parmigiano-Reggiano cheese, plus more for serving

Juice of 1 lemon

Heat the oven to 475°F.

Rub the cabbage quarters with the butter, season with salt and pepper, and arrange on a rimmed baking sheet. Roast in the hot oven until it's browned and crisped around the edges and slightly softened in the center, 10 to 15 minutes.

Sprinkle the saba over the cabbage quarters and toss lightly to season them, trying to keep them intact . . . though it's okay if the leaves start to separate.

While the cabbage is roasting, put the garlic in a small bowl and pour on ¼ cup olive oil. Add the walnuts, breadcrumbs, and Parmigiano. Season generously with salt, pepper, and 2 tablespoons of the lemon juice. Stir to mix and then taste and adjust the seasoning—you're making sort of a loose, sloppy salsa, which should be bright from the lemon, salty from the cheese, and toasty and crunchy from the walnuts and breadcrumbs.

Either leave the cabbage quarters intact or give them a rough chop. Arrange on plates or a platter and dress with the walnut salsa. Drizzle on a bit more saba, a sprinkling of lemon juice, and a shower of grated cheese. Serve soon.

Battered and Fried Cabbage with Crispy Seeds and Lemon

Looking for an appetizer that's out of the ordinary? Spicy, crunchy leaves of cabbage cooked tempura-style are fantastic with drinks and friends. Cooking them is a bit of a performance piece for your guests, however, because you need to eat these as soon as they're out of the pan. Serve them with a simple squeeze of lemon, or for a more substantial preparation, serve with a bowl of Tonnato (page 45) for dipping.

» *Serves 4 as an appetizer*

¼ head green cabbage	1 teaspoon fennel seeds
Vegetable oil or olive oil, for deep-frying	1 teaspoon cumin seeds
½ cup cornstarch	1 teaspoon coriander seeds
½ cup all-purpose flour	Dried chile flakes
1 cup sparkling water	Kosher salt and freshly ground black pepper
¼ cup poppy seeds	½ lemon

Cut away the dense cabbage core with a sharp paring knife and separate the leaves; it's fine that they are all different sizes, though you should tear any huge ones into smaller pieces. The cabbage leaves need to fit into your frying pot.

Arrange a double layer of paper towels on a tray or baking sheet and set it near your stove. Pour 3 inches of oil (vegetable oil or a mix of olive and vegetable) into a saucepan, making sure there are at least 3 inches of headroom (because the oil may bubble up a bit during cooking, and you don't want any spillovers—dangerous!). Slowly bring the oil up to 375°F on a thermometer. (Or fry a small piece of bread: When it takes 60 seconds to get nicely crisp and brown, but not burnt, your oil is just about right.)

As the oil is heating, whisk together the cornstarch and flour in a bowl. Whisk in enough sparkling water to make a thin batter. Whisk in the poppy seeds, fennel seeds, cumin seeds, coriander seeds, ¼ teaspoon chile flakes (or more, if you like things spicy), ½ teaspoon salt, and a bunch of twists of black pepper.

When the oil is ready, dip a cabbage leaf into the batter, let the excess drip off, and then carefully immerse it in the hot oil. If there's room in the pan for more than one leaf, fry more than one at a time, but don't overcrowd the pan or the oil temperature may drop, making the coating greasy rather than crisp. Fry until the coating is puffed and very light golden (these will not get deeply colored). Transfer to the paper towels to drain and continue frying the rest of the cabbage.

Once all the cabbage leaves are fried, turn off the heat under the oil and arrange the cabbage on a platter. Season with a bit more salt and a squeeze of lemon and serve right away.

Comforting Cabbage, Onion, and Farro Soup

This soup has a definite grandma vibe—warm, comforting, nourishing, and maybe just the tiniest bit old-fashioned, which is what you want on a cold or drizzly day.

» Serves 4

1 pound cabbage, savoy or green

Extra-virgin olive oil

1 medium onion, thinly sliced

Kosher salt and freshly ground black pepper

3 garlic cloves, smashed and peeled

1 healthy sprig rosemary or thyme

1 tablespoon red wine vinegar or white wine vinegar

⅔ cup farro

About 4 cups meat or poultry broth, homemade or low-sodium store-bought

1 tablespoon fresh lemon juice

1 cup freshly grated Parmigiano-Reggiano cheese

Cut out the cabbage core and finely chop it. Cut the leaves into fine shreds, either by slicing through the chunk of cabbage or by separating the leaves, rolling them into a cylinder, and slicing crosswise into ⅛-inch ribbons (called chiffonade).

Heat ¼ cup olive oil in a large pot or Dutch oven over medium heat. Add the onion and cabbage core, a pinch of salt, and a few twists of pepper. Cook, stirring frequently, until the onion starts to soften and become fragrant—but not at all browned—about 10 minutes. Add the garlic and cook for another 5 minutes until the garlic is soft too.

Add the shredded cabbage leaves and rosemary. Cover the pot and let steam for a bit to soften the leaves, then toss the cabbage to help it wilt and soften more. Cook, covered, until the cabbage is very tender and sweet, at least 30 minutes.

When the cabbage is ready, stir in the vinegar. Taste and adjust with more salt or pepper.

Meanwhile, in another saucepan, heat a glug of olive oil over medium heat. Add the farro and cook, stirring constantly, until the farro is lightly toasted and fragrant, 5 to 8 minutes.

Scrape the farro into the cabbage pot (or put the cabbage into the farro pot—whichever is bigger) and add 4 cups broth. Adjust the heat to a lazy simmer and simmer until the farro is tender and all the flavors are married, 25 to 35 minutes.

Stir in the lemon juice. The soup should be very thick, but if it seems like it needs more liquid, add another ½ cup water or broth. Taste and adjust with more salt, pepper, or lemon juice. Serve the soup in shallow bowls, with a shower of Parmigiano and a drizzle of olive oil on top, with more cheese passed at the table.

Cabbage and Mushroom Hand Pies

If serving fewer than eight people, freeze the extras: assemble the pies, chill well, and then slide—unbaked—into a freezer bag and freeze for up to 1 month. Bake the frozen pies, without thawing them, in a 350°F oven for 1 hour.

» *Makes 8 hand pies*

Extra-virgin olive oil

½ pound mushrooms, thinly sliced

Kosher salt and freshly ground black pepper

1 large leek, white and light green parts only, halved lengthwise and cut into ¼-inch-thick half-moons, cleaned well (about 2 cups)

4 cups lightly packed finely shredded savoy cabbage (from a ½-pound chunk of cabbage)

2 teaspoons balsamic vinegar

2 teaspoons Worcestershire sauce

2 teaspoons Dijon mustard

½ cup freshly grated Parmigiano-Reggiano cheese

½ lemon

Hot sauce

Very Flaky Pastry Dough (page 49)

All-purpose flour, for dusting

Heat a glug of olive oil in a large skillet over medium heat. Add the mushrooms, season lightly with salt and pepper, and cook, stirring, until very soft and fragrant, about 8 minutes.

Scoop the mushrooms out into a bowl. Add another 1 tablespoon oil to the skillet, add the leeks, season lightly with salt and pepper, and reduce the heat so that the leeks cook slowly. (If the leeks seem dry, you can cover the pan to capture the steam, which will help them soften up; add a spoonful of water if you need even more moisture.) Cook until they are fairly soft and fragrant, but not at all browned, about 3 minutes.

Add the cabbage to the skillet, season with salt and pepper, and pour in ¼ cup water. Cover the skillet and cook over medium heat until the cabbage has wilted, about 5 minutes. Uncover and cook the cabbage, tossing frequently,

until it's very tender and starting to turn golden, another 8 minutes or so.

Add the vinegar, Worcestershire, mustard, Parmigiano, a big squeeze of lemon juice, and a shake of hot sauce and toss to combine. Taste and adjust the salt, pepper, hot sauce, or lemon juice until the mixture is highly savory and delicious. Let the filling cool completely, preferably in the refrigerator (you can't assemble the pies if the filling is warm).

To assemble the hand pies, divide the dough into 8 pieces. Gently shape each piece into a round and flatten the round by pressing with your fingertips until you have a disk that's about 3 inches across. If the dough is sticking as you're doing this, dust it or your hands with flour.

Lightly flour the work surface and roll the disk into a round about 7 inches in diameter; it's okay if it isn't perfectly round. Scoop out one-eighth of the filling and pile it onto the lower half of the dough round, leaving a 1-inch border all around.

Brush the border lightly with water using a pastry brush or your fingertips. Fold over the top half of the dough round, tucking it nicely around the filling, then press gently to seal the two layers of dough. Starting on one end, fold the edge over in small pleats, pressing firmly to seal. Work your way around the edge until the pie is fully sealed. Repeat with the rest of the dough and filling. Alternatively, crimp by pressing the edges with a fork. (If your kitchen is warm, pop the finished pies in the refrigerator as you work on the rest.) Chill for at least 30 minutes.

When ready to bake, heat the oven to 375°F.

Cut three decorative slits into the top of each pie and arrange the pies on a heavy baking sheet. Bake until the pastry is an even, rich light brown (be sure to check the underside of the pies), 30 to 40 minutes. Some juices from the filling may bubble through the seams or slits; that's fine.

Let the pies cool on a rack and serve warm. You can bake ahead, cool, and then reheat for 10 minutes or so in a 375°F oven.

Celery Root

You're forgiven if you've passed up celery root in the market. Hairy and gnarled, it certainly doesn't advertise its virtues. But celery root is delicately flavored and really easy to cook with. Think of it as a subtly celery-flavored potato. Sounds pretty good, right?

Weight before beauty. The key is to choose a heavy-for-its-size root (hoist a few to compare), and one that isn't sporting too much root-y stuff. By the time you trim away the exterior, you want to have plenty of flesh left.

Prep right before using. Don't wash or trim your celery root until you're ready to cook it, because once cut, it will turn brown. If you want to prep it a few hours ahead of cooking, you can soak it in a bowl of water with lemon juice.

So versatile. As with most root vegetables, you can eat celery root raw (as long as you grate it or slice it very thin), you can boil or steam it for mashing, or you can toss it in oil and herbs and roast it the way you would roast potatoes.

Celery Root with Brown Butter, Oranges, Dates, and Almonds

Raw celery root has the assertive flavor of stalk celery, but with a flesh that's dense and way less fibrous. I create layers of flavor in this treatment by bringing in brightness from the oranges, salt from the almonds, and sweetness from the dates, and tying all that together with a mellow hit of nutty brown butter.

» *Serves 4*

2 navel oranges, preferably Cara Caras or blood oranges

1 small or ½ large celery root (about ¾ pound)

½ cup pitted dates, cut into quarters or smaller

¼ teaspoon dried chile flakes

Kosher salt and freshly ground black pepper

Extra-virgin olive oil

¼ cup Brined and Roasted Almonds (page 30)

1 small bunch chives, cut into 3-inch lengths

1 small handful flat-leaf parsley leaves

2 tablespoons unsalted butter

Grate the zest from one of the oranges, then squeeze the juice from half of that grated orange.

Cut a small slice from the navel and stem ends of the second orange and set the orange on the cutting board on one cut end. Using a sharp paring knife, cut away all the orange peel and the underlying white pith from top to bottom, working in strips around the orange. Slice off any remaining bits of pith. Halve the orange pole to pole (not through the equator). Set a half on the cutting board cut side down and cut crosswise into ⅛-inch-thick half-moons. Repeat with the other half and put all the slices in a large bowl.

Using a sharp paring knife, cut away all the tough exterior of the celery root; if there are dark fissures remaining, cut those away, too. Cut the whole thing in half, and if the circumference of the halves is still big and unwieldy, halve them again. Set one piece of celery root on the cutting board on a cut side, and slice as thin as you can. (A mandoline would make this easy, but you can do just fine with a sharp knife.) When the piece of celery root gets wobbly, turn to another side and keep cutting—it's okay if the slices are shaped differently. Put the celery root into the bowl with the oranges.

Add the juice from the orange half you squeezed, half the grated zest (reserve the other half), the dates, chile flakes, 1 teaspoon salt, and lots of twists of black pepper and toss. Taste and adjust the salt, black pepper, and chile flakes until the salad is very zippy. Add a glug of olive oil and toss again. Add the almonds, chives, and parsley and toss. Taste and adjust one more time.

Melt the butter in a small saucepan or skillet over medium heat. Cook the butter, swirling the pan every few seconds, until all the water inside the butter has sizzled off and the milk solids at the bottom of the pan begin to turn a pale golden color, 1 to 2 minutes. Cook the butter until it turns golden brown and smells nutty and delicious, another few seconds. When the butter looks and smells perfect, immediately—so that the butter stops cooking and doesn't get too dark—pour it into a little bowl.

Arrange the salad on plates or a platter and pour the warm brown butter over top. Sprinkle with the reserved orange zest and serve.

Mashed Celery Root with Garlic and Thyme

Beautiful on its own as an alternative for straight mashed potatoes, this recipe can be a launch pad for many other dishes, from gratins to soups.

» *Serves 4*

1½ pounds celery root

1 cup whole milk

6 garlic cloves, smashed and peeled

1 bay leaf

4 sprigs thyme

Kosher salt and freshly ground black pepper

2 tablespoons unsalted butter

Using a sharp paring knife, cut away all the tough exterior of the celery root; if there are dark fissures remaining, cut those away, too. Cut the cleaned root into chunks.

Put the celery root in a medium saucepan and add the milk, garlic, bay leaf, and thyme. Season with salt and pepper. Bring to a simmer, partially cover, and cook until the celery root is very tender, about 20 minutes (taking care that the milk doesn't boil over). At this point, the milk will look curdled, but don't worry.

Remove and discard (compost, please) the bay leaf and thyme. For a smooth texture, transfer the celery root and liquid to a food processor, add the butter, and puree until smooth. For a chunkier texture, add the butter and smash the celery root with a potato masher or a wooden spoon to the degree of chunkiness you like. Taste and season with more salt and pepper, if needed.

MORE WAYS:

Invite more roots: Swap out some of the celery root for potatoes and turnips to add both complexity and creaminess. If you have any truffle butter, this is the place to use it.

Bake with cheese: Spread the mashed celery root in a shallow baking dish, add a layer of Taleggio cheese, goat cheese, or Parmigiano-Reggiano, top with some breadcrumbs, and bake.

Make a smooth soup: After pureeing, loosen the puree with water, a touch of cream, or some broth (or a combination) to make a silky soup.

Celery Root, Cracked Wheat, and Every-Fall-Vegetable-You-Can-Find Chowder

Any and all fall and winter vegetables work well in this soup. The celery root puree keeps the overall flavors from becoming too sweet and one-note. You could use farro or another grain in place of the cracked wheat, but the soup's consistency will be thicker and more porridgelike . . . not necessarily a bad thing on a cold day.

» *Serves 8*

1 small celery root (about ¾ pound)	1 cup cracked wheat
½ pound onions, sliced	Several sprigs thyme
3 garlic cloves, smashed and peeled	1 stalk celery, diced
3 tablespoons unsalted butter	1 small carrot, diced
	1 big turnip, diced
Kosher salt and freshly ground black pepper	1 medium potato, diced
	2 cups shredded kale
2 tablespoons olive oil	1 big handful arugula or other spicy or bitter greens

Using a sharp paring knife, cut away all the tough exterior of the celery root; if there are dark fissures remaining, cut those away, too. Cut it into chunks.

Put the celery root, onions, 1 garlic clove, butter, and ½ cup water in a medium pot with a lid. Add 1 teaspoon salt and about 20 twists of pepper, cover, and bring to a simmer. Cook until everything is thoroughly soft, 20 to 25 minutes depending on the size of your chunks. Let this cool for a few minutes, then puree it in a food processor or blender. Set it aside.

Heat the olive oil in a big soup pot or Dutch oven over medium heat. Add the remaining 2 garlic cloves and gently toast for a few minutes to begin to soften the garlic. Add the cracked wheat, reduce the heat to low, and cook, stirring frequently, to gently toast the grain and deepen the flavor, 7 to 8 minutes—you'll smell the grain getting toasty; take care not to burn the garlic. Add the thyme to the pot.

Add the celery, carrot, turnip, potato, and 1 teaspoon salt. Cover and cook over medium heat, stirring occasionally, until the vegetables are soft and fragrant but not at all browned, 10 to 15 minutes.

Add just enough water to cover by ½ inch, adjust the heat to a lively simmer, cover, and cook until the vegetables are all tender, 15 to 20 minutes. Add the kale and cook for another few minutes—the kale should keep a bit of bite to it.

Stir in the celery root puree. The final soup should be nicely thick, but if it seems too thick and porridgelike, add more water. Taste the soup and add more salt if you like, then add lots and lots of pepper so the flavors are mellow and sweet from the vegetables with a bit of heat from the pepper.

Right before serving, reheat the soup and toss in the arugula. Serve hot.

Fried Celery Root Steaks with Citrus and Horseradish

Even without the salad on top, these golden crisp disks are scrumptious—they have the comfort-food appeal of fried mozzarella sticks but are infinitely more nutritious and refined. Serve them as a vegetarian main dish or a side dish to roast pork. The two-step cooking process may seem fussy, but it ensures the celery root is thoroughly cooked, and it minimizes the actual frying time.

» Serves 4

1 large celery root (about 2 pounds), peeled and cut into ¾-inch-thick disks

Extra-virgin olive oil

Kosher salt and freshly ground black pepper

1 cup all-purpose flour

1 egg, beaten

1¼ cups panko breadcrumbs

½ teaspoon ground coriander

1 cup citrus segments (see sidebar): choose from blood orange, tangerine, navel orange, or Meyer lemon to make a nice mix

½ cup lightly packed roughly chopped flat-leaf parsley leaves

¼ cup sliced pepperoncini

Fresh horseradish root, for grating

Heat the oven to 400°F.

Brush or toss the celery root steaks with some olive oil, season with salt, spread in an even layer on a baking sheet, and roast until tender but not at all mushy, 15 to 20 minutes. Let the steaks cool.

Meanwhile, set up your work station like this: a plate with the flour; a shallow bowl containing the beaten egg; a shallow bowl with the panko and ground coriander tossed together; a wire rack or small tray; a tray lined with paper towels; and the final serving dish.

Gently dip a celery root steak into the flour and then into the egg, letting the excess drip off. Next dredge through the crumbs so that it is fully coated, patting to encourage the crumbs to stick. (This process gets messy, so try to use only one hand.) Transfer to the rack and continue with the rest of the steaks.

Pour ¼ inch of oil into a medium skillet and heat to about 375°F. Add as many steaks as will fit comfortably and cook, turning once, until both sides are nicely browned, 2 to 3 minutes per side. Transfer to the paper towels.

Toss the segmented citrus with the parsley and pepperoncini. Season generously with salt and pepper. Arrange the celery root steaks on plates or a platter and top each with some salad. Grate a generous amount of horseradish over all and serve while the steaks are still hot and crisp.

Segmenting Citrus Citrus fruit is a wonderful companion to many winter vegetables, bringing both bright flavor and juiciness to the table. Use this same technique whether working with a softball-size grapefruit or a teeny Persian lime. Provided your knife is sharp, this is an easy and pretty cool technique.

Cut a slice off each end of the citrus fruit to flatten. Stand it on the work surface on one of its flat sides. With a sharp knife, slice away the peel, including all the white pith, cutting from the top to the bottom and following the contour of the fruit. Take your time and work in wide strips. If any white pith remains, just slice it off.

Cut out the citrus segments by holding the fruit in one hand and cutting along both sides of each segment to release it from the membranes. Do this over a bowl to catch the juices. Put the segments into another small bowl and then squeeze the "empty" citrus membranes to get out more juice.

DRIED CORN AND POLENTA

CORNMEAL

It might seem strange to include dried corn—in the form of cornmeal—in a book about vegetables, but dried corn is as much a product of its season as springtime's fava beans are. Drying corn and milling it into meal is the way to bring one season's bounty into the next. Plus, polenta is a natural partner for so many of the dishes in the book, and it's at the heart of the Italian cooking I love so much.

POLENTA

Polenta isn't simply a recipe, it's more like a religion. Fundamental, simple, and rustic, and yet a bowl of perfect polenta can be transformative. You'll hear varying ways to cook it and most will get you where you want to go, but I've made a lot of polenta in my life and this is what I believe.

Six Steps for Perfect Polenta

Find the good stuff. Freshly milled from a local grower is the best, but there are plenty of other decent commercial options. The deal-breaker? Instant polenta. Do not use it. It has the mediocre flavor and texture of convenience. I'm lucky enough to get polenta from Ayers Creek Farm in Gaston, Oregon, grown by Anthony and Carol Boutard. Anthony's a dried bean and dried corn guru in our region, and his flint corn polenta is as good as any I've had in Italy or elsewhere.

For the ratio of polenta to water, I use 5 parts water to 1 part polenta, which is wetter than you may see elsewhere. Too little water makes a thick, underhydrated mixture. When in doubt, add more water and then cook it longer, because if the polenta can't absorb any more water, the water will simply evaporate.

Add the polenta to boiling water, which will avoid lumps. Get your whisk in one hand, polenta in the other, let the polenta flow into the water in a thin steady stream, and whisk like crazy. I know there are other methods, but I believe in this one. And I make killer polenta.

Immediately reduce the heat to very low. This will prevent sticking and burning on the bottom, but most important, it will prevent the polenta from becoming a messy, hot, volcanic porridge that can bubble up and burn the cook.

Cook for a long time, and then cook some more. I cook polenta for hours, tasting along the way to determine doneness; a home-size batch might take as long as 2½ hours. I want every bit of crunch cooked out of the cornmeal, so that the finished result is soft—almost airy—moist, and creamy. Your goal is polenta that's spoonable but doesn't run to the sides of a plate. You can easily reheat polenta of this consistency by adding a little water and stirring over low heat.

Don't season until you're ready to serve it. Because you're cooking for a long time and your cooking water is both being absorbed and evaporating, controlling the amount of residual salt is tricky. I prefer to add a pinch of salt and some cheese and butter right before I serve it.

MORE WAYS:

Stir in fresh corn kernels and top with grated cheese: One of life's simple pleasures, doubled.

Mix with bits of savory ingredients: Cooked fish, chopped meats, pickles, and all kinds of different cheese. Fold in the ingredients, cool until stiffer, and then shape into little cakes and fry. Or make cakes with just cheese and butter, and serve alongside brandade, stewed meats, grilled fish, blue cheese, or runny cheeses of all kinds.

Top with a spoonful of ragu: And of course plenty of Parmigiano.

Top with braised greens and a poached egg: Add some smoky meat on the side, and don't forget to grab the hot sauce.

Create a layer for a baked casserole: Top with crumbled sausage, cooked greens, and cheese and a touch of tomato sauce.

Add mascarpone and maple syrup, and top with some stewed dates: This can be breakfast or dessert.

Kohlrabi

Funny name, funny shape . . . but a seriously delicious vegetable! Crisp and juicy, a bit like a love child of a turnip and an apple, kohlrabi truly will be a revelation to those who haven't cooked with it yet. I use it both raw and cooked, but even when I cook it, I like to maintain its juicy crunch.

Small is best. You'll find both purple and green ones, so pick your favorite color because flavorwise, there's no difference. Smaller is better because larger specimens can be woody or spongy inside. Sometimes you'll get kohlrabi with branches and leaves still attached. If they look fresh, use them as you would any braising greens, like collards, kale, or chard. And as with a lot of winter vegetables, some time spent in the cold means more accumulated sugars and therefore a sweeter eat.

Easy prep. Most often the only prep required is trimming away the outer layer if it's tough; very young kohlrabi don't need peeling or trimming. Then just grate or julienne it for crunchy-sweet slaws (apple is a natural partner), shave it into salads, or cube it up and add it to soups and stir-fries.

Kohlrabi with Citrus, Arugula, Poppy Seeds, and Crème Fraîche

Get ready to fall in love. This simple salad shows off how sexy and delicious raw kohlrabi is. If you can't find crème fraîche, sour cream will do just fine.

» *Serves 4*

1 pound kohlrabi, peeled and any gnarly bits cut away

½ cup crème fraîche

2 tablespoons poppy seeds

Kosher salt and freshly ground black pepper

4 large handfuls arugula

3 oranges, tangerines, or other sweet citrus, segmented (see page 344), juice reserved

2 to 3 tablespoons Citrus Vinaigrette (page 39)

Cut the kohlrabi into little wedges about the same size as the blood orange segments. Toss with 3 tablespoons of the crème fraîche and the poppy seeds. Season generously with salt and pepper.

Spread a nice swoosh of the remaining crème fraîche onto each plate. Quickly toss the arugula with the blood orange segments and juices and the citrus vinaigrette. Arrange the arugula and oranges on each plate and top with the kohlrabi.

Kohlrabi Brandade

When I worked at Four Season Farm, the ocean breezes and the seaweed we tilled into the soil linked kohlrabi with brininess for me, so adding kohlrabi to salt-cod brandade, though not French, makes sense. Serve the brandade on toasted bread rubbed with garlic, or as one of the variations that follow. Note that you'll need to start salt cod prep at least a day ahead.

» Serves 6 to 8

½ pound salt cod, thoroughly rinsed of all surface salt

1 pound kohlrabi, peeled and cut into ½-inch dice

¾ pound potatoes, peeled and cut into ½-inch dice

6 garlic cloves, smashed and peeled

Whole milk

Freshly ground black pepper

1 bay leaf

1 dried chile, such as chile de árbol

½ cup roughly chopped flat-leaf parsley

½ lemon

Extra-virgin olive oil

Bread, toasted or grilled and rubbed with garlic

Submerge the salt cod in water and soak for at least 8 hours, changing the water every couple of hours. You can also soak overnight in the refrigerator, drain, and then do another 2-hour soak. Cut the cod into 1-inch pieces.

Put the kohlrabi, potatoes, salt cod, and garlic in a large saucepan. Pour in enough milk to come higher than halfway up the ingredients. Season with several twists of black pepper, add the bay leaf and dried chile, and bring to a gentle simmer. Partially cover to allow some but not all of the steam to escape, and simmer gently until the kohlrabi and potatoes are very tender and the salt cod is falling into flakes, about 20 minutes. Set a sieve over a bowl and drain. Return the milk to the pan and set the other ingredients aside; discard (compost) the bay leaf and chile.

Cook the milk at a lively simmer until reduced to about 1 cup. Taste and season with some salt if it needs it (the salt cod will have added saltiness). Return the vegetables and cod to the pot and simmer everything, stirring and folding so the ingredients break apart and the mixture starts to get creamy. You're aiming for a chunky, creamy, stringy, lovely consistency.

Fold in the parsley. Taste and season the brandade with more salt if you like, plus lots of black pepper and a squeeze of lemon. Finish with a hefty splash of olive oil. Prepare the garlic-rubbed grilled bread, spoon on some brandade, and serve as a hearty snack or a light meal.

MORE WAYS:

Fry crisp brandade cakes: Mix the brandade with chopped rehydrated dried mushrooms, sliced pickled carrots or fennel, and an egg. Shape into hockey puck–size cakes and dredge through breadcrumbs. Shallow-fry, drain briefly on paper towels, and serve with simple wilted greens.

Bake brandade with a potato chip crust: Sauté some mushrooms and fold into the brandade; spread into a baking dish. Make a topping of 3 parts crunched-up potato chips to 1 part crushed torn croutons (page 29), a bit of chopped rosemary, and a handful of shredded sharp cheddar. Grate more cheese over the top and bake at 450°F until browned and bubbling.

Onions
(Storage)

If ever there were an unsung hero of the vegetable world, onion is it. And yet plain, late-season storage onions are brilliant. By "storage," I mean onions that are grown and cured (through drying) to have a long shelf life. Despite the stinging-eye thing, mature onions are full of sugars, and the texture of a slowly cooked onion is both silky and substantial.

By the time winter rolls around, most of what you'll see are the mainstream varieties—white, yellow, and red onions and shallots. In some markets, sweet varieties such as Vidalia and Walla Walla are still available, but they are much more perishable and therefore aren't year-round. (See page 106 for early-season onions.)

Get the right one for the job. White, yellow, and red onions can be used interchangeably, but each has its best purpose. White onions are a bit milder than yellow and finish with a clean bite, great for using fresh—think salsas and garnishes. Red onions are on par with white onions and best used fresh, especially since the anthocyanins that produce their red color can turn blue-gray unless mixed with something acidic, like vinegar. Best to save them for sandwiches, salads, and pickles. Yellow onions need no introduction: Sauté until translucent for a bright onion flavor, or cook long and slow to caramelize their sugars. And as for shallots, they're in a class of their own, with a complex flavor that hints of garlic.

Keep them dry. Choose onions that are hard, with no soft spots, and tight, dry, papery skins. Give them a sniff: There should be no odor. If they are starting to smell like onions (or worse), they've started to rot. Heat and moisture are onions' worst enemies, as heat causes them to sprout and moisture promotes mold. So keep them in a cool, dry place with plenty of ventilation—no plastic bags, no fridge. (Potatoes need similar conditions, but don't be tempted to mingle the two, as onions give off a gas that encourages potatoes to sprout.)

Onion and Pancetta Tart

Unlike a quiche, this savory tart is filled with very little custard in order to let the sweet onions dominate. This is delicious reheated the next day, so it's a good make-ahead dish for entertaining.

» Makes one 10-inch tart

All-purpose flour, for dusting	Kosher salt and freshly ground black pepper
⅔ recipe Walnut Dough (see Note)	1 egg yolk
Extra-virgin olive oil	½ cup heavy cream or crème fraîche
3 ounces pancetta, chopped	2 ounces Gruyère cheese, shredded (½ cup)
3 cups thinly sliced yellow onion (about 1 large)	

Heat the oven to 400°F.

On a lightly floured work surface, roll the dough to a 13-inch round. Gently roll the dough around your rolling pin, transfer to a 10-inch tart pan with a removable bottom, and unroll. Gently press the dough down into the corner where the base meets the sides, and press the dough up the sides, leaving some above the rim. Pinch the dough to form a tidy, evenly thick rim.

Line the dough with parchment paper or foil and fill with dried beans or pie weights. Bake until the dough is set and the rim is light brown, about 10 minutes. Reduce the oven temperature to 325°F. Carefully remove the parchment and beans, return the tart shell to the oven, and cook until the base looks dry and is light gold, another 20 minutes. Let the crust cool slightly. (Leave the oven on.)

As the tart shell bakes, heat a small glug of olive oil in a large skillet or Dutch oven over medium-high heat. Add the pancetta and as soon as it sizzles, reduce the heat and cook until the fat has rendered and the pancetta is starting to brown, about 7 minutes; don't let it get fully browned and crisp.

Add the onion, season generously with salt and pepper, and cook gently until the onion becomes very soft and fragrant and is a rich golden brown, stirring and scraping the pan frequently, about 30 minutes. Cool the onion to room temperature.

Whisk together the egg yolk and cream in a bowl. Season lightly with salt and pepper. Fold in the Gruyère and onion. Fill the tart shell with the mixture, smoothing the top.

Bake until the filling is just set, about 20 minutes. Let the tart cool to warm before cutting and serving.

Note: Make the Pecan Dough (page 49) with walnuts instead of pecans. You only need two-thirds of the dough here, so wrap and freeze the other one-third of the dough for another use.

Onion Bread Soup with Sausage

Taking inspiration from a classic *pappa al pomodoro* (tomato and bread soup), this soup is perfect with winter's storage onions. This soup came to be during the cold Maine winter months while I was working on the farm and has been a staple at the restaurants and at my home ever since. Note that it's easy to make it vegetarian simply by leaving out the sausage.

» *Serves 6*

1 tablespoon extra-virgin olive oil

1 tablespoon unsalted butter

5 pounds onions (use a mix of yellow and red if you can), cut into ⅛-inch-thick slices

1 pound sweet Italian sausage (optional), bulk or casings removed

Kosher salt and freshly ground black pepper

3 bushy sprigs thyme

1 bay leaf

1 cup dry, unoaked white wine

8 cups rich meat or poultry broth, preferably homemade (see Note)

Three 1-inch-thick slices stale country bread, crusts on, each torn into 5 or 6 pieces

2 cups shredded extra-sharp cheddar cheese

Fresh horseradish root, for grating

Heat a very large soup pot or Dutch oven over medium heat. Add the olive oil and butter and when the butter has melted, add all the onions. Let them cook undisturbed for several minutes until the bottom layer is beginning to give off some juice and get soft. Reduce the heat to medium-low. Stir and fold over the onions so that the raw ones are on the bottom now. Keep cooking the onions slowly, stirring and folding frequently, until they are completely soft and a nice rich brown color. If the juices on the bottom of the pot seem like they're going to burn, reduce the heat and add a little bit of water or white wine to deglaze. This process will take at least 30 minutes, probably more like 45 minutes.

Meanwhile, if you're using the sausage, crumble it into a skillet and cook over medium heat until it is no longer pink, about 5 minutes. Drain on paper towels and set aside.

Increase the heat under the onion pot to medium-high. Season the onions with 1 tablespoon salt and a generous dose of pepper. Toss in the thyme sprigs and bay leaf. Pour in the white wine and stir and scrape the pan to completely dissolve the onion juices on the bottom, and to slightly reduce the wine so the alcohol cooks off and the flavors concentrate, about 5 minutes.

Add the broth and simmer the soup over medium heat until the broth is nicely concentrated and flavorful, about 20 minutes. Add the sausage, if you're using it. Taste and adjust the seasoning.

Heat the broiler and adjust a rack so it's about 6 inches below the heating element.

Distribute the bread pieces among 6 ovenproof 2-cup bowls. (Put the bowls on a baking sheet for easy maneuvering, if you like.)

Ladle the soup over the bread and let sit for 3 to 4 minutes so the bread absorbs the liquid. Sprinkle the cheddar over the top and put the bowls under the broiler. Broil until the cheese is bubbling slightly, 2 to 3 minutes. Grate on some horseradish. Serve hot.

Note: You can use store-bought broth if you don't have homemade. A half-and-half mix of low-sodium chicken and beef works nicely.

In the field So-called sweet onions, such as Walla Walla or Vidalia, aren't actually sweeter than a plain old onion. Their sugar content is about the same, but the sweets are much lower in pyruvic acid, which is the sulfurous stuff that gives you teary eyes. Sweet onions are grown in low-sulfur volcanic soil, which is responsible for the reduced pyruvic acid.

Braised Beef with Lots and Lots of Onions

This is one of those miraculous dishes that uses only a few basic ingredients, doesn't require much technique or fussing, and yet produces a delectable and soul-satisfying dish that's superb on its own but lends itself to leftover improvisation.

» Serves 4 with lots of leftovers (which you will want)

3 pounds boneless beef chuck roast, cut into two or three large pieces

Kosher salt and freshly ground black pepper

2 tablespoons extra-virgin olive oil

2 tablespoons unsalted butter

2 pounds onions, sliced as thin as possible

6 garlic cloves, smashed and peeled

1 small handful thyme sprigs

1 cup dry, unoaked white wine

Season the beef generously with salt and pepper, set it on a plate, and leave on the counter for about 1 hour so it comes to room temperature.

Heat the oven to 300°F.

Heat a large heavy ovenproof pot with a lid, such as a Dutch oven, over medium-high heat. Blot the beef with paper towels to absorb any moisture.

Add the olive oil to the pot and carefully lay the beef into the pan. Reduce the heat just a touch and cook without moving the meat until the first side is deeply browned, about 6 minutes. Turn the beef pieces and continue browning all sides. Take care that the pan juices don't get too dark.

Once the meat is browned, add the butter, onions, garlic, and thyme sprigs. Season lightly with more salt and pepper. Stir everything around so that the butter and moisture from the onions deglazes the cooked-on juices. Scoot the onions so they're mostly underneath the meat,

and cook until the onions are very soft and fragrant, about 10 minutes. Don't let them actually get crisp and browned.

Add the wine and bring to a gentle simmer. Cover the pot and transfer to the oven. Cook until the meat is extremely tender and the juices are thick and tasty. This could take anywhere from 1½ hours to 3 hours, so be sure to allow enough time for thorough cooking.

When the beef is tender, transfer it to a cutting board and let it rest for about 15 minutes. Cut into thick slices, or pull apart into smaller portions, and arrange on a platter. Taste the onions, adjust the seasoning, and pour over the beef.

MORE WAYS:

Build a deconstructed stew: Cut the meat into pieces and fold everything with some boiled and smashed potatoes, celery root, and carrots. Add a touch of water or broth to loosen.

Make a hearty soup: Shred some meat, then combine in a pot with some of the onions and juices, thinly sliced turnips and carrots, and torn kale leaves. Add broth and simmer until all is tender. Serve with crusty bread.

Lay out a spread: Slice the beef and arrange on a platter, smothered with the onions and juices. Serve at room temperature with several different kinds of pickle, good prepared horseradish, and torn bread and butter.

Make my favorite Italian beef sandwich: Heat the beef and onions with their liquid, slice a baguette or roll in half, stuff with beef and onions, and dip it back into the liquid. This is a messy and perfect sandwich.

In the field To keep onions in good shape throughout the year, growers let them dry for about 3 weeks in a well-ventilated, warm spot until they lose some moisture and the outer skins separate from the onion and become dry and papery.

Parsnips

To think of parsnips as some sort of white carrot is like confusing a Canadian with an American. There are similarities, yes, but there are also fundamental differences. First of all, they're noticeably starchier than their carrot cousins. They're sweeter, too, with a nuttier flavor. But like carrots, they're excellent any which way—roasted, mashed or sautéed, shaved into salads, simmered in stews, or, yes, folded into tender, sweet cakes.

Winter is their best friend. Parsnips first start appearing in markets in fall, but they get even sweeter as temperatures drop in winter, when the cold triggers the starches to turn to sugar. Some farmers will even intentionally "overwinter" some of their crop until spring, for maximum sweetness. Pick out small to medium roots that are firm, not flabby. But avoid the big guys, which have an unpleasantly woody core (if you do get one, cut it out and toss it in stock). Stored in plastic bags in the fridge, parsnips will keep for weeks.

Don't peel. While I'll often peel fall carrots because their peels are a bit tough and bitter this time of year, I generally leave parsnips alone. Much of the root's flavor is right at the skin. Exposed surfaces of parsnips will darken when exposed to air, kind of like an apple or potato, so if you're not going to cook them right away, toss them in lemon-spiked water.

Parsnips with Citrus and Olives

If you have a mandoline slicer, use it, but you can get lovely parsnip ribbons using a simple vegetable peeler. A soak in ice water will enhance their already crisp texture. Big mature parsnips can be woody in the center, so look for smaller specimens. Start peeling the thicker end first for easier handling.

» Serves 4

1 pound parsnips, ends trimmed

¼ cup white wine vinegar

3 Cara Cara or other navel oranges

1 cup pitted black olives, smashed and roughly chopped

3 scallions, trimmed (including ½ inch off the green tops), sliced on a sharp angle, soaked in ice water for 20 minutes, and drained well (see page 53)

Kosher salt and freshly ground black pepper

Extra-virgin olive oil

Use a vegetable peeler to shave the parsnips into very thin ribbons; it's fine if they're not the same length, you just want them nice and thin. Put in a bowl of ice water with half the vinegar and soak for 30 minutes.

Meanwhile, grate the zest from one of the oranges. Segment all three over a bowl to catch the juices (see page 344).

Drain the parsnips very well (you don't want them wet at all, so use a salad spinner if you can). Toss the parsnip ribbons with the orange zest, the orange segments and their juice, olives, and scallions. Season with salt and pepper, toss again, and taste. Let the salad rest for about 15 minutes, so the parsnips macerate a bit. Finish with a generous drizzle of olive oil and toss again.

Parsnip Soup with Pine Nut, Currant, and Celery Leaf Relish

For this soup, you "sweat" the vegetables by cooking them slowly in a touch of fat and their own juices. This creates a sweet and delicate parsnip puree as the base for a constellation of zingy flavors in the relish topping.

» *Serves 2 as a main-dish soup,*
  4 as a starter portion

Extra-virgin olive oil

1¼ pounds parsnips, peeled and sliced into ½-inch-thick coins

1 large or a few smaller celery stalks, sliced into ½-inch pieces, leaves roughly chopped and reserved (about ¼ cup)

½ small onion, thinly sliced

2 tablespoons unsalted butter

Kosher salt and freshly ground black pepper

¼ cup currants

2 tablespoons red wine vinegar

¼ cup pine nuts, toasted (see page 31)

¼ cup roughly chopped flat-leaf parsley

1 teaspoon finely grated lemon zest

1 teaspoon fresh lemon juice

⅛ teaspoon dried chile flakes

Heat a splash of olive oil in a medium saucepan with a lid over medium-high heat. Add the parsnips, celery, onion, and butter, and season lightly with salt and pepper. Reduce the heat to low, cover the pot, and cook the vegetables slowly without browning them at all, until they are getting tender, 10 to 15 minutes.

Add water just to cover (about 2 cups). Increase the heat to a simmer, cover, and continue cooking until the vegetables are fully tender, another 5 to 10 minutes. Let the soup cool a few minutes and then puree it in a blender. Add enough hot water until you have a nice rich but pourable consistency. Taste and adjust with more salt or pepper, remembering that the topping will have some zing.

While the soup is cooking, put the currants in a small bowl and pour over the vinegar. Soak for at least 15 minutes.

Toss the pine nuts, currants with their soaking vinegar, parsley, reserved celery leaves, lemon zest, lemon juice, chile flakes, and salt and black pepper to taste. When the flavor is very bright, add a nice glug of olive oil and stir to mix.

Serve a big spoonful of the relish on each portion of soup.

In the field Some vegetables are hardy enough to "overwinter," meaning they start their growth in late summer or early fall and then stay dormant in the ground through winter. When spring comes, they are ready to harvest and are much larger and more mature than the new crop will be—and sweeter, too, as the cold increases their sugars. Root vegetables are ideal candidates, especially in snowy climates, where the blanket of snow acts as insulation.

Parsnip, Date, and Hazelnut Loaf Cake with Meyer Lemon Glaze

Zucchini bread, carrot cake—why not parsnip cake? The olive oil keeps this cake very moist so it stays fresh for days. To serve as a breakfast bread, just leave off the glaze.

» Makes one 8 x 5-inch loaf cake

Butter, for the pan

1¼ cups all-purpose flour, plus more for dusting

2 tablespoons fresh lemon juice

1 cup powdered sugar

2 teaspoons finely grated lemon zest

Freshly ground black pepper

½ pound parsnips, cut into 1-inch pieces

1 teaspoon baking soda

1 teaspoon kosher salt

½ cup chopped dates

2 large eggs

¾ cup granulated sugar

¼ cup packed dark brown sugar

1 teaspoon vanilla extract

⅔ cup extra-virgin olive oil

¾ cup hazelnuts, toasted (see page 31) and finely chopped

Heat the oven to 325°F. Generously butter an 8 x 5-inch loaf pan. Add a few spoonfuls of flour, shake to coat all the surfaces, and tap out any excess.

Stir together the lemon juice and powdered sugar in a bowl. Stir in 1 teaspoon of the lemon zest and several twists of pepper. Set the glaze aside.

Put the parsnips in a food processor and process until they are finely chopped, like the texture of couscous; you want to have about 1½ cups. (If you don't have a processor, you can grate the parsnips.) Return the parsnips to the processor if you've taken them out to measure them.

Whisk together the flour, baking soda, and salt in a medium bowl. Add the dates and toss until the dates are coated with flour so they don't clump together.

To the food processor, add the eggs, granulated sugar, brown sugar, vanilla, and remaining 1 teaspoon of the lemon zest and pulse until smooth and well blended. Pulse in the oil to make a creamy consistency. Pour the parsnip mixture into the dry ingredients and fold until blended. Add the hazelnuts and fold until there are no more bits of flour.

Pour the batter into the prepared pan. Bake until slightly risen and a pick or thin knife blade inserted into the center comes out clean, 35 to 45 minutes for a metal pan, longer for glass or ceramic. Let the cake cool in the pan for 10 minutes, then run a knife around the edges to release it from the pan. Set the warm cake on a rack set over a tray to catch the glaze. Drizzle the glaze all over the top while the cake is still warm.

In the field The "hunger gap" is the period between the end of winter and beginning of spring vegetables. You're either sick of winter vegetables or you've consumed them all (if you're eating from your own garden), and you can't wait for the first radishes and lettuces of spring to appear. But the gap period does provide a few delicacies—in particular, overwintered parsnips, which have grown sweeter during their long stay in the ground.

Potatoes *(Late Season)*

It's impossible not to love the tender, tiny new potatoes of spring, but they do have one drawback: They're too perfect to mess with. Mature potatoes, on the other hand, are perhaps the most versatile (and therefore inspiring) vegetables you can possibly have at your disposal. (See page 160 for early-season potatoes.)

Heavy or light starch? Whatever heat source or flavor profile you want to apply to your potatoes, they're up for it. The only thing you really have to consider is their starch content. Russet potatoes are high starch. Their flesh soaks up liquids and falls apart into a fluffy, mealy texture. This is exactly what you want for baked potatoes, mashed potatoes, potato soup, and French fries. But it's not what you want in, say, potato salad, hash, or gratins. Basically, if you want to end up with discernible potato pieces, don't go for russets. Instead, opt for medium- or low-starch potatoes, sometimes described as "waxy," like the common yellow and red varieties, as well as heirlooms like German Butterball.

Choose wisely. It's tempting to opt for one of those grab-and-go bags of potatoes, but don't. You can't really tell what shape the potatoes are in, and more often than not there are a few less-than-stellar specimens hiding inside. Instead, pick them out yourself, looking for those that are heavy and firm, with no soft spots or traces of green, which would indicate the presence of mildly toxic solanine, an alkaloid substance triggered by too much exposure to light.

Storage. Once you get them home, keep those potatoes tucked away in the dark, somewhere cool but not cold. Don't be tempted to put them in the fridge, where the low temps will turn the starches to sugar. If your potatoes do show signs of greening, peel off all traces before using. And keep them away from onions, which release a gas that encourages them to sprout. A few sprouts are fine to pick off, but once potatoes really start growing, they're best relegated to the compost—or planted in the garden.

Prep school. When boiling potatoes, it helps to keep the skins on to keep them from soaking up too much of the water. Medium- and low-starch potatoes have such thin skins they rarely require peeling anyway. But if you want to do any slicing and dicing in advance, keep the prepped potatoes in water spiked with acid, like lemon juice or vinegar, to keep them from turning brown.

Fried Potato and Cheese Pancake

Serve this crisp-on-the-outside and creamy-on-the-inside dish on its own as a savory side, or dress it up by topping with a drizzle of Spiced Green Sauce or Pickle Salsa Verde (page 44), or with spicy greens and herbs dressed in olive oil and lemon with a shower of cheese.

» Serves 2 as a main dish, 4 as a side

1 pound Yukon Gold potatoes (2 large), peeled and quartered

Kosher salt and freshly ground black pepper

Extra-virgin olive oil

1 cup thinly sliced onion

¼ pound Parmigiano-Reggiano cheese, finely grated (about 2 cups)

Put the potatoes in a large pot of water and add salt until it tastes like the sea. Bring to a boil, then reduce to a gentle simmer and cook until tender, 20 to 25 minutes. Drain well.

Meanwhile, heat a glug of olive oil in a medium skillet over medium heat. Add the onion and cook until soft and fragrant, about 8 minutes; do not brown.

Put the potatoes in a large bowl and crush them with a potato masher or a wooden spoon until they're fairly smooth; some chunks are fine, just not huge ones. Add the onion and Parmigiano, season generously with salt and pepper, and toss. Taste and adjust the seasoning.

Heat a glug of olive oil in a nonstick 9-inch skillet over medium-high heat. When the oil is hot, add a small spoonful of the potato mixture. If it sizzles on contact, add the rest and gently press into an even layer. (If not, let the pan heat up some more.) Adjust the heat so that the bottom browns nicely but doesn't burn. Cook until the pancake develops a deep golden crust and the potatoes are getting warm.

Gently slide the pancake from the pan onto a plate or other flat surface. Using hot pads, carefully invert the skillet over the pancake and, holding the pan and plate tightly together, quickly flip the assembly so the pancake falls into the pan. If it falls apart a bit, don't worry, just press it back together.

Return the pan to the heat and cook until the second side is lovely and crisp. If the pancake seems oily, you can blot briefly on paper towels, but this step isn't necessary. Serve right away.

Crushed and Fried Potatoes with Crispy Herbs and Garlic

Jacques Pépin made this dish popular, but you know it was developed by some frugal cook centuries ago, who simply wanted to use leftover potatoes and ended up creating a sublime experience of crisp and creamy potatoness.

» Serves 4

1½ pounds small medium-starch potatoes, such as Yukon Gold

Extra-virgin olive oil, for frying

2 garlic cloves, thinly sliced

1 tablespoon fresh rosemary leaves

1 teaspoon thyme leaves

Kosher salt and freshly ground black pepper

¼ teaspoon dried chile flakes

4 lemon wedges

Heat the oven to 400°F.

Spread the potatoes on a baking sheet and bake until fully tender when poked with a knife, about 30 minutes, depending on how big they are.

Let the potatoes cool enough that you can handle them, then crush each one with your palm or the back of a pan. You want to create a patty shape, with lots of craggy surface area to crisp up in the hot oil. If you have larger potatoes, tear them up into smaller pieces after smashing.

Heat ½ inch of olive oil in a large skillet until quite hot. Put a corner of a potato into the oil to test the heat; if it sizzles nicely, the oil is ready. Working in batches, fry the potatoes until nicely browned on one side. Flip and cook until both sides are browned, about 5 minutes total, but about 30 seconds before the potatoes are done, toss in some of the garlic, rosemary, and thyme. Transfer the potatoes to paper towels to drain. Continue frying the potatoes, scraping out the bits of garlic and herbs between batches so it doesn't burn.

Season with salt and black pepper and the chile flakes. Serve with a lemon wedge for each diner.

Rutabaga

A lot of cooks find roadblocks on the way to discovering this fine winter root. First, there's the name. To the untrained eye, rutabagas (also called swedes) look like big turnips. So rutabaga newbies inevitably find themselves standing in the produce aisle looking for rutabagas and all they see are turnips. No wonder they call the whole thing off.

But don't give up. Mild in flavor when raw, developing into a slightly sweet richness when cooked, rutabagas are definitely worth getting to know better. Try them roasted, either on their own with olive oil and herbs, or as part of a winter root medley with potatoes, carrots, parsnips, and the like. Or mash them up with plenty of butter and cream. They shine when accompanied by a dose of sweetness, whether it's a touch of maple syrup in a glaze or a handful of apples or carrots in a slaw or mash.

Pick the right root. Rutabagas are a cross between a cabbage and a turnip, hence the uncanny resemblance to turnips. But you'll know it's a rutabaga because it's usually bigger, with a yellow (rather than white) hue blending into the purple top. Pick roots that are firm and heavy for their size and store them in plastic bags in the fridge. They'll keep for weeks. You'll likely never see them at the market with their tops on, but if you do, treat the greens as you would beet or turnip greens. To prep, just give the roots a once-over with a vegetable peeler before slicing or dicing, especially since grocery stores often sell them coated in food-grade wax.

Mashed Rutabaga with Watercress and Watercress Butter

This recipe is very much a farmhouse dish—exactly the kind of food I crave in the winter. It's sweet and earthy, and a perfect easy dish to serve next to a pork roast, roast chicken, fish fillet, or in a big bowl on its own, as a bowl of comfort. You'll find yourself using the watercress butter on tons of other dishes—fish, grilled meats, and other roasted vegetables.

» Serves 4

Kosher salt and freshly ground black pepper

2 pounds rutabaga, trimmed, peeled, and cut into large chunks

Extra-virgin olive oil

1 big bunch watercress (about 2 ounces), roughly chopped

4 tablespoons Watercress Butter (page 36)

Fill a large pot with water and add salt until it tastes like the sea. Add the rutabaga, bring to a boil, reduce to a simmer, and cook until the rutabaga is completely tender when poked with a fork, 20 to 25 minutes.

Drain the rutabaga and return to the pot. Smash with a potato masher, a wooden spoon, or a large fork. The final texture of the dish will be like chunky mashed potatoes. Season generously with salt, pepper, and a glug of olive oil.

Add the chopped watercress and smash and fold everything together. Pile into a serving bowl and top with the watercress butter and another drizzle of olive oil. Serve hot.

Rutabaga with Maple Syrup, Black Pepper, and Rosemary

If steaming the rutabaga is more convenient, use that method, though roasting will add a slight toastiness to this mellow mix of flavors. This dish begs to be served with a pork chop.

Serves 2 to 3

1½ pounds rutabaga, trimmed, peeled, and cut into ½-inch wedges

Extra-virgin olive oil

Kosher salt and freshly ground black pepper

2 tablespoons apple cider vinegar

1 tablespoon pure maple syrup

½ teaspoon chopped fresh rosemary

⅛ teaspoon dried chile flakes

Heat the oven to 400°F.

Toss the rutabaga cubes with a nice glug of olive oil and season generously with salt and black pepper. Spread evenly on a baking sheet and roast until fully tender and lightly browned, 25 to 30 minutes.

Pile into a bowl, sprinkle with the vinegar, and toss to distribute. Let the rutabaga absorb the vinegar for a minute. Add the maple syrup, rosemary, and chile flakes and toss. Taste and adjust with more salt or black pepper.

At the market Look for Grade B maple syrup. The flavor is bolder and better.

Smashed Rutabaga with Apples and Ham

Rutabaga is not a sophisticated vegetable; it feels right at home with the country fixings of apples and ham. Pears in place of apples would be delicious, too.

» Serves 4 to 6

Extra-virgin olive oil

2 garlic cloves, smashed and peeled

1½ pounds rutabaga, peeled, trimmed, and cut into chunks or wedges

2 tart apples, such as Braeburn or Fujis, peeled and cut into chunks

Kosher salt and freshly ground black pepper

½ cup diced cooked ham

1 tablespoon apple cider vinegar

Put a nice glug of olive oil in a large skillet that has a lid and heat over medium heat. Add the garlic and cook slowly to toast the garlic so it's very soft, fragrant, and nicely golden brown—but not burnt—about 5 minutes.

Arrange the rutabaga and apples in the pan in an even layer—it's okay if the pan is crowded. Season with ½ teaspoon salt.

Increase the heat to medium, add about ¼ cup water, and cover right away. Steam the rutabaga and apples until tender, adding more water if the pan gets dry. You want enough water in the pan to steam, but not so much that the ingredients sit in water and get soggy. The whole process should take about 30 minutes.

When the rutabaga is fully tender (the apples should get tender first), transfer them to a bowl, add the ham and vinegar, and season generously with salt and pepper. Smash with a potato masher or wooden spoon; the texture should be quite chunky. Taste and adjust with more salt and pepper, and finish with a nice drizzle of oil.

Turnips
(Late Season)

While I opt for mild Japanese turnips for salads, slaws, and pickles each spring (see page 59), I reach for the more robust purple-top turnips come fall. In combination with other root vegetables that are in season this time of year, their hint of peppery spiciness adds some welcome dimension and complexity to all that mild-mannered sweetness. And they can match bold flavors bite for bite, so don't be shy about pairing them up with ingredients that pack a big punch.

How to choose. Unlike early in the year when you find small turnips with their greens still attached, winter markets will have only the bigger, more mature turnips with their leafy tops long gone. These will have to be peeled, as their skins have likely gotten a bit leathery, and you may have to trim away a bit of the flesh, too, if it's gotten woody near the surface.

Good keepers.
Turnips will keep in a plastic bag in the refrigerator for up to a couple of weeks. This time of year, it's always good to have a few on hand to roast along with chicken or pork, mash along with potatoes, or toss into soup.

Half-Steamed Turnips with Alla Diavola Butter

My inspiration for this dish is kimchi, with its garlicky-spicy pungent notes. I deliver the spiciness in a flavored butter, however, so the dish also has a note of luxuriousness.

» Serves 4

Extra-virgin olive oil

2 garlic cloves, smashed and peeled

1½ pounds turnips, peeled, trimmed, and cut into chunks or wedges

Kosher salt and freshly ground black pepper

4 tablespoons Alla Diavola Butter (page 33)

Put a nice glug of olive oil in a large skillet that has a lid and heat over medium heat. Add the garlic and cook slowly to toast the garlic so it's very soft, fragrant, and nicely golden brown—but not burnt—about 5 minutes. Arrange the turnips in the pan in an even layer—it's okay if the pan is crowded. Season with ½ teaspoon salt and several twists of pepper.

Increase the heat to medium-high, add a nice big splash of water (about ¼ cup), and put the lid on right away. Steam the turnips until tender, adding more water a few times. You want enough water in the pan to steam the turnips, but not so much that they sit in water and get soggy. The whole process should take about 10 minutes.

Pile the turnips in a bowl, add the diavola butter, and toss gently until the turnips are glossy with it. Serve warm.

Roasted Turnips with Caper-Raisin Vinaigrette and Breadcrumbs

The sweet-tart vinaigrette stands up nicely to the pungency of a late-season turnip.

» *Serves 4*

1½ pounds turnips, trimmed, peeled, and cut into ½-inch wedges (if the turnips are very large, halve them first so the wedges aren't too long)

Extra-virgin olive oil

Kosher salt and freshly ground black pepper

Juice of ½ lemon

⅓ cup Caper-Raisin Vinaigrette (page 39)

⅓ cup dried breadcrumbs (page 30)

Heat the oven to 450°F. Put a baking sheet in to heat too.

Toss the turnips with a small glug of olive oil and season with salt and pepper.

When the oven is at temperature and the baking sheet is very hot, carefully remove it and dump the turnips onto it. Spread them out evenly so they are all cut side down, return to the oven, and roast until the turnips are nicely tender and browned around the edges, 12 to 15 minutes.

Pile the turnips into a big bowl. Toss with the lemon juice and then with the vinaigrette. Taste and adjust with more salt or pepper. Toss with the breadcrumbs and serve.

Turnip, Leek, and Potato Soup

The soup pot is a good destination for turnips that may be a touch over the hill. This recipe is very flexible, so add more or less of the three vegetables, and leave the soup chunky or puree it until silky smooth; a big pat of butter would make a nice final enrichment.

» *Serves 4*

Extra-virgin olive oil

3 garlic cloves, thinly sliced

1 leek, trimmed, split lengthwise into quarters, cleaned well, and thinly sliced crosswise

1¼ pounds turnips

1 pound russet potatoes, peeled

1½ teaspoons chopped thyme

1½ teaspoons chopped fresh rosemary

1 bay leaf

¼ teaspoon dried chile flakes

Kosher salt and freshly ground black pepper

Heat a glug of olive oil in a large pot over low heat. Add the garlic and let it cook slowly for about a minute to let the flavor bloom. Add the leek and cook until soft and fragrant but not browned, about 6 minutes. Add the turnips and potatoes and cook everything gently for another 10 minutes.

Add 6 cups water, the thyme, rosemary, bay leaf, chile flakes, and 2 teaspoons salt. Bring to a simmer and cook until the potatoes are falling apart and the turnips are very tender, about 25 minutes. Season generously with black pepper. Taste and adjust the seasoning. Adjust the texture as you like—crush with a wooden spoon or potato masher for a chunky soup or blend for a smooth consistency, adding more water if the soup is too thick.

Freekeh, Mushrooms, Turnips, Almonds

Freekeh is an "emerging" grain, not quite mainstream, but worth seeking out. It's a young wheat that's been slightly smoked during the harvesting process, which adds a layer of complexity. The texture is chewy but not as dense as farro or barley.

» Serves 4 to 6

1 cup freekeh, cracked or whole

1 dried chile

1 bay leaf

Kosher salt and freshly ground black pepper

1 pound mushrooms (cremini or a mix of wild and cremini)

Extra-virgin olive oil

1 pound turnips, trimmed, peeled, and thinly sliced (halve or quarter first if large)

½ cup pickled onions, store-bought or homemade (page 59)

4 scallions, trimmed (including ½ inch off the green tops), cut thinly at a sharp angle, soaked in ice water for 20 minutes, and drained well (see page 53)

3 tablespoons red wine vinegar

Dried chile flakes

½ cup almonds, toasted (see page 30) and roughly chopped

Put the freekeh in a medium saucepan and add water to cover by 2 inches. Add the chile, bay leaf, and 1 teaspoon salt. Bring to a boil, reduce the heat to a simmer, cover, and cook until the freekeh is tender, 15 to 20 minutes for cracked freekeh, longer for whole. Drain in a sieve (compost the chile and bay leaf) and spread the freekeh out on a plate or tray to cool.

Heat the oven to 450°F.

Trim off any dried ends of the mushrooms (if you're using shiitakes, discard or compost the stems) and brush off any soil or pine needles. Cut any large mushrooms in half. Toss them with a glug of olive oil, season generously with salt and black pepper, and spread in a single layer on a rimmed baking sheet.

Roast the mushrooms until they are crisp around the edges and slightly dried out, 15 to 25 minutes depending on the moisture content of your mushrooms. You might want to stir them around once or twice during cooking. Set them aside to cool.

Put the turnip slices into a bowl of ice water to soak for at least 20 minutes, so they get crisp and a bit of the spiciness is tamed. Drain well and blot dry with paper towels.

To assemble the dish, put the freekeh in a big bowl. Add the mushrooms, pickled onions, scallions, and turnips. Add the vinegar and ¼ teaspoon chile flakes, season generously with salt and black pepper, and toss well.

Add ¼ cup olive oil and toss again. Taste and adjust with more salt, black pepper, vinegar, or olive oil until the salad is nicely balanced and very savory. Add the almonds and toss again. Serve at room temperature.

Winter Squash

The world of winter squash is wide, from sweet dumplings to big blue Hubbards. But they all have two things in common: Their flesh is orange and sweet. This means you can use them interchangeably (stringy spaghetti squash is one exception), although each variety has its nuances. Some, like kabocha, are more savory, while others, like delicata, have starchier flesh. Now's the time to cook your way through the market to see which varieties you like best.

Sugar or spice? One of the beauties of winter squash is its ability to move effortlessly between sweet and savory dishes. You can match its natural sweetness with ingredients like honey, browned butter, nuts, and sweet baking spices, or you can use it as a contrast to set off things like spicy chiles, grassy herbs, and tangy yogurt. Roast it, fry it, steam it, puree it, or, yes, finely slice it and eat it raw.

Peeling is (sometimes) optional. Winter squashes can be a challenge for two reasons: first because they are dense and firm and require a steady hand to trim or slice them, and second because many have shapes that don't make it easy to peel or portion. The most obliging squash is also one of the tastiest, I think, and that's the butternut. The skin is smooth and, while tough, can be easily sliced away with a paring knife or good vegetable peeler. Other varieties are lobed or ridged and are therefore difficult to peel before cooking. For something like an acorn squash, which has deep crenellations, you're better off roasting or steaming it first and then doing the cutting or scraping of flesh later.

If you don't like hacking away at your vegetables to get the peel off, you'll likely find the smaller varieties better suited to your temperament. Delicata and sweet dumpling are both pint-size with edible skins, which makes prep simple. Just scoop out the seeds and slice. The skins on other common varieties, like butternut, acorn, and kabocha, aren't really tender enough to be pleasant to eat. To make cutting into them easier, put the whole squash in the microwave to warm up for a minute or two.

To cut a winter squash, cut a thin slice off one side to create a flat surface and set the squash on the cutting board, flat surface down for stability. For very tough squash, you may need to push your knife point into the squash first and then pull the blade down to slice across it. In any case, keep your fingers out of the way of the knife, and hold the squash steady so it doesn't skitter away as you apply pressure.

Whether you peel before or after cooking, you'll want to remove the seeds before cooking. Use a sturdy soup spoon to scrape out the seeds and the fibers that hold them together. If you need something slightly sharper to make a clean surface, try a melon baller.

They don't keep forever. Although they can seem indestructible, winter squash do eventually rot, and they can certainly get dried out with age. Be sure to choose squash that have no bruises or brown spots, and they should feel heavy for their size.

Raw Winter Squash with Brown Butter, Pecans, and Currants

That's right—raw. Once you try this salad, you'll wonder why you haven't been eating raw squash all along. Serve it as soon as it's assembled so the brown butter doesn't cool and set up.

» Serves 4

½ cup dried currants

¼ cup red wine vinegar

1 pound pumpkin or butternut squash, peeled and seeded

3 scallions, trimmed (including ½ inch off the green tops), thinly sliced on an angle, soaked in ice water for 20 minutes, and drained well (see page 53)

½ teaspoon dried chile flakes

Kosher salt and freshly ground black pepper

¼ cup Brown Butter (page 36)

3 tablespoons extra-virgin olive oil

Butternut squash oil or pumpkin seed oil (optional)

½ cup lightly packed mint leaves

½ cup pecans, lightly toasted (see page 31), some roughly chopped, some crushed

Put the currants in a small bowl and pour over the vinegar. Soak for 30 minutes.

Use a vegetable peeler to shave the squash into very thin ribbons. If you have pieces of squash that are too hard to shave, just cut them into very thin julienne with a sharp knife. It doesn't matter if everything is the same shape; you just want the squash as thin and delicate as possible.

Pile the squash into a large bowl and add the currants and soaking vinegar, scallions, chile flakes, and a generous amount of salt and black pepper. Toss to combine. Taste and adjust the seasoning so it is balanced and vibrant.

Pour in the warm brown butter and toss again. Add the olive oil (and a drizzle of the squash oil, if using), toss again, and taste. Add the mint and pecans, toss, and serve right away.

In the field While most vegetables are best just-plucked from the ground, winter squash need time to cure outdoors in the field. The sunshine and airflow allows the flesh to grow sweeter and the skin to harden up. It's the smooth, hard skin that makes these such long-keepers.

Winter Squash and Leek Risotto

Butternut squash is perfect for this dish, as the big bulb of solid flesh is easy to grate. Adding the scraps to the broth doubles down on the lovely squash flavor.

» Serves 4

About 8 cups vegetable or chicken stock

2 pounds winter squash

2 tablespoons unsalted butter

Extra-virgin olive oil

½ teaspoon dried chile flakes

Kosher salt

2 cups carnaroli or other risotto-appropriate rice

1 pound leeks, trimmed, split lengthwise into quarters, cleaned, and thinly sliced crosswise

1 cup dry white wine

2 cups freshly grated Parmigiano-Reggiano cheese

¼ cup chopped flat-leaf parsley

1 tablespoon chopped sage

Put the stock in a soup pot. Peel the squash with a vegetable peeler or a sharp paring knife and split it lengthwise. Scoop out the seeds and fibers and add to the stock. Grate about 2 cups of the flesh using the large holes of a box grater and set aside. Roughly chop the rest of the squash and add it to the stock. Let the stock simmer slowly for at least 30 minutes so it takes on the squash flavor.

Melt the butter in a small glug of olive oil in a large skillet or Dutch oven over medium-low heat. Add half the grated squash, the chile flakes, and 1 teaspoon salt and cook for about 2 minutes. Add the rice and cook, stirring frequently, so that the rice becomes glossy and slightly darker golden, about 5 minutes. Add the leeks and 1 teaspoon salt and cook over medium-low heat until they are soft and fragrant, another 10 minutes or so.

Increase the heat to medium-high and add the wine, stirring and scraping to deglaze the pan. Simmer until all the wine has evaporated.

Start ladling in enough of the hot stock (don't let the solids get into the risotto pan) so that it just barely covers the rice. Adjust the heat so the liquid bubbles nicely but isn't boiling hard. Stir the rice occasionally, scraping the bottom of the pan. When most of the liquid has reduced, add more stock. Continue this process, stirring to encourage creaminess, until the rice is getting tender but still has a chalky center when you bite into a grain, about 10 minutes.

Add the remaining grated squash and a bit more stock and cook just until the squash is tender. The consistency of the risotto should be quite moist, because it will stiffen up as you add the cheese and as it cools.

Fold in 1½ cups of the Parmigiano, the parsley, and the sage and serve right away, passing the rest of the cheese at the table.

In the kitchen We're familiar with oils from many nuts—such as walnuts and peanuts—and seeds, such as rapeseed (canola oil) and sesame seed. But I recently discovered a new seed oil—pressed from toasted butternut squash seed, made by Stony Brook Wholehearted Foods (www.wholeheartedfoods.com). Similar to pumpkin seed oil, which is popular in Austrian cuisine, it's exquisitely nutty and intense, and I love to drizzle it over vegetables and onto soups.

Fontina-Stuffed Arancini

Typically, these fried risotto balls are made with leftover risotto, but they're such a fun party food that I approve of making the risotto just to make these. Serve them as is, or surrounded by a ribbon of tomato sauce or one of my salsa verdes (page 44).

» *Makes 32 arancini*

Winter Squash and Leek Risotto (opposite)

½ pound Fontina or other mild melting cheese, cut into 32 pieces

2 cups dried bread-crumbs (page 30) or panko

Vegetable oil, for frying

Make the risotto. Oil a baking sheet and spread the risotto out in a ½-inch layer to cool. When it's completely cool, use a ¼-cup ice cream scoop or two tablespoons to scoop and shape into 32 balls.

Push a piece of the Fontina into the center of each ball (don't worry if it's sticking out a bit at this stage). Now pull some risotto around the hole the cheese made and then roll the ball between your palms until the cheese is sealed inside. Set onto another baking sheet.

Heat the oven to 375°F.

Put the breadcrumbs in a wide shallow bowl. Roll each risotto ball in the crumbs to coat thoroughly, patting lightly so the crumbs stick.

Pour ½ inch of vegetable oil into a large skillet and heat to about 375°F. Working in small batches, fry each risotto ball for about 2 minutes, so it's nicely browned all over, and then transfer to a baking sheet. Once you have a panful, transfer to the oven and finish cooking the arancini until they are hot all the way through and the cheese has melted, 7 to 10 minutes (or up to 15 minutes if the arancini have been fried and sitting at room temperature for a while). Serve as soon as possible.

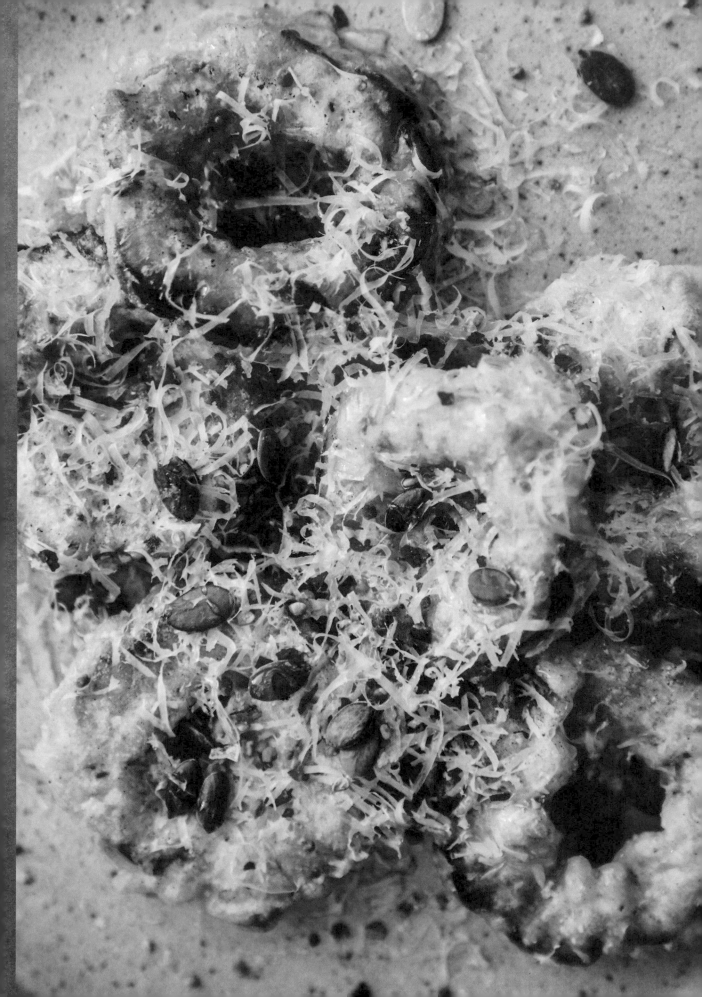

Delicata Squash "Donuts" with Pumpkin Seeds and Honey

This dish is one of the biggest hits at the restaurant—it's hard not to smile when served little rings of fried squash. Be sure to use good frying technique: Don't fill your pot with too much oil; you need room for it to bubble up.

» Makes about 20 two-bite appetizers

2 pounds delicata squash (2 medium)	Pecorino Romano cheese, for grating
Vegetable oil or olive oil, for deep-frying	Dried chile flakes
½ cup cornstarch	Toasted pumpkin seeds
½ cup all-purpose flour	2 tablespoons honey
1 cup sparkling water	Flaky sea salt, for serving
Kosher salt and freshly ground black pepper	Lemon wedges (optional)

Heat the oven to 400°F.

Trim the ends of the squashes and peel the skin in alternating strips using a sharp vegetable peeler. This will make the rings easier to eat (less skin) and will help them stay intact.

Cut the squash crosswise into ½-inch-thick slices (you should get about 10 per squash). With a spoon or a sharp paring knife, cut around the inside of each ring to remove the seeds and fibers. Arrange the squash rings on baking sheets and roast (with no oil) until they are tender but not mushy, about 20 minutes, depending on the density of the flesh. Let them cool. You can do this a few hours ahead of serving.

Arrange a double layer of paper towels on a tray or baking sheet and set it near your stove. Pour 2 inches of oil (vegetable oil or a mix of olive and vegetable) into a saucepan, making sure there are at least 3 inches of headroom (the oil may bubble up a bit during cooking, and you don't want any spillovers—dangerous!). Slowly bring the oil up to 375°F on a thermometer. (Or fry a small piece of bread: When it takes 60 seconds to get nicely crisp and brown, but not burnt, your oil is just about right.)

As the oil is heating, whisk together the cornstarch and flour. Whisk in enough sparkling water to make a thin batter. Season with some salt and black pepper.

When the oil is ready, dip a squash ring into the batter, let the excess drip off, and carefully immerse it in the hot oil. You can use tongs for this or, if you're handy with them, use wooden chopsticks. Fry the ring until the coating is puffed and very light golden. Transfer to the paper towels to drain. Continue frying, a few at a time now, but don't add too many at once because that will cause the oil temperature to drop and the rings will get greasy.

Once all the squash rings are fried, turn off the heat under the oil and arrange the rings on a serving platter. Shower with pecorino, a pinch of chile flakes, and pumpkin seeds. Drizzle with a delicate thread of honey and sprinkle with flaky salt. Serve right away while the rings are hot and crisp.

If you like, serve with a squeeze of lemon.

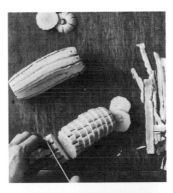

Roasted Squash with Yogurt, Walnuts, and Spiced Green Sauce

Such a stunning dish, and with so little work. I look for a mix of squash that will have differently shaped slices so that you get some drama on the platter.

» Serves 4

1½ cups plain whole-milk or low-fat yogurt

1 small garlic clove, minced

½ teaspoon finely grated lemon zest

Kosher salt and freshly ground black pepper

About 2 pounds winter squash (one kind or a mix)

Extra-virgin olive oil

2 tablespoons slightly sweet white wine vinegar, such as KATZ Sauvignon Blanc Vinegar (see page 18)

½ recipe Spiced Green Sauce (page 44)

¼ cup walnuts, lightly toasted (see page 31) and roughly chopped

Butternut squash oil or pumpkin seed oil (optional)

Line a sieve with some dampened cheesecloth and set over a bowl. (If you don't have cheese-cloth, you can use paper coffee filters, but the draining time will be slightly longer.) Put the yogurt in the cheesecloth and let it sit for at least 1 hour, so the whey drains out and the yogurt gets thick and creamy (save the whey to use in a smoothie or something; it's nutritious!). You can set this up in the fridge and drain overnight, if you like.

Mix the drained yogurt with the garlic, lemon zest, and ¼ teaspoon salt. Set aside.

Heat the oven to 400°F.

Trim off the top and bottom of the squash, then peel away the skin with a paring knife or sturdy vegetable peeler. Cut the squash in half, scoop out the seeds and fibers with a stiff spoon, and cut the squash into ½-inch slices.

Toss the squash, either in a large bowl or directly on a rimmed baking sheet, with 2 tablespoons olive oil and a generous seasoning of salt and pepper. Spread out on one or two rimmed baking sheets, and roast until tender and nicely browned on the underside, 20 to 40 minutes depending on the texture of the squash. Let the squash cool slightly on the baking sheet(s).

Arrange the squash slices on a platter, spoon a ribbon of yogurt on top, and then sprinkle with the vinegar. Drizzle/spoon the green sauce over the squash so it looks pretty. Scatter the walnuts on the dish and finish with a few drops of the squash oil (if using) or some olive oil. Serve warm or at room temperature.

In the kitchen To save time, instead of draining your own yogurt, you can use store-bought labneh or Greek yogurt, though I like the slightly looser texture I get when I drain my own.

Pumpkin Bolognese

Here, pumpkin replaces the tomato of a typical Bolognese sauce. The flavors are more mellow and rounded, so make sure you're generous with the black pepper.

» Serves 4

About 2 pounds pumpkin, unpeeled, cut into wide wedges, seeds scraped out

Extra-virgin olive oil

Kosher salt and freshly ground black pepper

1 pound ground beef chuck

½ pound ground pork (get ground shoulder, if you can)

1 cup finely chopped onion

½ cup finely chopped celery

½ cup finely chopped carrot

1 cup dry, unoaked white wine

1 cup whole milk

Cooked pasta of your choice (any short or long shape will be nice)

Freshly grated Parmigiano-Reggiano cheese, for serving

Heat the oven to 400°F.

Brush the pumpkin wedges with olive oil and season lightly with salt and pepper. Arrange on a baking sheet and roast, turning once, until fully tender, about 25 minutes.

Let the pumpkin cool, then scrape the flesh into a food processor. Blend until you have a smooth puree. Transfer the puree to a saucepan or large skillet and cook over medium-high heat, scraping frequently with a spatula, until the puree has lost a lot of its water and the pumpkin is thick and concentrated in flavor—like tomato paste, but with pumpkin. This could take 10 to 20 minutes, depending on the moisture level of your pumpkin.

Heat a glug of olive oil in a large skillet or Dutch oven over medium-high heat. Add the ground beef and pork, breaking up any big chunks, and cook until the meats are no longer pink, another 5 to 10 minutes. Take care to not brown the meat; you don't want crusty bits. Remove the meat.

Add the onion, celery, and carrot. Season with 1 teaspoon salt and lots of twists of pepper. As soon as the vegetables begin to sizzle, reduce the heat to medium-low. Keep cooking, stirring frequently, until they are soft and fragrant, but not browned at all, about 10 minutes.

Return the meat to the pan, then add the wine. Simmer until the wine has reduced to just a small amount of liquid, about 10 minutes.

Fold in the pumpkin mixture and the milk. Season with salt and pepper, and adjust the heat to a very low simmer, cover, and simmer the sauce until the flavors are all nicely married, another hour or so. Check on the sauce during cooking to be sure it's not drying out; if so, add a bit more water. You want the meat to be in very small bits and the meat fat should have separated out a bit. Taste the sauce and adjust with more salt and lots of pepper, if needed.

Serve with cooked pasta and lots of grated Parmigiano.

In the kitchen Rather than wrestling with unwieldy and tough-skinned pumpkin or winter squash, give it a blast in the microwave before cutting. You won't really cook it—you'll just soften it enough for your knife to penetrate more easily. Slit the squash and microwave for 3 minutes for a medium size, longer for a bruiser like a big kabocha or pumpkin. Let the squash cool, then either peel or cut open and into slices or chunks.

Acknowledgments

I would like to thank: Tom Petty, Bob Dylan, my mom and pops, Martha Holmberg, Ann Bramson, Laura Dart, Ashley Marti, A.J. Meeker, Michelle Ishay-Cohen, Renata Di Biase, Melinda Josie, Bella, Maine, Duane Sorenson, Sam Smith, Charlie Trotter, Andrew Fienberg, Mark Ladner, David Chang, Four Season Farm, Ayers Creek, Artisan, Dan Barber, Mario Batali, Alice Waters, Sean Brock, the River Café, Jamie Oliver, All-Clad, Le Creuset, Staub, Williams-Sonoma, Breville, all the farmers, farmers' markets, all the dishwashers, all the good jukeboxes, long roads and changing seasons. **—Joshua McFadden**

Warm thanks to collaborators Andrea Slonecker, Danielle Centoni, and Li Agen and to the genius team at Artisan. Huge affection and gratitude to our wise editor, Ann Bramson, who managed to gracefully wrangle us into making the best book we could. And thanks to Joshua McFadden for your infectious enthusiasm, for lots of pink wine, and for teaching me things about cooking that I thought I already knew. **—Martha Holmberg**

Index

Note: Page references in *italics* indicate photographs.

P.S.

Don't buy tomatoes in winter.

Love,
Joshua

Joshua McFadden is the chef/owner of the beloved trattoria Ava Gene's in Portland, Oregon. After years cooking in San Francisco (Lark Creek Inn, Roxanne's) and in New York (Franny's, Lupa, Momofuku, Blue Hill), he helped manage the trailblazing Four Season Farm in coastal Maine, an experience that transformed his approach to cooking. It was there that he learned to coax the best from vegetables at each stage of their lives, from root to leaf. The food he started cooking as a result is nothing short of a revelation. With a business partner, McFadden formed Submarine Hospitality, a burgeoning food empire that now owns both Ava Gene's and the Middle Eastern-inspired Tusk, with plans to create an agricultural complex that will host creative collaboration between farming, food, and design.

Collaborator **Martha Holmberg** is a former editor in chief of *Fine Cooking* magazine and has authored or coauthored eight cookbooks, including *Modern Sauces* and *The Bar Book*, with Jeffrey Morgenthaler. She lives in Portland, Oregon, where her day job is as the CEO of the International Association of Cooking Professionals.

Conversion Charts

Here are rounded-off equivalents between the metric system and the traditional systems that are used in the United States to measure weight and volume.

WEIGHTS

US/UK	METRIC
1 oz	30 g
2 oz	55 g
3 oz	85 g
4 oz (¼ lb)	115 g
5 oz	140 g
6 oz	170 g
7 oz	200 g
8 oz (½ lb)	225 g
9 oz	255 g
10 oz	285 g
11 oz	310 g
12 oz	340 g
13 oz	370 g
14 oz	395 g
15 oz	425 g
16 oz (1 lb)	455 g

VOLUME

AMERICAN	IMPERIAL	METRIC
¼ tsp		1.25 ml
½ tsp		2.5 ml
1 tsp		5 ml
½ Tbsp (1½ tsp)		7.5 ml
1 Tbsp (3 tsp)		15 ml
¼ cup (4 Tbsp)	2 fl oz	60 ml
⅓ cup (5 Tbsp)	2½ fl oz	75 ml
½ cup (8 Tbsp)	4 fl oz	125 ml
⅔ cup (10 Tbsp)	5 fl oz	150 ml
¾ cup (12 Tbsp)	6 fl oz	175 ml
1 cup (16 Tbsp)	8 fl oz	250 ml
1¼ cups	10 fl oz	300 ml
1½ cups	12 fl oz	350 ml
2 cups (1 pint)	16 fl oz	500 ml
2½ cups	20 fl oz (1 pint)	625 ml
5 cups	40 fl oz (1 qt)	1.25 l

OVEN TEMPERATURES

	°F	°C	GAS MARK
very cool	250–275	130–140	½–1
cool	300	148	2
warm	325	163	3
moderate	350	177	4
moderately hot	375–400	190–204	5–6
hot	425	218	7
very hot	450–475	232–245	8–9